D0206066

WITHDRAWAL

Challenging Boundaries

This edited volume is an important and key resource for managers, researchers, and policy makers in the field of higher education and further education. *Challenging Boundaries* offers international insights into a radical new way of organizing post-secondary education that directly promotes a social justice agenda and the widening of student participation.

Around the world, post-secondary education is divided between universities and community-based colleges. Universities are typically concerned with "higher" education, while community-based colleges focus on "further" and technical education. In response to a range of social and economic forces there has been a growth in the number of dual sector institutions ("duals") that span this divide. *Challenging Boundaries* brings together leading international thinkers, policy analysts, academic managers, and researchers who detail how duals can provide relevant education to students and appropriate graduates for the economy, while also extending access to a broader range of students. *Challenging Boundaries* provides an analysis of the potential of duals in North America, UK, Norway, South Africa, and Australasia.

This volume:

- Challenges conventional thinking about post-secondary education
- Demonstrates how a number of institutions internationally are addressing the organizational, managerial, and cultural challenges of operating as dual sector universities
- Combines the latest research in the field from a range of international scholars with operational insights from university leaders
- Provides a key resource for education policy makers and researchers and students of educational policy and management at the Masters and Doctoral level

Neil Garrod is Executive Director, Enterprise and Civic Engagement, at Glyndŵr University, Wrexham (Wales), Honorary Professor in the Faculty of Economics at the University of Ljubljana (Slovenija) and Associate at the Centre for Higher Education Studies at the Institute of Education, University of London (UK). He is a Director of the Equality Challenge Unit, Treasurer and Director of HERO UK and Chair of Open College Network, Oxford, Thames & Chiltern.

Bruce Macfarlane is Professor of Higher Education at the University of Portsmouth (UK) where he is also Head of Academic Development. His previous books include *Teaching with Integrity* (Routledge, 2003) and *The Academic Citizen* (Routledge, 2006). He is a Vice Chair of the Society for Research into Higher Education.

Challenging Boundaries
Managing the Integration of Post-Secondary Education

HARVARD UNIVERSITY
GRADUATE SCHOOL OF EDUCATION
MONROE C. GUTMAN LIBRARY

Edited by Neil Garrod and Bruce Macfarlane

Routledge
Taylor & Francis Group

NEW YORK AND LONDON

LC
1039
.C43
2009

XI/0058

HARVARD UNIVERSITY
GRADUATE SCHOOL OF EDUCATION
MONROE C. GUTMAN LIBRARY

First published 2009
by Routledge
270 Madison Ave, New York, NY 10016

Simultaneously published in the UK
by Routledge
2 Park Square, Milton Park, Abingdon, Oxon OX14 4RN

Routledge is an imprint of the Taylor & Francis Group, an informa business

© 2009 Taylor & Francis

Typeset in Minion by
RefineCatch Limited, Bungay, Suffolk
Printed and bound in the United States of America on acid-free paper by
Edwards Brothers, Inc.

All rights reserved. No part of this book may be reprinted or reproduced or utilized in any form or by any electronic, mechanical or other means, now known or hereafter invented, including photocopying and recording, or in any information storage or retrieval system, without permission in writing from the publishers.

Trademark Notice: Product or corporate names may be trademarks or registered trademarks, and are used only for identification and explanation without intent to infringe.

Library of Congress Cataloging in Publication Data
   Challenging boundaries : managing the integration of post-secondary education / edited by Neil Garrod and Bruce Macfarlane.
   p. cm.
   Includes bibliographical references and index.
   1. Post-compulsory education.   I. Garrod, Neil   II. Macfarlane, Bruce,
   LC1039.C43 2009
   370–dc22
   2008026337

ISBN10: 0–415–98931–0 (hbk)
ISBN10: 0–415–98932–9 (pbk)
ISBN10: 0–203–88514–7 (ebk)

ISBN13: 978–0–415–98931–2 (hbk)
ISBN13: 978–0–415–98932–9 (pbk)
ISBN13: 978–0–203–88514–7 (ebk)

March 30, 2009

For Sonja, Gala and Aran

Contents

Part III
Operational Responses

Foreword

In 1996 I was appointed by the UK government to chair a committee to advise on the way forward in higher education. Not one of the seventeen members came from the world of further education—the other arm of post-school education in Britain—and I cannot recall anyone suggesting this was odd. Perhaps stimulated by the appointment of my committee, the body responsible for funding further education appointed a committee under the chairmanship of Helena Kennedy, QC, also with seventeen members, to advise on widening participation in further education. That committee did include one member from higher education, from a former polytechnic, but—and this is the main point—no one suggested the committees talk to each other, and so far as I can recall, as the committees moved on to report within a month of each other, there was no contact between them.

That could hardly happen today, and the publication of this collection of commentaries and reflections on the emergence of the transbinary institution is a testament to that. But for most countries covered by the book it is still early days for transbinary institutions, and there is still a lot of learning from experience to be done.

It would be the easier to make sense of a binary system if there were a solid, widely accepted definition of higher education differentiating it from vocationally oriented education, as the historically distinct purpose of the College of Further Education (further education in the UK and technical and further education in Australia) in serving students looking to advance their knowledge beyond the traditional academic curriculum of the school. It would be the more achievable if the role of higher education were static, but in its rapid migration from serving an intellectual elite to the provision of higher education for a mass system, its role has inevitably accommodated to the breadth of the students it serves and to the developing needs of society. In making this accommodation its institutions have become increasingly diverse in their missions. And yet the distinction between higher and further education exists strongly in the minds of the public, employers, and students, and most significantly in the minds of government and academics themselves.

In part the difference is reputational. In England, a notoriously class-conscious society, a well-known television sketch has three characters standing in a row, one remarkably tall, one equally remarkably short, and one in the middle of intermediate stature. The middle man, looking to Mr. Tall, comments that he is "higher than me," and "I look up to him," while the other is "shorter than me," and "I look down on him," or words to that effect. That describes the positional difference in attitudes to academic, technical, and trade education and training. This ranking of forms of education is probably more pronounced in England than elsewhere, but as the chapters of this book demonstrate, it is a positional differentiator that causes the institution of further education and the transbinary institution to have a tendency to transmute, albeit to varying degrees, towards what is perceived as, and financed, as higher education, with the associated possibility of the award of much-coveted funding for research. This is well illustrated by experience in Norway (chapter 4), Australia (chapter 5), and Canada (chapter 7), and by the introduction to the vocabulary of education of the term "isomorphism"—a term used frequently in this study—to recognize the tendency to move towards the more esteemed form of study, that is higher education.

Isomorphism is not unique to tertiary education. In the 1990s, in advising the British government on qualifications for sixteen- to nineteen-year-olds in the interests of lifting the standing of vocational awards, I recommended the merger of the two bodies responsible for overseeing academic and vocational awards and moving towards a common nomenclature. It was not long before the stronger, more esteemed culture of academic awards began to influence the character of learning for vocationally oriented awards to the detriment of an approach to learning that had proved apt for the pupils choosing the vocational route.

Chapter 6 describes the process by which the merger of Thames Valley University (a former polytechnic) and Reading College and School of Arts & Design (a further education college) came into being and the difficulties encountered. Following the demise of efforts to merge two institutions in Bradford with a long tradition of joint working, and the difficulties in another merger across the binary divide, it is hard to have foreseen the merger described in this chapter taking place unless both institutions had found themselves in crisis at the same time, and it is noteworthy that the staff in both were little involved in the process until it was a fait accompli. A true coming together of the two cultures is proving difficult to achieve, and the fact that the campus of the large Further Education College is at a considerable distance from that of the merging university gives grounds for hoping that the phenomenon of isomorphism will not readily overwhelm the much needed traditions and distinctiveness of further education.

The prospect for colleges of further education in Britain increasingly engaging in higher education and some of them reaching the tipping point suggested of 20 percent (see chapter 5) to become a truly transbinary institution have been enhanced, first by the introduction of a two-year foundation degree that can be offered by a college of further education under the academic supervision of the university that makes the award, and more recently by legislation making it possible for colleges that have an established reputation in this degree to obtain awarding powers in their own right. It will also be helped by the UK government's wish to extend the availability of higher education on a small scale to sizeable towns where it is not currently available. Where such towns have a college of further education, it may be that they will be able to bid successfully, perhaps in partnership with a university, to be the provider.

As to the English universities, in response to the acute national need to lift the proportion of the working population with skills at the level of the foundation degree, and the pressure on them for expansion to be led by employer demand rather than by their traditional mission, many universities, in response to the influence government can exert through funding, may offer more of the consciously "instrumental learning," especially for part-time students, that is the traditional territory of the colleges.

In fact, from experience I would suggest that while there are fundamental differences in emphasis between further and higher education in their missions in teaching, the difference does not necessarily derive intrinsically from differences in subject matter. It is rather a difference that derives from style and purpose. Accepting all the dangers of seeking to compress this into a few words, while higher education is distinctively concerned with "debating why," further education is more concerned with "learning how." To illustrate the point that an intrinsic difference does not necessarily lie in subject matter but rather in the way in which it is treated, a fleeting experience of the very practical subject of accountancy demonstrated to me that while mastering a skill, a body of knowledge, and "a rule book" is one demanding approach, another approach may distinctively concern itself with the whys and wherefores. It might be added that both in their distinctive ways may guide the student to a common understanding that, important as the Balance Sheet and the Profit and Loss Account are, the notes to the accounts, and what they say and do not say, merit a great deal of attention! Of course some disciplines lend themselves more fully to one approach than the other, but the essence of the difference lies in the objective of the study.

Those concerned with education know that no simple definition such as mine of the difference between higher and further education can be satisfactory, not least because what goes under the name of higher education is increasingly diverse. But what matters increasingly is how institutional structures can best meet the needs of society, and traditional names and boundaries, while powerful influences, will inescapably respond to these developing needs. Taking sectors as a whole as opposed to commenting on individual institutions, the traditional boundaries will need, for example, to be responsive to the imperative for lifelong learning, and ease of access for all, particularly those in work. Such considerations point to increasing provision across the binary line and to a place for the transbinary institution.

The value of this book lies in its distillation of experience to date for policy makers in government, managers in institutions, and forward-thinking leaders of staff associations, helping them to anticipate the very real issues that arise in creating such institutions. Perhaps one lesson is that purposive evolution within institutions is the most reliable formula; another that diversity of missions between institutions in both sectors is a strength; and a third that success in creating sustainable transbinary institutions depends on those forming public policy and managing institutions realizing that they need to create a framework that coheres with the aspirations of institutions and the staff within them.

Lord Ron Dearing
House of Lords, April 2008

Preface

Around the globe, post-secondary education is typically organized across two sectors, often described as further education (or vocational and technical education) and higher education. However, in an age of mass participation in post-secondary education such a divide appears anachronistic and ill-suited to the needs of modern economies or raising aspirations among disadvantaged and low-participation groups. In response to a range of social, economic, and political forces, there has been a growth in the number of "dual sector" or "comprehensive" post-secondary institutions that span this divide, for example in Australia, Canada, New Zealand, Norway, South Africa, and England. These institutions are frequently characterized and benchmarked by reference to others that do not attempt to bridge the boundary. This results in comprehensiveness being overlooked as a distinctive characteristic of a growing number of twenty-first-century post-secondary education institutions that, in many respects, renew and revitalize the civic mission of the university.

In this book, these distinctive characteristics are identified, discussed, and evaluated for the first time. In the process, the contributors question the conventional division between "further" and "higher" education and what a "university" is for. The chapters draw on the very latest research findings in this area from around the globe. Specifically the book:

- brings together a unique collection of case studies demonstrating how a range of institutions internationally are addressing the organizational, managerial, and cultural challenges of operating as comprehensive post-secondary institutions;
- combines the latest research in the field from a range of international scholars with operational insights from institutional leaders; and
- provides a key resource for education policy makers, researchers, and students of post-secondary policy and management at master's and doctoral level.

Contributors

The Editors

Neil Garrod is Executive Director, Enterprise and Civic Engagement, at Glyndŵr University, Wrexham (Wales), Honorary Professor in the Faculty of Economics at the University of Ljubljana (Slovenija), and Associate at the Centre for Higher Education Studies at the Institute of Education, University of London (UK). He is a Director of the Equality Challenge Unit, Treasurer and Director of HERO UK and Chair of Open College Network, Oxford, Thames & Chiltern.

Bruce Macfarlane is Professor of Higher Education at the University of Portsmouth, where he is also Head of Academic Development. His previous books include *Teaching with Integrity*, *The Academic Citizen*, and *Researching with Integrity*. He is a Vice Chair of the Society for Research into Higher Education and a Senior Fellow of the UK Higher Education Academy.

For the period 2004–2008, Neil Garrod was Deputy Vice-Chancellor and Bruce Macfarlane was Head of Educational Development at Thames Valley University.

The Contributors

Roger Barnsley was President and Vice-Chancellor of Thompson Rivers University, Canada, from 1998 to 2008.

Lord Ron Dearing is a former Chancellor of the University of Nottingham and Chairman of the University for Industry. In 1996–7 he chaired the National Committee of Inquiry into UK higher education.

Robert Fleming is Associate Vice President Academic, Kwantlen Polytechnic University, Canada.

Svein Kyvik is a Senior Researcher at the Norwegian Institute for Studies in Innovation, Research, and Education (NIFU STEP), Norway.

Gordon R. Lee is Vice President Strategic Services, Kwantlen Polytechnic University, Canada.

Gavin Moodie is Principal Policy Advisor, Griffith University, Australia.

Bronte Neyland is General Manager, Marketing and Recruitment, at Victoria University International, Victoria, Australia.

Martin Oosthuizen is Professor and Senior Director of the Centre for Planning and Institutional Development, Nelson Mandela Metropolitan University, South Africa.

Romulo Pinheiro is a Research Fellow at the Institute for Educational Research (PFI), The Faculty of Education, University of Oslo, Norway.

John Sparks is Associate Vice-President, Legal Affairs, Thompson Rivers University, Canada.

Leslie "Skip" Triplett was President of Kwantlen University College (redesignated Kwantlen Polytechnic University in 2008), Canada, until his retirement in 2008.

Liz Warr is Director of Educational Development, Writtle College, UK.

John Webster was the President of Unitec, New Zealand, until his retirement in 2007.

Leesa Wheelahan is senior lecturer in adult and vocational education at Griffith University, Australia.

John White is Emeritus Professor of Philosophy of Education, Institute of Education, University of London, UK.

Acknowledgements

The book results from a project about the challenges of dual sector management, which has been supported by the Leadership, Governance and Management fund of the Higher Education Funding Council for England. The project was informed by a network of other dual sector institutions both in England and internationally. In particular, we would like to acknowledge the collaboration of institutions and colleagues in Australia, Canada, New Zealand, Norway, and South Africa, and the insights they gave us into post-secondary arrangements in these countries.

We would also like to thank Alice Chan and Becky Sadler for their help with proofreading the manuscript.

Acknowledgments

I
Challenges

1

Further, Higher, Better?

NEIL GARROD AND BRUCE MACFARLANE

Introduction

Post-secondary education is on the move. Statistics from the Organisation for Economic Co-operation and Development (OECD) indicate the global expansion in student numbers and achievement at the tertiary level (OECD 2006). This expansion reflects a widening of access to new groups of students that have historically been excluded from post-secondary education and the changing needs of a global, knowledge-based economy. Both are reflected in the diversity of institutional form adopted to meet this growing demand. Universities are typically distinguished from other institutions that exclusively or mainly provide "further," "technical," "vocational," or "trades" education. Nomenclature varies, as the authors contributing to this book from Australia, Canada, New Zealand, Norway, South Africa, and England help to illustrate. In this chapter we use the term "post-secondary" while authors of other chapters use, variously, "post-school," "post-compulsory," "comprehensive," "transbinary," and "tertiary." These differences of language aside, the further–higher distinction, in most educational systems across the world, is reflected in a pyramid of institutional forms with universities sitting at its apex. This book sets out to explore the validity of this fundamental divide on the basis of its rationality and its implications for economic and social progress in the twenty-first century. It aims to challenge this conventional boundary.

A Fuzzying Divide

Around the globe, post-secondary education is typically organized across two sectors, often described as further education (or vocational and technical education) and higher education. But why should this division persist? In an age of mass participation in post-secondary education this historic divide appears anachronistic, based largely on a bureaucratic rather than philosophical rationale (White, chapter 2). In other words, entrenched administrative arrangements appear to separate post-secondary education in a way that is not justified from a knowledge-based or epistemological perspective.

Until comparatively recent times, with a few notable exceptions such as in the United States, receiving a higher education has been an opportunity restricted to the elite in society. In the last twenty years higher education in many developed countries has opened up to greater participation, and previously elite systems have been redefined as mass or universal as a result (Trow 1974). In England, more than 40 percent of eighteen- to thirty-year olds now go to university. In Europe, participation has grown tenfold since the mid-1950s (White 2001), and rapid expansion is also now taking place in many developing countries such as those in central and southeast Asia. The logic of the division between further and higher education looks more tenuous in an age of mass or universal higher education. Going to university is increasingly seen as a right rather than a privilege and the historic, class-based inequalities that underpin the distinction between further and higher education are looking out of step with this expansion.

There are other trends that make the further–higher education distinction questionable. The university has become a place where the development of student skills, attributes and professional competences for the workplace takes place as much as the pursuit of "pure" or "academic" disciplines. Universities have expanded their provision of vocational subjects that might previously have been offered at a sub-bachelor's degree level. Such incorporation has a long history. In the nineteenth century subjects like engineering were included in the university curriculum; business and management studies took their place in the 1960s, while in the 1990s the nursing and allied health professions were incorporated. While universities have always responded to new social and economic conditions by expanding and modernizing their range of provision, we have now reached a stage at which it is no longer accurate to talk of "vocational" education taking place separately from the university. Indeed, it has never really been accurate to talk in these terms as many universities, from medieval times through to the Victorian age, were institutions that trained clerics, medics, and lawyers.

At the same time that universities are broadening the vocational and practical nature of their provision, there are more further education or community colleges offering higher education programs, often in partnership with universities. In England it is estimated that around one in nine students, or 12 percent, experience higher education within a further education context. The percentage in Scotland is higher still (Parry 2005). The UK government sees so-called "mixed economy colleges," containing both further and higher education teaching provision, as playing an important role in expanding higher education, especially at sub-degree level (Department for Education and Skills 2003). Recently, as a result of the *Further Education and Training Act* passed in 2007, the UK government has also decided that colleges of further education should be allowed to offer their own two-year foundation degrees, the equivalent of associate degrees in the United States. Outside the UK, the former community colleges of British Columbia in Canada, along with two other post-secondary providers, have been recently redesignated as universities while in other countries, such as Australia and Norway, stratified or binary systems have collapsed in recent years. The divide between further and higher education is clearly fuzzying.

There are economic as well as social reasons for questioning the division between further and higher education. A modern economy needs graduates who are able to blend academic knowledge with the skills and attributes required by employers (Leitch 2006; Department for Education and Skills 2003). In an ever more competitive global business environment, graduates need intercultural competence and an adaptable mind-set as much as a conventional knowledge base. This makes it dubious whether it is still appropriate to separate "knowledge" from "skills" by different types of post-secondary institution. Such trends are recognized through national reports on post-secondary education that express the view that skills are an integral part of higher education (National Committee of Inquiry into Higher Education 1997; Leitch 2006). In turn, the integration of knowledge and skills signaled by these reports raises fundamental issues for curriculum design and credit recognition (Biggs 1999). This all suggests that it is more realistic to think of post-secondary education as a continuum of learning rather than neatly divided into separate further and higher education sectors. In short, the idea of what it means to be a university is being reshaped by social and economic change.

Considerable efforts have been made to harmonize the higher education curriculum in Europe through the Bologna process (European Commission 2007). This has been designed to make it possible for students to transfer between systems and for the mutual recognition of qualifications. Although originally intended as a Europe-wide initiative, forty-six countries from within and beyond Europe are now involved and it is cited as a contributory factor in major academic restructuring in jurisdictions as distant as Australia (University of Melbourne 2007). However, while considerable effort has gone into the Bologna process, curriculum integration is required *vertically* between further and higher education forms of tertiary education as well as *horizontally* between universities across the world.

Widening Participation

Despite the rise in student numbers in higher education, governments in many developed and developing country contexts have expressed a desire to see participation expand still further. In the UK, the government has expressed a commitment to increase the percentage of eighteen- to thirty-year olds in higher education to 50 percent by the year 2010. Elsewhere in the world, and despite the costs, governments are seeking to expand their provision of higher education from more modest foundations to tackle skills shortages. In South Africa, the goal is to have a 20 percent participation rate by 2015 (MacGregor 2007).

However, there are barriers to further expansion of higher education. Much of this growth has taken place as a result of more middle-class students and those from aspirational groups within the lower socioeconomic classes going to university. If governments are to succeed in further expanding higher education, and addressing deep-rooted social disparities in participation, it is necessary to find a way of encouraging greater involvement from more groups within society that have been conventionally excluded from higher education or for whom university is still beyond their expectations in life. In some national contexts, notably Canada, Australia, and New Zealand, indigenous or "first nations" groups have historically been disadvantaged and participate at much lower levels in higher education (Wheelahan, chapter 3; Webster, chapter 8; Neyland and Triplett, chapter 12). Effective responses need to be found to ensure equality of opportunity for groups that are under-represented in tertiary education if governments are to succeed in their objectives to achieve target participation rates and thereby improve social cohesion and support economic growth. Moreover, students drawn from disadvantaged backgrounds are less likely to be able to relocate to study. Here, the geography of countries such as Canada and Australia is an important consideration in any strategy to improve participation rates in post-secondary education. In creating five new universities in British Columbia in 2008 following a review of tertiary provision (Plant 2007), the state premier referred specifically to the importance of these institutions in meeting the educational needs of particular geographic regions as well as providing applied and professional programs that will serve the entire province (Palmer 2008).

The Emergence of "Duals"

In response to these social, economic, and political forces, there has been a growth in the number of "dual sector" or comprehensive post-secondary institutions that span the divide between further and higher education in countries such as Australia, Canada, New Zealand, South Africa, and England. These institutions are frequently characterized and benchmarked by reference to others that do not attempt to bridge the boundary. This can result in comprehensiveness being overlooked as a distinctive characteristic of a growing number of twenty-first-century post-secondary education institutions that, in many respects, renew and revitalize the civic mission of the university to serve its communities by providing access to educational opportunity for all.

These new institutions have evolved either through mergers between existing universities and other tertiary and further education providers, such as in Australia, England, and South Africa, or through the redesignation of institutions that originated as further education or community colleges, as in Canada or, to some extent, in England and the UK more widely. Many duals have emerged from contexts where there has been a desire to address economic, social, and racial inequalities. In South Africa, the merger of a number of research universities with technikons is part of a process of educational restructuring that also addresses the elimination of racial divisions in the post-apartheid era.

What is meant by a "dual"? Many universities have small pockets of further education work, perhaps as a result of language and other community exchange programs. A number of further education, community, or junior colleges contain elements of higher education provision, especially in English mixed-economy colleges. On this basis, most post-secondary institutions worldwide could lay claim to duality. In explaining the dual identity of Thames Valley University, the first English dual, Garrod (2005: 57) argued that it had an "equal commitment given to both higher and further education." This implies that the numbers of student registrations, while not necessarily equal, should at least demonstrate that both sub-degree and degree-level studies are central to the institution's mission. This is a theme taken up by Moodie (chapter 5), who also considers the question of a dual's commitment to research. He defines a dual as an institution that has a substantial number of sub-degree students as well as higher education provision *and* awards a minimum number of doctoral degrees per year. He sets the benchmark at 20 percent provision in both sectors and at least 20 doctoral graduate completions per annum. Moodie draws on Grodzins's (1958) metaphor of a "tipping point" to argue that a dual is characterized by this "20:20" rule. The importance of research and scholarship implicit in this 20:20 rule would appear critical if duals are to effectively challenge the existing boundary rather than simply relocate it (Garrod and Macfarlane, chapter 11; Garrod and Warr, chapter 13).

The Challenges

Duals are faced with significant challenges in an environment still dominated by the conventional division between further and higher education. They must cope with strategic issues related to both their internal and their external environments. Externally, duals must often deal with separate government funding and audit arrangements for further and higher education. Internally, they must develop seamless curriculum pathways to foster student progression (Garrod and Warr, chapter 13), structure career paths for faculty that traverse the boundary between further and higher education (Garrod and Macfarlane, chapter 11), and develop a system of governance for the whole institution (Barnsley and Sparks, chapter 10).

Duals face a large number of practical problems. Probably the most important practical issue is ensuring that the institution provides a "seamless" route through qualification levels that maximizes the potential for student progression. The nature of this progression, however, should not be understood as just upward. Many learners return to educational institutions to undertake a professional or trades qualification having previously obtained a "higher" academic qualification. Duals may be particularly well placed to offer a suitable environment for this type of adult returner.

The creation of seamless pathways for students also depends on a dual being able to meet the demands of a range of external audit and validation authorities. All universities or colleges must meet such requirements, but a dual has an additional set of such bodies with which to cope (Garrod and Warr, chapter 13). Meeting the formal requirements of quality assurance of the curriculum makes seamless pathways available. A number of contributors argue that institutions containing both further and higher education are handicapped by the need to account to separate funding, standards, and quality agencies. Writing about the New Zealand context, Webster (chapter 8) highlights that even within a formally unified tertiary sector boundaries remain.

Even where it is possible for students to progress within a single institution between different academic levels, it does not automatically follow that they will take up such opportunities (Garrod, chapter 6). Higher education involves a different set of assumptions about the level of independence, the nature of learning, and the maturity of the learner than does further education. As a result, universities can sometimes appear to offer a cold and uncaring environment for students used to more contact time with teachers and lecturers (Christie *et al.*, 2006). Furthermore, university teachers may see themselves primarily as researchers and not regard teaching as their principal or preferred occupation (Becher and Trowler 2001). For these academics, research will rate as a higher priority, linked to their self-identity as researchers and their future career prospects.

Wheelahan (chapter 3) argues that one of the major barriers facing dual sector universities in Australia is culture. She highlights the key role of academic staff as "boundary spanners" able to connect further and higher education and smooth student progression opportunities in the process. However, in reality few academic staff tend to be "literate" across the conventional boundaries of post-secondary education. Their identities, and their academic careers, are shaped by one or other of the post-secondary sectors. Here there are issues of equality of opportunity for faculty as well as students in a dual in gaining access to and support to pursue research and scholarship. This is about contractual arrangements but also about creating an environment that is inclusive (Garrod and Macfarlane, chapter 11).

One of the most important decisions facing duals is their organizational formation. By definition, most such institutions are relatively recent either in being formed or in the re-designation of their mission. Elsewhere we have suggested that duals are faced by a critical decision when determining the extent to which they develop a *unitary* organizational form by integrating faculty, services, campuses, and governance arrangements or opting to maintain a *binary* divide between their further and higher education provision (Garrod and Macfarlane 2007). This is a complex decision to make and much will depend on the nature of the circumstances in which the institution may find itself. Merging institutions and the processes and personnel within each former institution is, however, only the first step to creating a new common culture. In his chapter on the creation of the first English dual sector university through a merger between a university and an English further education college, Garrod reflects on the considerable cultural challenges this entailed (chapter 6).

Finally, duals are faced with the challenge of justifying and explaining their very distinctiveness. They do not fit conventional classification as either a further or a higher education institution. Nor is their mission necessarily captured by monochromatic adjectives such as "teaching-led" or "research-led." This poses a challenge for communicating the distinctive mission of a dual through lobbying government, working with other universities, and engaging the community (Neyland and Triplett, chapter 12)

Academic Drift

Perhaps the central challenge facing duals, particularly those that have origins as community or further education colleges, is to avoid the risk of mission or "academic drift." The term "academic drift" refers to a process whereby lower status, non-university institutions aspire to and work towards becoming more like universities (Pratt and Burgess 1974). The tendency was first noted in relation to British polytechnics seeking to ape the defining features of universities in the 1970s and has also been recognized in relation to the former Australian colleges of advanced education and South African universities of technology (Harman 1977; Kraak 2006). Arguably, the same process goes back even further and may be applied to the drift of many English civic universities away from their founding intentions as mainly vocationally oriented (Macfarlane 2007). Thus the definition of a university has changed and developed over time. As older institutions have moved away from their vocational roots, this has left a vacuum that has been filled by new forms of post-secondary institution.

At a broader level of analysis, organizational theorists refer to this phenomenon as "mimetic isomorphism" whereby organizations facing similar environmental conditions tend to model themselves on comparators that they perceive to be successful (DiMaggio and Powell 1983). For example, the globalization of higher education has encouraged technical and vocational post-secondary institutions, not formally titled as universities, to adopt the more widely understood nomenclature of "university." An illustration of this phenomenon is the way that polytechnics in Finland have recently started to refer to themselves, in English, as "universities of applied sciences," also representing a shift towards a stronger research focus (Dobson 2008). Why, it might be asked, should duals be any different from their predecessors in drifting away from their original intentions to retain equal commitment to further as well as higher education? After all, education is a positional good, the possession of which confers status on individuals and affords them a place in the social hierarchy (Moodie, chapter 5).

Academic drift or isomorphism is a particular concern of a number of contributors to this book. Fleming and Lee (chapter 7) identify the dangers of isomorphic tendencies for comprehensive post-secondary institutions in British Columbia, Canada. The temptation to drift away from commitment to the roots of such institutions as vocationally focused community colleges is a risk associated with their gradual redesignation as universities with degree-awarding powers. Similarly, Pinheiro and Kyvik (chapter 4) comment on the way that within the Norwegian tertiary sector the student transfer system has had the unintended consequence of leading to the academic drift of the colleges and a weakening of their distinctive vocational mission. The same tendency may be occurring in a South African context, where Oosthuizen (chapter 9) remarks that the boundary between comprehensive universities and universities of technology is becoming increasingly indistinct.

The United States was the first major economy to develop a system of mass education. Led by California, where so-called "junior colleges" were created in the early twentieth century as extensions of senior public high schools, a mass system of post-secondary education was developed by the mid-1930s. The rest of the United States was to follow by the end of that decade (Douglass 2004). Mission drift has been prevented by the preservation of institutional diversity and the development of strong connections between the junior and community college system and the universities (Douglass 2004). Dual sector universities face the major challenge of achieving mission extension while avoiding mission drift. They will thereby occupy territory that represents a new type of tertiary education, one that continues to be responsive to community needs in the coming era of universal higher education.

The Chapters

The book is organized in three sections. The **first section** will identify the challenges that face institutions and policy makers looking to develop systems and universities that unify post-secondary education. These challenges include perceptions with respect to the aims of further as opposed to higher education institutions, the nature of academic identity, the impact of post-secondary education arrangements on wider social issues, and the response of institutions to these issues in the formation of comprehensive universities.

The **second section** includes a number of case studies from Norway, Australia, England, Canada, New Zealand, and South Africa. Through them is charted the way in which the separate sectors interact; the emergence of dual sector universities; the importance of their title and status; and the impact of government and the market on the location of sector boundaries. The chapters also reflect the experiences of comprehensive post-secondary universities managing across structural and policy boundaries between further and higher education within these different national contexts.

The **third section** focuses on the operational challenges of managing a comprehensive post-secondary institution. It includes contributions from institutional leaders and academic managers on the key leadership and operational issues of governance, curriculum, culture, and community. A variety of ideas and strategies for developing a coherent institutional identity across sector boundaries are presented.

Conclusion

It is ironic that, in various parts of the world, elite pathways through educational systems from elementary school through to university are often the most integrated. In England, the leading public schools continue to dominate admission into Oxford and Cambridge universities (Ward 2007). In 2006, over a third of all students leaving Eton, one of England's top public schools, were accepted into Oxford or Cambridge universities (Eton College 2008). In other countries, elite universities even have their own formally designated feeder schools on campus, which practically guarantee student progression. In Japan, the country's oldest private university, Keio, gives places to 99 percent of students from its own senior high school (Keio University 2008). However, these examples of well-integrated educational arrangements largely serve to do the opposite of that intended by dual sector institutions, by perpetuating rather than breaking down economic and social inequality.

The challenge for duals is to make the progression of students from socially disadvantaged backgrounds as seamless as for those from privileged minorities. This is a hard task but one that is vital for the future social and economic well-being of modern society. The contributors to this collection indicate the breadth and depth of the challenges faced by institutions seeking to bridge the divide between the sectors. These are organizational, structural, political, financial, and, above all perhaps, cultural. The modern challenge is to achieve mission expansion without mission drift by enabling students to move seamlessly through different phases of post-secondary education. Addressing this challenge is essential if duals are to resist the temptations of academic drift in seeking to mimic elite universities. In short, they must remain committed to transcending, and not just challenging, the boundaries.

References

Becher, T. and P. Trowler. 2001. *Academic Tribes and Territories: Intellectual Enquiry and the Cultures of Disciplines*, Buckingham: Society for Research into Higher Education/Open University Press.

Biggs, J. 1999. *Teaching for Quality Learning in University*, Buckingham: Society for Research into Higher Education/Open University Press.

Christie, H., V.E. Cree, J. Hounsell, V. McCune and L. Tett. 2006. From college to university: looking backwards, looking forwards, in *Research in Post-Compulsory Education*, 11:3, 351–65.

Department for Education and Skills. 2003. *The Future of Higher Education*, London: Department for Education and Skills.

DiMaggio, P.J. and W.W. Powell. 1983. The iron cage revisited: institutional isomorphism and collective rationality in organizational fields, *American Sociological Review*, 48, 147–60.

Dobson, I. 2008. Finland: polytechnics call themselves universities, *University World News*, 13 April, http://www.universityworldnews.com/article.php?story=2008041014313989 (accessed April 20, 2008).

Douglass, J. 2004. A Transatlantic persuasion: America's path to access and equity in higher education. In *Understanding Mass Higher Education: Comparative Perspectives on Access*, ed. I. McNay, London/New York: Routledge, pp. 211–46.

Eton College. 2008. *Destinations of Leavers*, http://www.etoncollege.com/default.asp (accessed March 20, 2008).

European Commission. 2007. *The Bologna Process*, http://ec.europa.eu/education/policies/educ/bologna/bologna_en.html (accessed May 22, 2008).

Garrod, N. 2005. The building of a dual sector university. In *The Tertiary Moment: What Road to Inclusive Higher Education?*, ed. C. Duke, Leicester: NIACE, pp. 57–73.

Garrod, N. and B. Macfarlane. 2007. Scoping the duals: the structural challenges of combining further and higher education in post-compulsory institutions, *Higher Education Quarterly*, 61:4, 578–96.

Grodzins, M. 1958. *The Metropolitan Area as a Racial Problem*, Pittsburgh: University of Pittsburgh Press.

Harman, G. 1977. Academic staff and academic drift in Australian Colleges of Advanced Education, *Higher Education*, 6, 313–35.

Keio University. 2008. *Keio University: A Tradition of Excellence*, Tokyo: Keio University.

Kraak A. 2006. "Academic drift" in South African universities of technology: Beneficial or detrimental?, *Perspectives in Education*, 24:3, 135–52.

Leitch, S. 2006. *Prosperity for all in the Global Economy: World Class Skills*, http://www.hm-treasury.gov.uk/media/6/4/leitch_finalreport051206.pdf (accessed March 12, 2008).

Macfarlane, B. 2007. *The Academic Citizen: The Virtue of Service in University Life*, Abingdon: Routledge.

MacGregor, K. 2007. Wanted: 100,000 more students, *World University News*, http://www.universityworldnews.com/article.php?story=200711300951265 (accessed March 14, 2008).

National Committee of Inquiry into Higher Education. 1997. *Higher Education in the Learning Society: Report of the National Committee*, London: The Stationery Office.

OECD (Organisation for Economic Co-operation and Development). 2006. *Education at a Glance*, Paris: Organisation for Economic Co-operation and Development.

Palmer, V. 2008. Campbell makes universities in name, not necessarily in money, *Vancouver Sun*, 30 April.

Parry, G. 2005. Why the English are different. In *The Tertiary Moment: What Road to Inclusive Higher Education?*, ed. C. Duke, Leicester: NIACE, pp. 117–32.

Plant, G. P. 2007. *Campus 2020: Thinking Ahead: The Report*, Province of British Columbia: Ministry of Advanced Education.

Pratt, J. and T. Burgess. 1974. *Polytechnics: A Report*, London: Pitman.

Trow, M. 1974. Problems in the transition from elite to mass higher education. In *Policies for Higher Education*, ed. Organisation for Economic Co-operation and Development, Paris: OECD, pp. 51–101.

University of Melbourne. 2007. The Making of the Melbourne Model, *The University of Melbourne Voice*, 1:3, http://uninews.unimelb.edu.au/articleid_4131.html (accessed March 21, 2008).

Ward, D. 2007. More pupils from top public schools getting in to Oxford, *The Guardian*, March 5, p. 7.

White, T. 2001. *Investing in People: Higher Education in Ireland from 1960 to 2000*, Dublin: Institute of Public Administration.

2

Further and Higher: A Philosophical Divide?

JOHN WHITE

Introduction

Post-compulsory education in England has long been based on the division between higher and further education. We have come to accept it as an indelible part of the educational landscape. But is it?

In the past, other distinctions made in the educational system have also seemed unquestionable—for instance, the separation of children into "academic" and "non-academic." What made the latter division apparently unchallengeable was its alleged basis in the psychology of intelligence. This grounding is now almost universally discredited. What seemed like an innate—and therefore unalterable—difference turned out to be nothing of the kind. The academic discipline of psychology had been used to lend credence to a division introduced for political reasons.

It is becoming clearer with the years that the higher–further dichotomy is also not set in stone. The recent growth of dual sector universities (or "duals") in different parts of the world testifies to this—especially those duals organized on unitary rather than binary lines, that is, where distinctions between the higher and further aspects of the institution are broken down at point after point (Garrod and Macfarlane 2007).

Yet the idea that there is something special about higher education that marks it neatly off from further education is still strong. Once again we find reliance on an academic discipline to justify the distinction—in this case, not psychology, but philosophy. The first part of this chapter examines the most celebrated philosophical defense of the uniqueness of higher education, that by Ronald Barnett in his 1990 book *The Idea of Higher Education* and in related articles. The second section moves on to more recent philosophical arguments in the same vein. The final part of the chapter discusses the accepted view that school education should ideally, for students judged suitable for it, be followed immediately by a university education. It also argues, more broadly, for a unitary, and less age-related, system of post-compulsory education.

Barnett's Argument

The core of Ronald Barnett's case is that there are aims that any institution of higher education worthy of the name must embrace, aims built into our understanding of what higher education is. In Barnett's view higher education is "emancipatory." It liberates students from the narrow intellectual perspectives that would constrain them if confined to their specialism, enabling them to think critically about its assumptions and to see it in relation to other areas of thought. Since knowledge is culturally situated, this process gives students insight into the nature of their own society and so into themselves, making them better capable of acting in the world.

> Key elements in "emancipation" are self-understanding and self-empowerment.
>
> (Barnett 1990: 199)

> In the higher education sketched out here, students come into themselves. The challenge on the educator is to provide an experience in which the student can be released into herself.
>
> (Barnett 1994: 191)

Drawing on Habermas, Barnett contrasts his emancipatory conception of higher education with other approaches favoring discrete disciplines on the one hand and service to the economy on the other. *All* students in higher education, not only those with a particular predilection for such things, are to be inducted into discipline-transcending reflection and ultimately into a more adequate self-understanding. Why?

Basically, Barnett's grounds rest on an appeal to the nature of higher education itself. If we examine this, we see that it cannot but be emancipatory. Provided, therefore, that a student of French or forestry is intent on acquiring a higher education and not some more limited kind of training or initiation, he or she is logically committed to embracing its liberating aims.

There are two types of argument on which Barnett relies to make his case: the first philosophical, the second historical; the former focusing on an analysis of the concept of higher education, the latter on how higher education has developed over time.

The Philosophical Argument

The philosophical argument revolves round the embedded meanings in the two linguistic components of higher education, the terms "higher" and "education." On "education," Barnett has been influenced by R. S. Peters's view (1959) that education does not have aims outside itself. It is not a means to some external end, but something worthwhile in itself. "In my view," says Peters, "many disputes about the aims of education are disputes about principles of procedure rather than about 'aims' in the sense of objectives to be arrived at by taking appropriate means" (p. 90). The progressive who objects to the traditionalist's aim of molding boys into Christian gentlemen, for instance, is really arguing against "treating children as little manikins, as material to be poured into an adult mode. A child . . . should be treated with respect as a person" (p. 91).

In Peters's view, what the aims of education are can be discovered, at least in part, by reflection on what the concept of education logically implies. Respect for the pupil as a person is one such embedded element, helping to distinguish education proper from activities like indoctrination or manipulation. Since educating, in Peters's view, also necessarily involves initiating pupils into intrinsically worthwhile activities, expanding their understanding and reasoning abilities and encouraging them to take a synoptic view of the knowledge they have across several domains ("cognitive perspective"), it is clear how what might seem at first blush external educational goals, like giving pupils a thorough grounding in the pursuit of knowledge for its own sake, or encouraging them to bridge the arts–sciences divide, are in fact derivable from the content of the concept of education itself.

Although he is not committed to all the elements that Peters sees as necessarily embedded in the concept of education, Barnett adopts a similar position to him on aims. He sees himself as doing for the aims of higher education what Peters did for the aims of education in general, holding that reflection on the nature of higher education will reveal aims implicit in it (Barnett 1988: 239). This leads him to focus on what is implied in the term "higher":

> "[H]igher education" is essentially a matter of the development of the mind of the individual student. It is not just any kind of development that the idea points to. An educational process can be termed higher education when the student is carried on to levels of reasoning which make possible critical reflection on his or her experiences, whether consisting of propositional knowledge or of knowledge through action. These levels of reasoning and reflection are "higher," because they enable the student to take a view (from above, as it were) of what has been learned. Simply, "higher education" resides in the higher-order states of mind.
>
> (Barnett 1990: 202)

> [T]he massing of units of information is not a higher order mental act constitutive of *higher* education. For that, mental acts have to take place which give individuals power to deploy and manipulate such items of information. The mental acts marked out by such terms as analysis, synthesis, evaluation, criticism and even imagination are higher order acts.
>
> (Barnett 1994: 85)

As these quotations show, Barnett sees higher education as conceptually requiring higher-order, critical thinking about the knowledge one already possesses, enabling one to see it in larger contexts.

An assessment of the philosophical argument must start from Peters's views on the aims of education. These are far from trouble-free. A main difficulty, now widely acknowledged by philosophers of education, is that Peters's purportedly objective "analysis" of the concept of education hides value judgments, which not all would share, about the directions in which educators should proceed (Dray 1973). Peters's vision of education belongs to the tradition—always especially strong in Britain—that promotes the pursuit of knowledge and understanding for its own sake. This aim has its rivals—empowering pupils, for instance, to lead a self-directed life not just intellectually but more globally. If one writes "aiming at learning for its own sake" into one's definition of education from the start, it is easy to see how such aims can be derived from reflection on the concept. But for those who do not make this first move, the conclusion cuts no ice.

Barnett's model for deriving the aims of higher education, then, is unpropitious. His own contribution to this derivation is, unfortunately, no more convincing. He proceeds, as Peters does, via seeing what is embedded in a concept—in Barnett's case, the concept "higher" as used in "higher education." Barnett sees this as connoting higher-order thinking; and this leads him to the "emancipatory" aim. There are three problems about this.

First, why take "higher" as implying higher-order thinking? Higher education is certainly at a different level from school education. If we like, we can say it is at a higher level. But this rests on an administrative, not an epistemological, distinction. Junior school education is higher than infant school and secondary school education is higher than junior school. Higher education is simply a further stage. We could have used, and sometimes do use, a different term for it: "tertiary," or "university" education. Nothing hangs on the term "higher" as such. Thus allegedly necessary features that are peculiar to "higherness" cannot be milked out of it. The Italians' term for higher education is *insegnamento superiore*, where *superiore* also has the connotations of the English word "superior." Could an Italian philosopher then try to make a case that higher education is *more valuable* than school education? The suggestion is ridiculous.

Nothing, as I say, hangs on the use of the word "higher." Yet Barnett sees an important—logical, rather than administrative—difference between higher education and further education:

> [Higher education] is not "further education": it is not simply more of what has gone before. Rather, the term is a reference to a level of individual development over and above that normally implied by the term "education." There is, therefore, a conceptual distinction between the two processes actually built into our language.
>
> (Barnett 1990: 6)

It is not clear why "further" education should be taken to imply more of the same. But this is really beside the point. Britain has various sorts of post-school institutions, falling under different sets of regulations, and it makes obvious sense to give the different sectors special names. With different political arrangements, the post-school structure could be quite otherwise. There is no essence to further education, just as there is no essence to higher education: any line between them is bureaucratic, not Platonic. (My Spanish dictionary translates them both as *educacion superior!*)

The first problem with Barnett's account, then, is that there is nothing about our administrative preference for the word "higher" that should lead us to think that higher education is distinguished by its reliance on higher-order thinking.

The second is that higher-order thinking, as described, is not peculiar to higher education and can be found in school and indeed home education. In academic contexts, older schoolchildren are often encouraged to think about the epistemological bases of the history or science that they are studying, while a feature of good personal and social education, even for younger children, is getting children to reflect on their own actions, desires, and emotions in the interests of winnowing out those less worthy or otherwise inadequate. There is nothing in the nature of higher-order thinking that associates it particularly with over-eighteens. Indeed, Harry Frankfurt (1988), in a well-known argument in ethics, has made the capacity that human beings have for second-order desiring (*wanting*, for instance, to be the sort of person who does not *want* to smoke, be unkind, etc.) the defining feature that sets us apart from other animals. As they grow up, children are inducted into such higher-order thinking as part of their normal upbringing. Barnett may reply to this that it is not just any kind of higher-order thinking that he sees as associated with higher education, but only that which takes as its object elements in academic disciplines. But even this, as just mentioned, is present in school education, even in some cases below senior secondary level. In so far as it is present, according to Barnett's criteria, these children are experiencing "higher education" while still at school. We could talk in this way if we wanted to, but it would amount to a massive—and potentially confusing—revision of our usual practice.

Third, there is a gap between higher-order thinking, even construed more narrowly as reflecting upon the academic knowledge one has at the first order, and Barnett's "emancipation," key elements of which are self-understanding and self-empowerment. My higher-order mental powers may indeed enable me "to take up a stance in relation to discrete units of information, to discriminate between them, to classify them, to see relationships between them and to set them in a larger context" (Barnett 1994: 85). As a student of Russian, I can think about the Russian word for "mother"—*mat* (genitive *materi*)—and wonder just what connections it has with the Latin *mater*. But this kind of higher-order thinking need have nothing to do with self-knowledge or self-empowerment. True, self-knowledge must involve higher-order thinking of some kind, but higher-order thinking does not necessarily imply self-knowledge.

For these three reasons, Barnett's attempt to derive general aims of higher education from the fact that it is *higher* fails.

Before we leave Barnett's philosophical argument, there is one further point. It is about the scope of conceptual analysis as a philosophical procedure. Barnett has attempted a conceptual analysis of "higher education," just as Peters attempted one of "education" in general. But are these the *kinds* of concepts one can usefully investigate in this way? Not all concepts are susceptible to this kind of probing. There is nothing philosophically interesting to say, for instance, about the concept of a pencil or the concept of broccoli. Is "higher education" more like these two concepts than it is like the concepts of "time" or "truth" or "liberty," whose suitability for philosophical investigation no one could doubt?

Why are the latter so obviously suitable? This has to do with the deep embeddedness of ideas like these in our conceptual schemes and their interrelatedness with others of similar status. Higher education is not a concept fundamental to our thinking. It is an administrative category, found useful in a society like my own, British, for certain purposes. It is not difficult to imagine its absence. Rather than making a distinction among forms of post-compulsory education between "higher" and "further" and perhaps other kinds of education, a society could operate with some more inclusive notion. Reference has already been made to dual sector institutions, or duals. These could well presage a more general rejection of the dichotomy and the creation of a unified system of post-compulsory education in its place. The final section of the chapter will say somewhat more about this.

Given the problems to which Barnett's philosophical thesis give rise, it is best abandoned. In this area, a more fitting role for philosophical argument lies in critique of current assumptions about the divided nature of post-school learning than in an attempt to shore them up.

The Historical Argument

As well as appealing directly to what he sees embedded in the notion of higher education, Barnett supports his views about its aims via historical evidence. In his 1988 article, this was drawn from the ideas about university education of Newman, J. S. Mill, Huxley, Jaspers, and Leavis:

> [W]hat might be described as the "emancipatory" concept of higher education . . . appears to underlie the history, over the last 150 years, of the western idea of higher education itself. These notions are now so built into our understanding of higher education that they become constitutive of the concept of higher education. They are not so much aims of higher education as essential conditions of it.
>
> (Barnett 1988: 245)

In Barnett (1990) the historical net is cast further back in time, embracing

Plato and the medieval university as well as Newman and Jaspers. What is caught is of the same species: the "emancipatory" concept.

But there are difficulties in his position. First, suppose his historical account is accurate. What does this show? It cannot be used to show that we should continue on traditional lines since there may be all sorts of good reasons for rejecting the tradition. For hundreds of years boys' education has been seen as more important than girls', but we have now *rejected* this view in favor of something more just.

Secondly, doubts have been cast on the accuracy of the historical claims themselves. Aviram (1992: 190) has criticized Barnett for failing to justify his selection of the latter historical examples, hinting that he has chosen them to support an already adopted position. Among other things, Barnett has underplayed the vocational functions of the university, which have been there since the middle ages and are still massively present today. It is here that the attempt to make a conceptual rather than administrative distinction between higher and further education is particularly implausible.

I have tried to show that neither Barnett's philosophical nor his historical arguments succeed in showing that higher education must have emancipatory aims. This raises the question of whether the claim mirrors a value-judgment on Barnett's part rather than conceptual reality. Anticipating this thought, in a short section of his 1990 book devoted to replies to objectors, he writes:

> It could be said that *the* idea of higher education worked out here is simply *an* idea of higher education. I have not, in other words, escaped the accusation "that's only your view."
>
> (Barnett 1990: 204)

He has two responses. The first is that "the emancipatory conception of higher education does in fact have its roots in the whole history of the thought and practice of higher education" (Barnett 1990: 204). We have already seen the shortcomings of this move. The second is:

> that there is an inherent openness in the emancipatory concept of higher education; and so, characterizing this concept as simply one of several partial alternatives is misleading . . . The reflective processes prompted by the emancipatory concept even provide for critical evaluation about the concept itself. There is no question, therefore, about the emancipatory concept being imposed arbitrarily.
>
> (p. 204)

While it is true that once students are working along emancipatory lines they can question—and presumably reject—their involvement in this, Barnett's argument does nothing to meet the charge put by someone faced with mandatory emancipatory studies: "Why should I have to do this when all I have come to university for is to pursue my chosen specialism?" Despite what Barnett says, there may well be a danger of emancipation being imposed arbitrarily.

Other Defenses of "Higher" Education

Since Barnett's work on the concept of higher education in the early 1990s, there have been several similar attempts by philosophers to define higher education (or the university) in such a way that other forms of education are explicitly or implicitly excluded.

In 1996 David Hamlyn argued, in *Philosophy*, that a university is characterized not only by the pursuit of learning (i.e. research), as an earlier paper by Griffiths (1965) claimed, but also by "the enablement of that pursuit's being carried on both *now and in the future*, via future graduates" (Hamlyn 1996: 215; his italics). So a research institute could not be a university, given "that it had no teaching function enabling it to produce graduates who could forward its research" (p. 215). The immediate implication of Hamlyn's view, as he recognizes, is that many of the new universities recently created in Britain "by what is in effect a simple fiat" (p. 207) do not deserve the name since the teaching they do is not geared into and does not subserve the institution's pursuit of learning. He adds: "it might be suggested that what I have said amounts to an elitism. If it does, well and good" (p. 216). Hamlyn's argument is explicitly non-essentialist (p. 211) and in this differs from Barnett's. He sees himself as putting forward a *recommendation*, albeit one based on good grounds (p. 216).

If one accepts his point that the pursuit of learning via teaching future graduates is an important social enterprise both now and in the future, this does not mean that there must be a system of quite distinct institutions— Hamlyn's "universities"—devoted to this end. One might think, rather, in terms of a continuum of post-compulsory teaching institutions, in some of which the contribution of graduates to the pursuit of learning is a major aim, and in others of which it has a minor role, or possibly no role at all. (I am not at this point advocating this system, only pointing out that it is a conceivable one.) Hamlyn seems to be making the unfounded assumption that only some institutions, his "universities," can pursue the aim he picks out, while no other institution can have any hand in this. Like Barnett's argument, Hamlyn's fails to show that one can draw a philosophically defensible line between one type of post-compulsory institution and another.

In their discussion of UK higher education after the Dearing Report of 1997 (National Committee of Inquiry into Higher Education 1997), Blake *et al.* (1998) include a chapter on "Aims, purposes and principles" (ch. 3). This begins by asking: "What does Dearing think higher education is for?" It outlines the four purposes that Dearing picks out—to do with personal development, knowledge for its own sake, economic needs, and democratic society—and says that the Report subsumes these purposes under the overarching aim of enabling "society to make progress through an understanding of itself and of its world," an aim that Dearing takes as equivalent to "sustaining a learning society" (National Committee of Inquiry into Higher Education 1997: 51).

While the three authors make useful comments about Dearing's celebration of instrumental thinking, especially in the service of economic ends, when they turn to their own view of what higher education is for (pp. 63–4) their response is disappointing. They say that the question is not a technical one that instrumental reason alone can answer. What is needed is something broader—something like Aristotle's notion of "rational deliberation," involving judgment, sensitivity to ethical considerations on the one hand and the diverse particularity of the world on the other. This is a disappointing answer, because it is so general. Aristotelian judgment is something we need in many aspects of our lives—in our personal relationships, jobs and home-making, for instance. No doubt if we assume that higher education is a category worth hanging on to and that it must have defensible aims, the same kind of judgment must be put to work in deliberating about what these should be. Blake *et al.* tell us what the *form* of the answer should look like, but they say nothing about its *content*. At the same time, they appear to be presupposing that it is a valuable question to ask what the aims of higher education should be. But is it? If, as is becoming clear, there is no non-bureaucratic way of demarcating higher from further education, we may well do better to scrap these two terms and redraw the map of post-compulsory education as a continuum, or a series of continua, of different kinds of learning, taking place in a variety of institutions, some of which, like the more unitary duals, deliberately seek to break down traditional divides.

A more recent book (Walker and Nixon 2004) includes philosophical arguments on the nature of the university by Michael Peters and also by Ronald Barnett. These are not, like the arguments of Blake *et al.*, associated with UK developments but are more general.

Peters argues that "three ideas of the university dominate the modern era: the Kantian idea of reason, the Humboldtian notion of culture, and now the technological idea of excellence" (Peters 2004: 70). In Peters's opinion there is no point in adopting a unitary view of what characterizes a university. "We might substitute for a single unifying idea (like 'reason' or 'culture') a constellation or field of overlapping and mutually self-reinforcing ideas of the liberal university, based on family resemblances" (p. 79); and again, "for a single governing Idea I substitute [the Wittgensteinian] notion of a constellation based on family resemblances" (p. 80).

Later in the same volume, Barnett questions whether the idea of a liberal university is indeed a family resemblance concept. He does this on the grounds that there are now just such a great number of accounts of what a university is—going far beyond Peters's tally—that the question arises: "are their family resemblances such that the members of this particular family have anything in common with each other?" (Barnett 2004: 197).

I believe this response is misconceived. Barnett is working within the same frame of reference as Peters. They are both looking for the special characteristics that make a university a university. It is in the light of such an account that one can distinguish universities from other things—technical colleges for instance. But what this approach underplays is the role of human decisions to name things in one way rather than another. University X is now a university because it was made one in 2002; before that it was a college of higher education. The more stress one puts on such bureaucratic, often politically motivated, decisions rather than on allegedly special features, the more the arbitrariness of the distinction between universities and other institutions becomes apparent. It is no advance to move, as Peters does, from a search for *common* features of universities to the *widely shared* features of the family resemblance model. This makes it, indeed, even more unlikely that one can find features that belong to universities alone and not at all to further education colleges.

In the same chapter of the book, Barnett reiterates his arguments from the early 1990s. He still hopes to "reclaim" the idea of the university, despite the "runaway world" in which we all now operate, in which the proliferating notions of what a university is have got wildly out of hand. He is attracted by the idea of a "meta-narrative under which many different kinds of ideas of the university could find shelter and support," suggesting that the idea of "ethically based freedom" might provide this "meta-narrative" (Barnett 2004: 199). This freedom is "anchored in some sense of allegiance to another (whether communities, society, disciplines or even institutions such as universities)."

I am not sure I follow all this. It seems to be a resurrection, or a relic, of the link Barnett made in 1990 between the university and emancipation. What is clear is that this is yet another attempt to find what lies at the heart of being a university, and that it brings with it problems we have already encountered. Like Blake *et al.*'s account, it is extremely general. As such, it means that all sorts of institutions can creep under the same umbrella—not only those currently called universities but also all sorts of other post-compulsory educational institutions (as well, perhaps, as monasteries, political parties, sports clubs, and commercial firms). We are still a long way from discovering what makes a university a university.

Rethinking Post-Compulsory Education

As should be plain by now, this whole project is in my view misguided. I see no good reason to believe that there is something distinctive (except bureaucratically) about universities in contrast with other post-compulsory institutions, or higher education as compared with further. There are reasons enough, if not necessarily good ones, if you want to keep the post-compulsory status quo. Institutions designated universities, and thus in the higher education category, have advantages that further education colleges lack in finance and in status. It is not surprising that people want to hang on to these—and one way of doing this is to show, as incontrovertibly as possible, why universities are unique and worth preserving. I am not ascribing this motive to the writers I have discussed above. At the same time, the powerful forces in our culture that support current arrangements ensure a permanent and favorable audience for theorizings of this sort, the more philosophical—and hence seemingly the more grounded in necessity—the better.

But should the status quo remain? The alternative is to treat post-compulsory education in a more inclusive way, deliberately to blur boundaries between different kinds of institutions rather than to make hard divisions between them. There is a good case for radically rethinking post-compulsory studies. Until now we have seen these in the light of a certain tradition. For several centuries an elite of young people, until recently all men, has been able to continue formal education beyond school, in academies and universities. Often this has been for vocational reasons, to prepare them to be doctors, lawyers, clerics, or scholars. But sometimes these teenagers have not yet decided what they are going to do in life: for these, higher education has consisted in extra years tacked on to the end of school education and sharing some of its features. Some students have diligently focused on study, while for others this has been more like a period of freedom from the rigors of schooling until a way ahead becomes clearer.

The idea that higher education is a lengthy, full-time period of learning end-on to school is still widely accepted today. But are there good reasons for it? In earlier times there was, in some quarters, a religious rationale. For a devout protestant—a seventeenth-century Calvinist, for instance—the acquisition of knowledge was a religious duty. To come closer to God, one needed as comprehensive as possible an understanding of God's created universe in all its wondrous heterogeneity. Ignorance was a sin; knowledge, a condition of personal and communal salvation. Its systematic assimilation, the more all-embracing the better, was a high obligation. Pedagogy was rethought, by Comenius and other reformers going back to Ramus in the sixteenth century, so that learning could take place as efficiently and pleasantly as possible (Hotson 2007).

In such a culture, which continued into the eighteenth century and beyond, it made obvious sense for young protestant men from relatively privileged backgrounds to continue their studies beyond their schooldays, especially because, even though some of them might not yet have found their divinely appointed vocation, the religious assumption that any knowledge acquired had to be used for the betterment of God's world meant that their four or five years of diligence could not but be well spent.

In Britain, this tradition persisted through the eighteenth century in the Dissenting Academies in England and the Scottish universities, based as they were on a modern curriculum in a wide range of disciplines (White 2006, ch. 5). The two English universities, Oxford and Cambridge, were still based largely on the classics, and their clientele, especially from the landed classes, rarely had the seriousness of purpose that typified the former group. For many of them, their time at university was an idle, fun-filled period of socializing until other things came along. It was part of the established way of life of the upper classes, and hard to justify from a utilitarian point of view. In this latter feature it differed from the higher education of the radical protestant, intended to facilitate both individual salvation and social improvement.

The modern curriculum and seriousness of purpose of the dissenting tradition became dominant in university circles in the nineteenth and twentieth centuries, even though the religious rationale for this type of higher education progressively fell into the background. The University of London, later University College London (UCL), was originally founded in 1826 with dissenters prominent among its sponsors. Its general course was based on a wide gamut of compulsory studies like those found in the Dissenting Academies and Scottish universities. Other colleges, often in the big industrial cities, and soon to become universities themselves, were modeled on it (White 2006: 120–1).

In the later nineteenth century, the idea that universities existed to provide a broad course of study—similar in its range to the modern curriculum found in schools in the dissenting world—gave way to the notion of specialized degrees. Although the older pattern had its advocates in the twentieth century—notably A. D. Lindsay at Keele, brought up as he was in the Scottish tradition—specialization has won out. This has meant a further erosion of the old rationale for higher education as an end-on continuation of schooling. This rationale had been influenced by the encyclopaedism so prominent in radical Protestantism under Alsted, Comenius and others (Hotson 2007). While early upbringing could provide the kind of schematic initiation into a comprehensive grasp of academic disciplines that one finds in Comenius's illustrated text-book *Orbis Sensualium Pictus* (1658), an engaging encyclopedia in miniature for younger children, his ideal of *pansophia* could be fully realized only once the student had acquired a detailed, rather than embryonic, understanding of a similar range of disciplines. It was the function of dissenting higher education, and of early UCL and its offshoots, to provide this.

Against this background, the rationale for end-on university education is perfectly intelligible. But by the twentieth century the rationale had virtually disappeared. Not only had the religious background necessary to it largely fallen away, but so also had the idea that the non-vocational, general course in higher education institutions should be encyclopedic rather than specialized.

In our own time it is still taken as read that, for the most part, and ignoring gap years, university should be end-on to school, and that undergraduate work should be heavily specialized. It is also largely taken as read—and this marks a departure from the tradition—that it is desirable that a very large proportion of school-leavers go on from school to university. Is there any good rationale for this to replace the one that has withered away?

It is hard to see what this might be. I am talking about *good* reasons. No doubt there are *reasons* why this kind of pattern is widely favored, but they may not be justifiable ones. I mentioned above the hedonism of eighteenth-century Oxbridge student life. Some of this has filtered through into our own age—and not merely in these elite universities, but in all others (perhaps there may be a few exceptions) that have been influenced by this model.

Not all find their undergraduate experience a fun time. Some find the regime disenchanting. Like myself, they may have been led at school to expect no greater felicity than the progress from the semi-specialization of their last two years at school to the even greater specialization of university. But why think in this way? Why should it be considered that spending three years of one's youth on advanced mathematics, German studies, or medieval English history is a good thing for most students? It may suit a tiny minority who for some reason spontaneously have this kind of passion at eighteen— that is, without the gentling towards it that the rest of us undergo at school. For the non-aficionado, there must surely be a less disappointing way forward.

Realistic undergraduates both enjoy themselves and do what work is neces- sary for the kind of degree they want, knowing that with luck they are in line for a decent job and a comfortable way of life once they have come down—not necessarily one closely linked with their specialism. And what, it may be asked, is wrong with that? Old justifications for three or four post-school years of studenthood may now have crumbled, but that does not mean new ones can- not take their place. Students are able to sort themselves out before plunging into the world of work. They have space to explore relationships, try this or that pursuit, learn from one another. Education is not only discipline-based: people can learn so much informally as well as formally.

These kinds of point are often put. But they do not add up to a justification for the status quo. We live in a democratic age, in which equality of respect is, in theory at any rate, a guiding principle. Why should only a section of the eighteen-year-old age group have this three years' mélange of fun, self- discovery, networking, and some study? Why should so many of their con- temporaries have to buckle down to hard, often unwelcome, work with little space for themselves? If three years of the time of your life is good for some, why is it not good for all?

There must be a better way of organizing things. We need, as I said earlier, to reconceptualize our ideas of post-school learning. First, we need to question the view that the age of eighteen or nineteen is for the most part a good time for people to go to university full time. Post-compulsory learning should be encouraged at any time of life, with extensive opportunities for everyone to pursue courses of study or practical activity that they have a great desire to follow, for whatever reason. Factors making for social divisiveness—such as the distinction between higher and further education, the gift of several years'

full-time emancipation from the labor market to some but not to others—
should be eliminated.

Conclusion

Post-compulsory learning should be predicated much more on passion, on
enthusiasm. Those of us who have got much more out of a part-time course
later in life on something we have really wanted to do than out of a full-time,
post-school course on a specialist subject to which we had a half-hearted commitment know what a difference there is between the two. Rather than putting
so much money and other resources into conventional patterns, there could be
more support for part-time study, such as by reducing working hours for those
so engaged and making grants and loans easily accessible. Investigations could
be launched into how far *all* post-school study could reasonably be made part-
time, and how far there still needs to be full-time courses in some areas to keep
up the supply of essential services. These and other measures would help in the
creation of a post-compulsory system more function- than status-orientated
compared to the one we have now, a system more sensitive to the equality of
respect that lies at the heart of a decent democracy.

There would be one other advantage—and a huge one. The last few years of
schooling up to eighteen are dominated by pressures to get places at university.
The specialization the latter requires is mirrored in the somewhat less full-
blooded specialization of the upper secondary school years. If it were no longer
taken as read that successful school students go directly on to university, the
curriculum of the upper secondary school could be transformed. And so it
should be. It is a tragedy that, as things are now, students are so often steered
unremittingly into unnecessary and often unwelcome scholarship. These adolescent years are a time of strong feelings, yearnings, a new receptiveness to art,
to politics, to philosophical questions about what we are, what we should do
with our lives, and how we should relate to others. Especially if, as now seems
likely, compulsory schooling in the UK will last until eighteen, these imperatives of the adolescent years could figure in a vibrant new curriculum for later
secondary school—a curriculum that young people could enjoy rather than
put up with. It would have affinities with Ronald Barnett's "emancipatory"
studies, and with his "self-understanding" and "self-empowerment." He is
forced to put them into the university curriculum because, as things are, there
is little place for them in school programs. He is right about their importance.
They are so important, indeed, that they should be for everybody, not only for
those able to get into higher education. He is right about their importance, but
not about the stage of education in which they should figure.

Notes

My critique of Barnett's argument first appeared, in a slightly different form, in *Studies
in Higher Education*, 22:1 (March 1997). It is partly on the same broad lines as, but

differently argued in detail from, the article by Aviram (1992) and the book reviews by Standish (1991) and Winch and Merriman (1994). I am indebted to all three of my predecessors.

References

Aviram, A. 1992. The nature of university education reconsidered (a response to Ronald Barnett's *The Idea of a Higher Education*), *Journal of Philosophy of Education*, 26, 183–200.

Barnett, R. 1988. Does higher education have aims?, *Journal of Philosophy of Education*, 22, 239–50.

Barnett, R. 1990. *The Idea of Higher Education*, Buckingham: Society for Research into Higher Education/Open University Press.

Barnett, R. 1994. *The Limits of Competence*, Buckingham: Society for Research into Higher Education/Open University Press.

Barnett, R. 2004. Epilogue: Reclaiming Universities from a Runaway World. In *Reclaiming Universities from a Runaway World*, eds. M. Walker and J. Nixon, Maidenhead: Society for Research into Higher Education/Open University Press, pp. 195–208.

Blake, N., R. Smith and P. Standish. 1998. *The Universities We Need: Higher Education after Dearing*, London: Kogan Page.

Comenius, J. 1658. *Orbis Sensualium Pictus* (republished 1896), London: Pospisila.

Dray, W.H. 1973. "Commentary" on Peters, R.S. "Aims of education—a conceptual enquiry." In *The Philosophy of Education*, ed. R. S. Peters, Oxford: Oxford University Press. pp. 34–9.

Frankfurt, H.G. 1988. Freedom of the will and the concept of a person, in *The Importance of What We Care About*, ed. H. G. Frankfurt, Cambridge: Cambridge University Press, pp. 11–25.

Garrod, N. and B. Macfarlane. 2007. Scoping the duals: the structural challenges of combining further and higher education in post-compulsory institutions, *Higher Education Quarterly*, 61:4, 578–96.

Griffiths, A.P. 1965. A deduction of universities. In *Philosophical Analysis and Education*, ed. R. D. Arachambault, London: Routledge and Kegan Paul, pp. 187–207.

Hamlyn, D.W. 1996. The concept of a university, *Philosophy*, 71, 205–18.

Hotson, H. 2007. *Commonplace Learning: Ramism and its German Ramifications 1543–1630*, Oxford: Oxford University Press.

National Committee of Inquiry into Higher Education. 1997. *Higher Education in the Learning Society: Report of the National Committee*, London: The Stationery Office.

Peters, M.A. 2004. Higher education, globalisation and the knowledge economy. In *Reclaiming Universities from a Runaway World*, eds. M. Walker and J. Nixon, Maidenhead: Society for Research into Higher Education/Open University Press, pp. 67–82.

Peters, R.S. 1959. Must an educator have an aim? In *Authority, Responsibility and Education*, ed. R. S. Peters, London: Allen and Unwin, pp. 83–95.

Standish, P. 1991. Review of "The Idea of a Higher Education," *Journal of Philosophy of Education*, 25, 143–8.

Walker, M. and J. Nixon. (eds) 2004. *Reclaiming Universities from a Runaway World*, Maidenhead: Society for Research into Higher Education/Open University Press.

White, J. 2006. *Intelligence, Destiny and Education: The Ideological Roots of IQ Testing*, London: Routledge.

Winch, C. and L. Merriman. 1994. Review of Ronald Barnett's "Improving Higher Education: total quality care," *Journal of Philosophy of Education*, 28, 275–9.

3
Post-secondary Education and Social Justice

LEESA WHEELAHAN

Introduction

Elsewhere, the editors of this book argue that "duals represent a distinct type of modern university" (Garrod and Macfarlane 2007: 579). They explain that even though dual sector universities are differentiated by their national policy and social contexts, origins, and sectoral relationships, the principal reason given for their creation "is the desire to develop 'seamlessness' within the post-secondary education system in the interests of social justice by improving progression opportunities into higher education" (p. 579). Despite their national differences, the duals "offer the potential to realize the vision of lifelong learning crossing the boundary between the sectors that exist in post-secondary education" (p. 579). While other universities may proclaim social justice as part of their defining mission and ethos, the notion of *seamlessness* distinguishes dual sector institutions from other tertiary education institutions through providing the mechanism for achieving social justice, democracy, access, and opportunity. The possibility of seamlessness promises to transcend boundaries between educational sectors; between academic and vocational preparation; and between theoretical knowledge and skill.

Do dual sector institutions fulfill this promise? Is there anything intrinsic about dual sector institutions that enables them to make a unique contribution to social justice? This chapter argues that dual sector institutions have the potential to make a distinctive contribution to social justice because of their dual sector character, but this identity is not a guarantee that they will do so. They can also contribute to social stratification by entrenching differences between types of qualifications and sectors, and by contributing to hierarchical relations within and between sectors. While duals may provide more *access* to higher education (HE), it may be to qualifications and a system that is more differentiated by hierarchies in status, outcomes, and access to social power. The extent to which they contribute to social justice or social stratification depends in large part on the broader social and policy context in their country.

This chapter addresses these issues through differentiating between the *intrinsic* purpose or logic of dual sector institutions, and the *institutional* logic that shapes the way in which the different sectors engage at the systemic and institutional level. It argues that while the intrinsic logic of dual sector institutions promotes seamlessness and boundary-crossing, the institutional logic often undermines these objectives. It identifies the nature of the tertiary education field and positional differentiation within the field as an important causal mechanism in shaping patterns of opportunity and the extent to which the duals are able to realize their intrinsic logic. Finally, it considers the way in which dual sector institutions can make a distinctive contribution through identifying systemic and institutional approaches that can be implemented to support social justice outcomes.

The Intrinsic Logic of the Duals

Young (2003) uses a framework developed by Raffe and his colleagues to distinguish between the intrinsic and the institutional logics of educational reforms and systems. The intrinsic logic of educational reforms reveals the political rationale for explicit policy objectives, "that is independent of the actual context in which the reform might be implemented" (Young 2003: 201). The intrinsic logic provides the basis upon which reforms are justified by supporters or attacked by critics. In contrast, the institutional logic reveals the drivers of educational systems and the political, social, and institutional contexts that mediate if and how reforms are implemented (p. 201).

Young elaborates Raffe's model by differentiating between the macro and the micro aspects of institutional logics. The macro refers to "forms of stratification and power relations and the pattern of institutions," whereas the micro refers to "the specific practices, patterns of interaction and values" that underpin the trust and credibility of systems, qualifications, and educational outcomes (Young 2003: 201). His distinction between the macro and micro aspects of institutional logics can be used to analyze and differentiate between the systemic or macro logic of dual sector relations within systems of tertiary education, and the way in which these are mediated at the micro level within dual sector institutions. This distinction is useful because it facilitates an analysis of the iterative and emergent relationship between the systemic and institutional, while also defining a space for the relative autonomy of the institutional from the systemic. The systemic matters because it provides the degrees of freedom that the duals operate within, thereby limiting the outcomes that can be achieved; however, the duals can still make a difference and contribute to achieving social justice objectives, even if the policy environment within which they operate is not as conducive as it could be.

With the advent of mass and then universal systems of tertiary education, participation in, and pathways through, the different sectors of tertiary education came to be linked to social justice, access, and equity. This provides the intrinsic logic of dual sector institutions. Participation in tertiary education took on functions hitherto associated with secondary education in mediating access to employment outcomes and in providing people with the knowledge and skills they needed to successfully participate in society. Scott (2003: 74) explains that "those who are excluded from participating in a mass higher education system are much more disadvantaged than those who are excluded from elite systems." This is because access to, and the capacity to succeed in, HE mediates access to a much wider range of jobs than in the past, and to the lifestyle and culture associated with high levels of education. The Organisation for Economic Co-operation and Development (OECD) explains that "[a]ccess, therefore, is not merely to an institution but to a way of life, not for the few but for all" (OECD 1998: 37).

Pathways between the sectors consequently matter because they provide access to HE for students from the "second" sector of tertiary education, which are, in the examples used in this chapter, further education (FE) in England and technical and further education (TAFE) in Australia. Students from FE and TAFE are more likely to come from disadvantaged backgrounds than are HE students (Foley 2007; Foster 2005). Foster (2005) explains that FE colleges contribute more than a third of undergraduate entrants to HE and that FE is the main route to HE for adults from low socioeconomic backgrounds in England. In Australia in 2003, almost 14 percent of all students commencing bachelor degrees in HE had a prior TAFE diploma or advanced diploma as their highest previous qualification; however, this rose to 30 percent for students aged over twenty-five (Stanwick 2006: 17).

This policy context provides the rationale for the duals; they constitute one mechanism for navigating the boundaries between qualifications, sectors, and the occupations they are linked to, and for providing social access to these qualifications and occupations for students from disadvantaged backgrounds. This is as a consequence of their dual sector character. Garrod and Macfarlane (2007: 586) explain that the overwhelming majority of the duals they surveyed "claim that their academic structures facilitate student progression within the institution between further and higher education programmes" and that "[t]his is, perhaps, the defining characteristic of a dual." They also explain that educational provision in most of the duals they surveyed was in vocational and professional areas, and this is perhaps another important characteristic of the duals (pp. 589–90).

Institutional Logics

The intrinsic logic of duals is, however, often undermined by macro and micro institutional logics and the political, institutional, and epistemological problems that arise as a consequence (Raffe 2005). The macro institutional logic shaping relations within and between sectors in countries such as England and Australia and the other countries included in this book is competitive education markets. The creation of markets has resulted in informal hierarchical differentiation of universities in which the distinguishing features are status, prestige, and resource levels. The HE market is characterized by student competition for positional goods (social position, status, power, and jobs), and students compete for the limited supply of the high-status goods at high-status universities (Marginson 1997). This competition structures relations between universities and between the sectors. It creates a hierarchy between HE and FE/TAFE so that the latter are lower status, and within HE so that elite universities are at the top. The social stratification and differentiation within and between tertiary education sectors means, as Grubb explains, that:

> equality of opportunity in practice means greater chances of enrolling in tertiary education, but not equality in the resources invested in different students, nor equality of the probability of completing a degree, nor equality of occupations for which students are being prepared.
>
> (Grubb 2006: 32)

It is more accurate, as Bathmaker and Thomas (2007: 2) argue, to see "the current system as an elite, mass and universal system all at the same time, with different parts of the system functioning in different ways." Bathmaker and Thomas (p. 2) situate the duals within the "universal" component of the system because of the range of qualifications they offer, and, we may add, their location in the HE status hierarchy. For example, two of the five dual sector universities in Australia are in the middle of the status hierarchy, and the remaining three are towards the lower end of the hierarchy.[1] None can be defined as elite universities. All five dual sector universities are "new" universities that were created when Australia merged its HE colleges of advanced education and universities into a "unified" HE system in the late 1980s and early 1990s. Garrod and Macfarlane (2007: 593–4) say that most of the dual sector institutions they surveyed were from "teaching-led" cultures, rather than "research-intensive" ones.

Maclennan et al. (2000) distinguish between "selecting" universities that are high-demand elite universities and select the "most qualified" students from the available pool, and lower-demand "recruiting" universities that must actively compete with each other for students. Selecting universities are more likely to focus on school leavers with high tertiary entrance scores based on their senior school certificate results, while recruiting universities must draw from a wider and more diverse pool and market for prospective students. Recruiting universities have more flexible entry requirements, provide flexible study options and more credit for prior studies (particularly for FE/TAFE studies), and emphasize vocational relevance and outcomes for students. They are more likely than elite universities to admit students from low socioeconomic backgrounds and to admit students from FE/TAFE. In Australia the selecting universities are the elite Group of Eight universities and the remaining universities are all, to varying degrees, recruiting universities, even though they are organized into groupings that are differentiated by status and levels of demand. In 2005, the Group of Eight admitted around nineteen school leavers for every TAFE graduate they admitted, while the recruiting universities admitted around three school leavers for every TAFE graduate they admitted (derived from DEST 2007a).

Moodie (2003: 5) compared the "unified" university systems in Australia and Scotland with the more formally segmented systems in three states in the United States, which comprise community colleges (the analogues of FE and TAFE), moderately selective universities, and elite doctoral-granting universities. In the states he examined, student transfers and levels of credit transfer between community colleges and universities were specified by state policy. He found that the elite universities in these states admitted one community college graduate for every two the less selective universities admitted. In contrast, the elite Australian universities admitted one TAFE graduate for every four the recruiting universities admitted, and the elite Scottish universities admitted one FE graduate for every five the recruiting universities admitted. This shows the extent to which the unified systems are informally, but powerfully, differentiated by status, and that apparently hierarchical, differentiated systems such as those in the US can actually provide more access, even if they have not definitively solved the problem of differential status hierarchies between community colleges and the rest of the HE system (Grubb 2006).

This informal hierarchy structures relations within and between sectors so that lower-status HE institutions gain relative positional advantage by being higher in status than FE or TAFE institutions. The struggle for positional advantage may also characterize relations *within* dual sector institutions, depending on the way in which these boundaries are navigated. This is because relations within dual sector institutions are contextualized by the broader policy context and the institutional logic at the macro level. This is shown in table 3.1, which demonstrates that the mere existence of a dual sector institution does not guarantee better outcomes for students. In 2000, while the dual sectors admitted considerably more students on the basis of prior TAFE studies compared to the elite Group of Eight, the percentage they admitted was still similar to that in other single sector universities.[2] Table 3.1 also shows that the duals *can* provide students with greater access; by 2005 the dual sector universities admitted more than 18 percent of students on the basis of prior TAFE studies. The reasons for this are discussed later in the chapter.

Bathmaker and Thomas's (2007: 2) analysis of dual sector institutions in England draws on Bourdieu's notion of habitus to argue that organizational cultures are linked to the wider tertiary education field and the way in which this is hierarchically structured. An institutional habitus provides the framework of assumptions and expectations about the normal, the possible, the contested, and the settled as the basis for differently situated perspectives within the field. It is an emergent outcome of the interplay between (institutional)

Table 3.1 Admission to bachelor degrees on the basis of
         prior TAFE qualification in 2000 and 2005 (%)

	2000* (%)	2005# (%)
Group of Eight	2	3
Duals	9	18
Other universities	8	12
Total	7	10

*Source: derived from Moodie (2007: 3)
#Source: derived from Department of Education, Science and Training (2007a)

agency and broader structure, but always within the context of the power of the field (Bathmaker and Thomas 2007: 2).

Raffe (2005) identifies three barriers to the creation of unified systems of post-compulsory education, and these are political, institutional, and epistemological. Arguably these contribute to shaping relations between the sectors at systemic and institutional levels, and it is useful to consider how their interplay helps to shape the institutional habitus within dual sector institutions. Bathmaker and Thomas (2007: 2) explain that the duals they studied did not have a single institutional habitus or culture, but instead they had an HE *and* an FE culture. These different cultures are expressed internally within the institution but reflect the broader sectoral relations within the field, the political structuring of these relations, and the way in which these relations are mediated in sectoral policies and practices, and expressed as epistemological differences in the types of programs offered in each of the sectors.

A key systemic political problem that arises in dual sector relations is the search for a territorial imperative that distinguishes FE/TAFE from HE on the one hand, and from schools on the other (Rushbrook 1997). In England this occurred through designating FE as one provider within the broader learning and skills sector (Parry *et al.* 2006: 11), and in Australia through designating TAFE as one provider within a vocational education and training (VET) sector that delivers skills needed for work (Wheelahan and Moodie 2005). While the role of FE in providing HE has been affirmed in England, this is as part of a broader strategy that designates FE's primary purpose as the delivery of skills needed for work (Parry *et al.* 2006: 21–2). A key difference between England and Australia is the greater scope FE colleges have in *how* they do this. FE colleges in England are funded to deliver two-year, vocational HE foundation degrees and other short-cycle HE programs, as well as a range of "second-chance" programs including basic adult education, and academic programs for senior school students and adults. They are also funded to deliver non-HE vocationally specific programs that include, but are not limited to, competency-based National Vocational Qualifications (Parry 2005: 5). In contrast, in Australia publicly funded provision in VET *must* be based on competency-based training packages that consist of "industry-specified" units of competency. The provision of publicly funded adult and community education is increasingly marginalized.[3] The only way TAFE can at present offer HE programs is through offering them as full-fee programs.

Political problems also arise between the sectors at the systemic level and within dual sector institutions because of struggles over control of curriculum, as a consequence of different regulatory regimes, and different funding, reporting, and quality assurance arrangements, often involving different government departments. In Australia as in England, the sectors fund, report, and count students differently, and have different student fees arrangements, industrial awards, quality assurance regimes, regulatory bodies, curriculum models, and accreditation processes; in Australia the sectors also report to different levels of government (Parry *et al.* 2006; Wheelahan and Moodie 2005). The different purposes and missions of the sectors are emphasized and used as an argument against sectoral collaboration. For example, an often heard argument in sectoral skirmishing in Australia is that pathways are not so important because TAFE qualifications are designed to be an outcome in their own right by preparing students for work.[4]

Institutional problems arise as a consequence of the way in which the sectors are constituted and they overlap with political problems. Even where there is good intent, institutional problems often arise as an unintended consequence of the way institutions work (Raffe 2005). This is because the dead weight of administrative requirements is an almost irresistible counterforce to policy that seeks to deepen and extend collaboration. Different student management information systems, timetabling, quality assurance and course review cycles, staff industrial awards, funding rates, and associated problems make it difficult to establish integration, particularly where this is compounded by requiring the sectors to answer to different regulatory regimes and government masters.

These political and institutional problems are often disguised as epistemological problems. For example, industrial issues are often masked as disputes over philosophy, teaching style, and standards, but upon closer examination are often just as much about preserving jobs and status in each sector. However, epistemological problems are among the most under-theorized problems in dual sector relations and this means that problems cannot be adequately addressed. Epistemological differences are asserted by sectoral separatists who insist on the separate missions of the sectors so that the focus is on the *purpose* of the sectors, even though both sectors seek to develop broadly educated citizens for a changing society and world of work. Arguably, this is the way in which epistemology is used as a cover for political and industrial issues because fundamental differences in purposes cannot be demonstrated.

More problematic is the *denial* of epistemological problems by dual sector champions, as this prevents the development of policies that can overcome epistemological differences through creating a coherent and consistent curriculum across the sectors so that there is a shared knowledge base underpinning qualifications. For example, Gabb and Glaisher (2006: 10) argue that much of the cross-sectoral literature in Australia tacitly suggests "that cross-sectoral pedagogy is unproblematic, or at least much less problematic than the institutional and structural barriers." Yet there are epistemological differences that make seamlessness much more problematic, at least in Australia. As explained earlier, all publicly funded qualifications in TAFE must be based on a competency-based training curriculum that specifies the outcomes of training independently of processes of learning, and in which knowledge and skill is tied to specific workplace roles and tasks. There are concerns that TAFE students do not have sufficient access to the disciplinary knowledge underpinning vocational practice in their field. This leads to the marginalization of underpinning knowledge in VET qualifications and provides a poor basis for articulation to HE (Wheelahan 2007). In contrast, HE qualifications are mostly derived through specifying curriculum and inputs, and are developed through shared understandings of stakeholders about the syllabus, processes of learning and assessment, and outcomes (Young 2005b).

Epistemological problems are perhaps less of an issue in England and Scotland because each delivers HE awards as the basis of progression to degrees, but this does not, however, remove the charge of epistemological incongruence. This is because of the smaller classes, highly structured curriculum and more supported learning environments in FE (Parry *et al.* 2003: 15) that result in differing levels of depth, complexity, and engagement with theoretical knowledge (Young 2006a). In other words, epistemological boundaries must be explicitly navigated rather than ignored, if students are to be supported in crossing them. Moreover, while FE may teach one in nine HE students in England, they are concentrated in a minority of FE colleges and HE provision in FE is only a small component of provision within FE overall (Parry 2005: 4). If pathways are to act as a mechanism for social justice then they also need to be developed explicitly between vocational qualifications in FE and qualifications in HE. At the systemic level this requires emphasizing the *educational* content and purposes of vocational qualifications to a greater extent, so that they provide the basis for progression and curricular coherence for students moving between qualifications and sectors (Young 2006b; Grubb 2006).

The combined effect of these political, institutional, and epistemological problems can be that barriers are placed in the way of student progression between sectors, even when the qualification is based on an HE curriculum, as in England. In their study of dual sector institutions in England, Bathmaker and Thomas (2007) found internal progression between the FE and HE divisions to be highly problematic, even when appropriate provision was available.

They found little communication between FE and HE lecturers as a result of separate teaching spaces, identities, and cultures. Woodley *et al.* (2005) identify selection practices within an Australian dual sector university where HE staff in some fields of education only choose TAFE articulators from within the university as a last resort, while others are glad to take TAFE students usually as a consequence of established relationships and high levels of trust between TAFE and HE staff (see also Milne *et al.* 2006).

There seems to be an important difference in the way in which dual sector relations are navigated and expressed in dual sector *universities* and in dual sector *institutions* (mainly FE Colleges or TAFEs) that are building their HE provision. Dual sector universities seek to transcend sectoral boundaries, whereas dual sector institutions seek to establish them. The emphasis in the latter is on how to engender an HE "ethos," student learning experience, and culture that is distinguished from the FE culture and practices (Bathmaker and Thomas 2007; Burns 2007). England has more experience of this than Australia because of FE's long-standing role in delivering HE, even if its role has been ambiguous and only brought into a coherent HE policy framework in recent years (Parry *et al.* 2006). In Australia, TAFE is beginning to embark on delivering HE but as a private HE provider. While there is not a great deal of research on the way in which HE is being constructed in TAFE because it is so new, anecdotal evidence suggests that similar processes are taking place, so that TAFEs emphasize the *distinctiveness* of their HE provision *within* the institution, in contrast to their VET provision.

In part, the emphasis on the distinctiveness of HE within FE or TAFE in both countries seems to be a consequence of national policies that require "appropriate" HE governance, quality assurance, curriculum, and learning environments, with "appropriately" qualified staff (Parry *et al.* 2006). However, it also seems to be about positioning within the field, through replicating hierarchies *within* institutions that reflect the broader sectoral hierarchies. This establishes HE provision within these institutions as higher-status provision and provides the basis for constructing HE identities that are differentiated from FE identities. For many students, this can provide the basis of their emerging identity as an HE student (Burns 2007), and we should not underestimate the importance of such "identity work" (Young 2006a: 3). However, the danger is that constructing large "mixed economy" providers in FE/TAFE may reproduce the binary divide within these institutions, but with HE in FE/TAFE even lower in status than the "new" universities. Bathmaker and Thomas seem to share this concern:

> The processes that we have found may change the current higher education system, but they do not appear to fundamentally challenge the power relations that are embodied in it. The work that transition currently appears to do, is to create a more detailed nuancing of existing

stratifications and inequalities within the system. Whether this might eventually allow opportunities for greater access to the more powerful parts of the higher education field is unclear.

(Bathmaker and Thomas 2007: 8)

Realizing the Potential of the Duals

The duals *can* make an important and distinctive contribution to social justice, but this requires paying attention to the boundaries at the systemic and institutional levels, rather than downplaying their significance. This includes national policy as well as boundaries within the duals, focusing on institutional policy, culture, programs, and curriculum. Most importantly, there must be attention to students' experiences of crossing the boundaries and the development of policies and practices that recognize the difficulties they experience (Milne *et al.* 2006).

The status of the duals will increase *if* pathways provide access to *elite* HE as well as to universal HE. FE/TAFE will always be lower in status than HE within Anglophone marketized tertiary education systems that are stratified because of the different access they provide to positional goods such as jobs, status, and social power. Wishing it were otherwise will not make it so. The status of FE/TAFE will be increased if they provide a "climbing framework" to these positional goods via pathways to HE (Lolwana 2005).[5] So while FE/TAFE qualifications are an outcome in their own right because they prepare students for particular occupations, they should also provide the basis for educational progression to HE. This is an honorable and important role that FE/TAFE plays, and arguably is the cornerstone of social justice policies that are concerned with *distributional justice* based on *equitable* participation in, and outcomes from, HE. Schools are likewise valued for the outcomes they produce in their own right but also for the access they provide to tertiary education. Moreover, *all* tertiary education qualifications need to provide two outcomes: the first is a vocationally specific outcome, and the second the knowledge and skills needed to study at a higher level within the field. This is what lifelong learning means in practice and it should underpin national lifelong learning policies.

It is clear, however, that the duals cannot by themselves ensure equitable access to elite HE in the absence of national policies designed to facilitate this outcome, even though they may make some inroads. Gallacher (2006: 54) argues that "an important challenge for policy is to ensure that opportunities for entry and progression within HE are not limited in ways which reinforce patterns of inequality." This is a policy challenge because the market has not worked as an equitable method for allocating elite HE places for FE/TAFE graduates and it is unlikely to do so.

Despite its commitment to the "free market," the United States has a different balance between planning and markets as distributive mechanisms for places in HE. Arguably it is this that accounts for the US's better relative performance in admitting community college students to elite universities compared to Scotland or Australia, which rely almost exclusively on markets. However, there are also important differences within the US itself (Moodie 2007). Wellman (2002) compared six US states that rely heavily on community college student transfers as an entry mechanism for low-income students to four-year degrees. She compared three states that did well on student retention and degree completion and three that did not. All six states had similar academic policies concerned with admission, curriculum, progression, and credit transfer that were "designed to influence the internal business of alignment between students, programs, and courses within and across institutions" (Wellman 2002: 38).

The main difference between the three high-performing and the three low-performing states was around statewide structural policies, which concerned "governance, institutional and sector mission and differentiation, statewide information system capacity, funding, planning capacities, and accountability strategies" (Wellman 2002: 38). Compared to three low-performing states, the three high-performing states had stronger statewide structural policies and coordinating mechanisms and used data as a tool to improve transfers and provide feedback to institutions about their relative performance. However, Wellman (2002: vii) finds limitations in all six states, one of which is that "[t]he accountability structures typically focus on two-year college transfer performance instead of also looking at the responsibilities of the four-year institutions." This is a key consideration in developing policy to increase access to elite HE. The conclusion that Moodie (2003: 5) draws from his comparative analysis of patterns of student transfers in Scotland, Australia, and the United States is that the elite universities have to be either "bribed or coerced" to accept transferring students. The evidence seems to support this argument, and the US experience shows that such policy is not beyond the bounds of possibility, however shocking it may seem to universities in other Anglophone countries.

However, individual dual sector institutions can make a difference, even if the policy environment is not as conducive as it could be. While macro institutional logics limit the possible and the probable, the duals have some degree of autonomy. This accounts for the dramatic increase in the percentage of students admitted to Australian dual sector universities from 2000 to 2005, as illustrated in table 3.1. Of the five dual sector universities, four substantially increased the percentage of students they admitted on the basis of prior TAFE studies in that time. This was because they began to emphasize their dual sector character and the opportunities open to students through pathways, and to develop policies to support these outcomes. RMIT increased its intake of TAFE students from 9 percent to 21 percent from 2000 to 2005, while Swinburne University of Technology increased its intake from 13 percent to 25 percent over the same period. Both are middle-ranking Australian universities.[6]

The example of Swinburne is particularly instructive because the university has developed a strong institutional strategy to increase articulation from its TAFE to its HE division (Young 2005a, 2007). The outcome of Swinburne's strategy was to increase its TAFE intake and decrease its school leaver intake, thereby increasing the tertiary entrance rank (TER) school students needed to enter its degrees. TERs are based on results in the senior school certificates. Swinburne's strategy had the effect of increasing the status of its degrees and thereby the status of its positional goods because it only admitted school leavers with a TER that placed them in the top 20 percent of students in that state (Young 2005a). At the same time, it put in place transition strategies to support students moving from a TAFE to an HE learning environment, particularly to account for problems in aligning the competency-based curriculum in TAFE with the HE curriculum, and it emphasizes the way in which pathways can act as a mechanism for social justice.

The academic progress and retention rates of TAFE students are similar to those for school leavers studying Swinburne degrees. While this is also the case at other universities (Abbott-Chapman 2006; Milne *et al.* 2006), the comparison is not usually between TAFE articulators and school leavers that are in the top 20 percent of the state. The percentage of students Swinburne admitted from a low socioeconomic background increased marginally from 2001 to 2005 (DEST 2007b), and while we cannot say this is as a consequence of their policy on TAFE articulation, the policy certainly has not had an adverse outcome on participation rates for special education students. Swinburne's vice-chancellor actively campaigns for national policy to support TAFE articulation, to overcome problems associated with VET competency-based qualifications, for funding and policy support for transition strategies, and for TAFE to become a provider of short-cycle HE programs that provide the basis of articulation to HE (Young 2005a, 2007).

The Swinburne experience shows that a focus on boundaries and the development of mechanisms to support transition across the boundaries facilitates such transition, and that institutional policies matter a great deal. We can also learn from the extensive literature in the United States about students' experiences of "transfer shock," which identifies the personal, social, cultural, and pedagogic hurdles that community college students experience when they transfer to four-year universities (Laanan 2007). A literature is beginning to emerge around students' experiences of transition in Australia that identifies problems associated with moving from a competency-based curriculum in TAFE to an HE curriculum as well as the "traditional" problems associated with transition shock. This literature shows that student transition is supported when there is an attempt to develop a coherent learning environment between sectors, and when TAFE *actively* prepares students for HE studies (Milne *et al.* 2006). Similarly, Bathmaker and Thomas (2007: 7) found in their institutional research that students needed support at the boundaries in applying to transfer to HE, and that they relied on their FE lecturers for information, support, and advice.

Conclusion

Coles and Oates (2005: 12) argue that "zones of mutual trust" (ZMT) consist of agreements between "individuals, enterprises and other organizations" to recognize and evaluate different types of qualifications between institutions and sectors. They explain that ZMTs "exist through the behaviour of people who are participating in them, operating through, or anticipating, common values and concerns. ZMTs cannot be imposed, they are dependent on processes of consensus and on voluntary participation" (Coles and Oates 2005: 13). Raffe explains:

> At its simplest a zone of trust may exist between two institutions, working in partnership to allow students to transfer in one discipline; at its most complex, a zone might extend across a network and cover a range of programmes, disciplines and levels.
>
> (Raffe 2005: 36)

The Australian cross-sectoral literature insists that pathways, credit transfer, and student articulation is based on trust between the sectors, and that resources must be invested in developing relations of trust (Wheelahan and Moodie 2005; Phillips 2006). While it is possible that ZMTs may arise serendipitously within institutions and regions and between sectors, they are more likely to do so if supported by strong systemic and institutional policies. Such policies are needed to support those who *do* wish to develop pathways and other collaborative relations and to overcome problems arising from the different ways in which the sectors are constituted and structured, and underpinned by relations of status within marketized tertiary education systems. Policy matters at the systemic level and within institutions.

Policy needs to be supported by resources invested to develop such relationships at the systemic level and within institutions. The macro and micro institutional logics of separate sectors mean that it is extremely expensive to develop collaborative relations to underpin the development of pathways. Such outcomes are facilitated when resources are invested in staff who act as "boundary spanners" who can understand the FE/TAFE and HE cultures, and the demands, requirements, and realities of each, and who can develop collaborative arrangements based on an understanding of the possible, which is in turn shaped by the political (Wheelahan and Moodie 2005). Such investments allow attention to be paid to the boundaries based on recognition of their importance, so that appropriate scaffolding can be put in place to support a "climbing framework" between the sectors (Lolwana 2005). It is this that will allow the intrinsic logic of the duals to be realized, so that they can make a distinctive contribution to supporting social justice outcomes for students, rather than reproducing sectoral hierarchies within the institution that limit students' options.

Notes

1. RMIT and Swinburne University of Technology are in the middle of the status hierarchy of universities in Australia, while the remaining three—Victoria University, the University of Ballarat, and Charles Darwin University—are towards the lower end of the status hierarchy (Marginson 1997).
2. The basis of admission underestimates the percentage of students with prior TAFE qualifications in HE because it does not take into account students' multiple enrollments in both sectors (Moodie 2005).
3. In Australia in 2005, 78.24 percent of outcomes achieved by students were based on training package units of competency, and 21.75 percent were based on modules that are not necessarily competency-based (DEST 2006: derived from table 1.10).
4. See Bathmaker and Thomas (2007) and Milne *et al.* (2006) for illustrations drawn from institutional research.
5. For example, Griffith University, a single-sector university in Queensland in Australia, has developed a range of "dual offers" with its partner TAFEs that consist of a guaranteed pathway from a TAFE diploma to a related degree at Griffith. Our TAFE partners tell us that there is much higher demand for dual offers than for the same diplomas that do not have a guaranteed place at a university attached to them. Developing dual offers has been an important focus of the Griffith–TAFE partnerships, and the Queensland Tertiary Admissions Centre guide listed fifty-seven Griffith–TAFE dual offers available to prospective students in 2008.
6. Derived from Commonwealth Department of Education, Science and Training Student Statistical collections, various years. See http://www.dest.gov.au/sectors/higher_education/publications_resources/statistics/publications_higher_education_statistics_collections.htm#studpubs—accessed 20 January 2008. In 2006, Swinburne admitted 28 percent of students to undergraduate degrees on the basis of prior TAFE studies (Young 2007: 7).

References

Abbott-Chapman, J. 2006. Moving from technical and further education to university: an Australian study of mature students, *Journal of Vocational Education and Training*, 58:1, 1–17.

Bathmaker, A.M. and W. Thomas. 2007. Positioning themselves: an exploration of the nature and meaning of transitions in the context of dual sector FE/HE institutions in England, *4th International Conference, Centre for Research in Lifelong Learning, "The Times they are a-changin'—researching transitions in lifelong learning,"* University of Stirling, Scotland, June 22–24 2007.

Burns, D. 2007. Conceptualising and interpreting organizational boundaries between further and higher education in "dual sector" institutions: where are they and what do they do?, *4th International Conference, Centre for Research in Lifelong Learning, "The Times they are a-changin'—researching transitions in lifelong learning,"* University of Stirling, Scotland, June 22–24 2007.

Coles, M. and T. Oates. 2005. *European Reference Levels for Education and Training Promoting Credit Transfer and Mutual Trust,* Cedefop Panorama series, 109, Study commissioned to the Qualifications and Curriculum Authority, England, Luxembourg: Office for Official Publications of the European Communities, http://www2.trainingvillage.gr/etv/publication/download/panorama/5146_en.pdf (accessed January 20, 2008).

Department of Education, Science and Training (DEST). 2006. *Annual National Report of the Australian Vocational and Technical Education System 2005,* November 29, Canberra: Department of Education, Science and Training. http://www.dest.gov.au/sectors/training_

skills/publications_resources/profiles/annual_national_report_australian_vtesystem2005. htm (accessed January 20, 2008).

Department of Education, Science and Training (DEST). 2007a. *2005 Basis of Admission for Domestic Students Commencing a Course at Bachelor Level or Below by State, Higher Education Provider and Basis for Admission to Current Course, Full Year 2005 Unpublished Data*, Canberra: Department of Education, Science and Training.

Department of Education, Science and Training (DEST). 2007b. *Institutional Student Equity Performance Data 2005*, Canberra: Department of Education, Science and Training. http://www.dest.gov.au/sectors/higher_education/publications_resources/statistics/student_equity _in_higher_education.htm (accessed January 20, 2008).

Foley, P. 2007. *The Socio-Economic Status of Vocational Education and Training Students in Australia*, Adelaide: National Centre for Vocational Education Research. http://www.ncver.edu.au/ publications/1690.html (accessed January 20, 2008).

Foster, A. 2005. *Realising the Potential: A Review of the Future Role of Further Education Colleges* (The Foster Review), Ref 1983–2005DOC-EN, November, Annesly: Department for Education and Skills. http://www.dfes.gov.uk/furthereducation/index.cfm?fuseaction=content. view&CategorID=20&ContentID=18 (accessed January 20, 2008).

Gabb, R. and S. Glaisher. 2006. *Models of Cross-Sectoral Curricula: TAFE and HE*, Postcompulsory Education Centre, Victoria University, Victoria. http://tls.vu.edu.au/PEC/reports.htm (accessed January 20, 2008).

Gallacher, J. 2006. Blurring the boundaries or creating diversity? The contribution of the further education colleges to higher education in Scotland, *Journal of Further and Higher Education*, 30:1, 43–58.

Garrod, N. and B. Macfarlane. 2007. Scoping the duals: the structural challenges of combining further and higher education in post-compulsory institutions, *Higher Education Quarterly*, 61:4, 578–96.

Grubb, W. N. 2006. Vocationalism and the differentiation of tertiary education: lessons from US community colleges, *Journal of Further and Higher Education*, 30:1, 27–42.

Laanan, F.S. 2007. Studying Transfer Students: Part II: Dimensions of transfer students' adjustment, *Community College Journal of Research and Practice*, 31: 35–9.

Lolwana, P. 2005. *National Qualifications Frameworks and the Further Education and Training/ Higher Education Interface*, Pretoria: South African Qualifications Authority.

Maclennan, A., K. Musselbrook and M. Dundas. 2000. *Credit Transfer at the FE/HE Interface: Widening Opportunities*, Edinburgh: Scottish Higher Education Funding Council/Scottish Further Education Funding Council.

Marginson, S. 1997. *Markets in Education*, St Leonards: Allen and Unwin.

Milne, L., S. Glaisher and S. Keating. 2006. *Making Articulation Work: TAFE to Higher Education at Victoria University*, Postcompulsory Education Centre, Victoria University, Victoria. http:// tls.vu.edu.au/PEC/reports.htm (accessed January 20, 2008).

Moodie, G. 2003. Comparative national and international transfer rates from TAFE/further education/community college to university, *Enhancing University-TAFE Partnerships*, University of New England, November 21, 2003.

Moodie, G. 2005. Reverse transfer in Australia, *14th National VET Research Conference*, Wodonga Institute of TAFE, July 8, 2005, http://www.griffith.edu.au//vc/staff/moodie/pdf/05ncver paper1.pdf (accessed January 20, 2008).

Moodie, G. 2007. Improving transfer from vocational to higher education: lessons from abroad, *4th International Conference, Centre for Research in Lifelong Learning, "The Times they are a-changin'—researching transitions in lifelong learning,"* University of Stirling, Scotland, June 22–24 2007.

OECD (Organisation for Economic Co-operation and Development). 1998. *Redefining Tertiary Education*, Paris: Organisation for Economic Co-operation and Development.

Parry, G. 2005. The Collegiate and Transfer Functions of Further Education Colleges in the United Kingdom, *Annual Conference of the Council for the Study of Community Colleges*, Boston, Mass., USA.

Parry, G., P. Davies and J. Williams. 2003. *Dimensions of Difference: Higher Education in the Learning and Skills Sector*, London: Learning and Skills Development Agency, Department for Education and Skills.

Parry, G., A. Thompson and P. Blackie. 2006. *Managing Higher Education in Colleges*, London: Continuum.

Phillips, K.P.A. 2006. *Stage 1 Report: National Study to Improve Outcomes in Credit Transfer and Articulation from Vocational and Technical Education to Higher Education*, February, Canberra: Department of Education, Science and Training, Canberra.

Raffe, D. 2005. *National Qualifications Frameworks as Integrated Qualifications Frameworks*, November, Pretoria: South African Qualifications Authority.

Rushbrook, P. 1997. Tradition, pathways and the renegotiation of TAFE identity in Victoria, *Discourse: Studies in the Cultural Politics of Education*, 18:1, 103–12.

Scott, P. 2003. 1992–2002: Where next?, *Perspectives: Policy and Practice in Higher Education*, 7:3, 71–5.

Stanwick, J. 2006. *Outcomes from Higher-Level Vocational Education and Training Qualifications*, Adelaide: National Centre for Vocational Education Research, http://www.ncver.edu.au/publications/1702.html (accessed January 20, 2008).

Wellman, J. V. 2002. *State Policy and Community College–Baccalaureate Transfer*, National Center Report #02–6 August, Washington D.C.: The National Center for Public Policy and Higher Education. http://www.highereducation.org/reports/transfer/transfer.pdf (accessed January 20, 2008).

Wheelahan, L. 2007. How competency-based training locks the working class out of powerful knowledge: a modified Bernsteinian analysis, *British Journal of Sociology of Education*, 28:5, 637–51.

Wheelahan, L. and G. Moodie. 2005. Separate post-compulsory education sectors within a liberal market economy: interesting models generated by the Australian anomaly. In *A Contested Landscape: International Perspectives on Diversity in Mass Higher Education*, eds. J. Gallacher and M. Osborne, Leicester: NIACE, pp. 18–46.

Woodley, C., F. Henderson, M. De Sensi and R. Gabb. 2005. *Selection Processes and Pathways: TAFE to Higher Education*, 12 October, Postcompulsory Education Centre, Victoria University, Melbourne. http://tls.vu.edu.au/PEC/reports.htm (accessed January 20, 2008).

Young, M. 2003. Comparing approaches to the role of qualifications in the promotion of lifelong learning, *European Journal of Education*, 38:2, 199–211.

Young, I. 2005a. Articulation at Swinburne University of Technology: intersectoral in our approach, *Business Higher Education Round Table Symposium: "Bridging the Gap,"* Melbourne, May 18, http://www.swinburne.edu.au/chance/vc/documents/opinionpieces/Articulation%20at20Swinburne%20University%20of%20Technology%20BHERT.doc (accessed January 20, 2008).

Young, M. 2005b. *National Qualifications Frameworks: Their Feasibility for Effective Implementation in Developing Countries*, Geneva: International Labour Organization.

Young, M. 2006a. Further and higher education: a seamless or differentiated future?, *Journal of Further and Higher Education*, 30:1, 1–10.

Young, M. 2006b. Reforming the further education and training curriculum: an international perspective. In *Knowledge, Curriculum and Qualifications for South African Further Education*, eds. M. Young and J. Gamble, Cape Town: Human Sciences Research Council, pp. 46–63.

Young, I. 2007. *Building Better Pathways to Higher Education*, Melbourne: Swinburne University of Technology. http://www.swinburne.edu.au/corporate/marketing/mediacentre/core/content/pathways.pdf (accessed January 20, 2008).

II
Systems Responses

4

Norway: Separate but Connected

ROMULO PINHEIRO AND SVEIN KYVIK

Introduction

In Norway, the tertiary education system has been the target of a wide variety of reforms since the mid-1960s, mostly as a consequence of the large growth in student numbers (Aamodt and Kyvik 2005). As in many other countries, recurrent questions have been raised about how this system should be organized in order to maintain diversity. The dominating opinion, as expressed by Clark (1983), has been that mass systems must be more differentiated than elite ones because they enroll a more heterogeneous student body, respond to new demands from the labor market, and attempt to cover a wider range of knowledge. In accordance with this view, diversification at the system level and the introduction of binary models became the guiding principle and strategy of higher education policy in most member countries of the Organisation for Economic Co-operation and Development (OECD) (Furth 1992). In many countries it was a basic idea that professional schools should only provide lower-degree vocational courses without the possibility for transfer to the universities. Short vocational courses were to be a clear alternative to a long university program, and there would be a watertight division between the two.

In Norway important reform efforts have been directed at establishing distinct educational sectors with different aims and purposes, while at the same time building bridges across the sectors, in particular to enhance possibilities for student transfer. The boundaries between these sectors have, however, not been commonly agreed upon, and repeated discussions have taken place on how the tertiary education system should be organized.

The nature of the research problem addressed in this chapter is twofold. First, our inquiry aims at exploring the ways through which the boundaries across the tertiary system have been established. Secondly, we want to shed light on the major implications of the adoption of a policy of transferability. The first part of the chapter provides contextual elements on the Norwegian tertiary education landscape. In the second part, an overview of the developments aimed at bridging the divide among the different types of institutions is given. Drawing upon theoretical insights from the new institutional view on organizations (DiMaggio and Powell 1983; Powell and DiMaggio 1991), we speculate on the possible driving forces for the recent developments across the sector. The chapter concludes by raising awareness, among policy makers and institutional leaders alike, of the implications of pursuing a policy of integration without paying adequate attention to the dynamics of the system and the unintended effects of particular policy measures, such as student transfers.

Tertiary Education in Norway

The Norwegian post-secondary education system constitutes three sectors corresponding to particular types of educational provision and institutional profiles: the vocational school sector, the college sector, and the university sector. Of these, only colleges and universities are recognized as being part of the higher education system. Although there are clear legal boundaries between these three sectors, there are also close links between the different parts of the tertiary education system.

The Vocational School Sector

In Norway, vocational education at the post-secondary level is regulated by a separate Act of 2003 and provided by a wide variety of institutions in domains such as technical education, maritime education, secretarial work, arts and crafts, economics and administration, computer technology, and health and tourism, with full-time courses lasting from six months to two years. There are currently close to 200 vocational schools, public as well as private (Brandt 2007). In total, there are about 12,000 students in this sector. Technical schools rank highest in popularity and number (about fifty), offering two-year vocational training courses to students who have either completed upper-secondary schooling, or possess a minimum of five years of working experience within a given trade. These schools provide training in such areas as building construction, electronics, chemicals and processing, and engineering, and are under the supervision of one of Norway's (nineteen) county authorities or administrative regions. Most importantly, successful completion confers on graduates the professional title of "technician" and enables them to access engineering studies at university or college level.

The College Sector

The emergence of a college sector can be traced back to the early 1970s, when district colleges providing vocationally oriented studies as well as some basic university courses were established across the country (Kyvik 1981; Bleiklie *et al.* 2000: 92–4). Throughout the 1970s, the upgrading of professional schools (e.g. for teacher training, engineering, maritime education, social work and nursing) to higher education status also contributed to the gradual development of a college sector. In 1994 this sector underwent a major reorganization when ninety-eight colleges were merged into twenty-six state university colleges (Kyvik 2002, 2008). The purpose of the reorganization was fourfold, namely to enhance the quality of administrative functions and academic work through the creation of larger administrative and academic units; to facilitate contact and cooperation between staff across different study programs; to create better organizational conditions for the development of new types of study programs; and to make the college sector more cost-efficient through economies of scale. In addition to the state university colleges, which today have around 87,000 students, there are twenty-five private colleges enrolling close to 29,000 students. The college sector offers study programs mainly at a bachelor's level, but to an increasing extent also master's programs as well as PhD programs in some areas.

The University Sector

This sector is composed of seven universities and six specialized university institutions (economics and business administration, veterinary science, sport and physical education, music, architecture). Until 2004 Norway had four universities, but the government then decided that colleges and specialized university institutions that fulfill certain minimum standards could apply for accreditation to university status. In the years 2005–2007, two university colleges and one specialized university institution were awarded university status. In total, about 92,000 students are enrolled in this sector, of which 850 attend a private institution.

The Relationship Between the Vocational School Sector and the College Sector

As will be shown in the following sections, the question of whether post-secondary vocational courses should be offered within separate schools or within the framework of university colleges has caused political disagreement among the various stakeholders at the system level.

The development of a vocational school sector in the education system—that is, institutions in the border area between upper secondary schools and higher education institutions—was first taken up systematically in the OECD report *Alternatives to Universities* from 1991 (OECD 1991). The report stated that these schools were essentially privately managed and financed, and offered short, strictly vocationally oriented education courses, but frequently without a state overall perspective of the need and use of this supplement to the public education system. These market-oriented schools were not really visible in the majority of countries, but had nevertheless a much greater number of students than were acknowledged, and the OECD went so far as to suggest that these schools could eventually develop as a real competitor to the established institutions in higher education. The reason was that new and non-traditional educational establishments had captured contemporary requirements in the labor market more quickly and more effectively than the colleges and universities, and frequently in niches that were not regarded as of interest by the established institutions. The OECD included this sector in a later report, *Redefining*

Tertiary Education (OECD 1998), with the intention of revealing and discussing its place within the overall education system.

As a direct consequence of the OECD report, a Norwegian governmental-appointed commission, the Berg Committee, was set up with the mandate to investigate the state of affairs of the vocational school sector and the possibility for strengthening its legal framework. The committee's recommendations included the development of a separate Act for vocational education; devising a mechanism for quality assurance; setting criteria for the public recognition of vocational schools; and clarifying roles and responsibilities with respect to the administrative and financial oversight of the sector (Norges Offentlige Utredninger 2000).

On the basis of the Berg Committee's recommendations, the Ministry of Education and Research presented a parliamentary White Paper in which it was determined that formalizing a vocational school sector served little purpose. Instead, the technical schools should be maintained as part of the responsibility of the county authorities. In addition, the Ministry expressed the view that the university colleges would have to take a greater degree of responsibility for shorter vocational courses and to integrate these as part of their study programs.

The consideration of this proposal by the parliamentary committee for educational affairs illuminates the political disagreement about the status of this part of the educational system. The committee's members from the Labor Party argued that responsibility for the short vocational courses should be the responsibility of the university colleges. It was pointed out that the college sector had the necessary capacity and teaching competence within most of these areas. The liberal/conservative majority on the committee, on the other hand, argued that there was a need for a vocational education level in the education system that could function as an alternative to higher education. A practical and vocational offer parallel to higher education would give the technical schools and other practically oriented courses a natural and permanent place in the education system. This would result in several new courses being offered, for example within health and social care, and enhance the practical relevance of such courses. In the view of the majority, a separate sector would also improve the status of vocational education, provide it with an identity, and present this level of education as a viable alternative to higher education. The majority also considered that a special Act should be prepared, and a request to government to present such a bill to Parliament was made.

The underlying reason for establishing a distinct vocational educational sector was the belief that the requirements of the market for qualified labor at this level would be met more appropriately outside the college sector than as part of it. In order to maintain and to further develop the variety of educational courses beyond upper secondary school, the committee members argued, a formal three-level education system should be developed to meet a variety of purposes. If, in accordance with the intentions of the Labor Party, vocational training should be accorded to the state colleges, a likely development would be that very short vocational courses in some regions would become university courses—at least in name.

As a result of consequent discussions in Parliament, and despite the initial reluctance of the government regarding the formalization of the sector, the Act on Vocational Education was passed in 2003. The Act formally established vocational education as a short and directly work-related alternative to higher education at universities and university colleges, as initially recommended by the majority of the Berg Committee's members.

Thus, through the establishment of an appropriate legal framework, Parliament made sure that a clear sector-wide demarcation would continue to exist between vocational education at vocational schools and higher education at the university colleges. By fostering the accreditation and quality recognition of practical courses at the vocational schools by Norway's accreditation agency (NOKUT), the Act not only guaranteed the legitimacy of the sector per se, but also enabled the latter to play a more prominent role in broader tertiary educational provision.

Despite the legislation, the structural barriers to progression into higher levels of education have not yet been entirely removed. The Ministry of Education and Research has recently stated that a lot remains to be done in clarifying the links between vocational schools and higher education institutions. When entering higher education, those with vocational school qualifications must undergo an individual assessment of skills acquired if part of their competence and skills is to be recognized as being at the higher education level. Part of the problem is related to the lack of a system of credit points in the vocational colleges, making it difficult to assess the scope and depth of education taken and, especially, making comparability with higher education more difficult (Ministry of Education and Research 2005: 84). Against this background, the latest OECD review of tertiary education in Norway has suggested integration to support student movement:

> We believe that there would be merit in linking or combining some vocational colleges with university colleges—so as to promote cooperation between vocational subjects and business studies or engineering and to facilitate the movement of students in either direction.
>
> (OECD 2006: 11)

The Relationship Between the College Sector and the University Sector

A key aspect of the relationship between the college and the university sectors has been the possibility of the transfer of students across sector boundaries, a process that can be traced back to the mid-1960s and the work of a committee on the future of post-secondary education in Norway (Bleiklie *et al.* 2000). According to the committee, the post-secondary education system should be as tightly integrated as possible, allowing the mobility of students from district colleges and professional schools into university education. This meant, among other things, that the institutional mission of the district colleges was not only to provide practical, short-term education for the labor market (their core purpose), but also to train and qualify students for higher-level studies at universities. Concerns regarding the feasibility of simultaneously accomplishing vocational and theoretical training were initially raised by Parliament, but the Ministry of Education supported the committee's recommendation nonetheless (Kyvik 1981).

In order to meet the requirements of universities, adaptations in the curricula offered by the district colleges were devised. Between 1973 and 1979, up to 15 percent of all graduates from the district colleges enrolled in a university program in the following semester (Kyvik 1981). By the early 1980s, with one exception, all two- to three-year degree programs at the district colleges had been accepted by universities as the equivalent of one and a half years of university studies. However, the increasing adaptation of curricular structures in line with the programmatic offers of the universities resulted in a decline of innovative efforts and regional orientation from the side of the colleges. Rather ironically, this process was, to a great extent, intensified by the district colleges themselves as they pressured the Ministry and the universities for the establishment of a transfer system between the two sectors.

In the early 1980s, a new Act on Examinations and Course Grades would extend the provision of university preparation to the professional colleges, in addition to the district colleges. Also during this period, the colleges were legally entitled to award a first-degree qualification corresponding to those offered by universities, thus fostering the possibility of student transfer between the two sectors. By 1981, a flexible credit transfer system had been successfully established, allowing graduates from the college sector to further their education at the university level. The study areas most affected by these developments were the programs in (i) engineering and (ii) economics and business administration. Vertical integration schemes between three-year engineering programs in colleges and five-year civil engineering programs were further enhanced. During the 1990s, close to 25 percent of all students graduating from three-year college degree programs in engineering enrolled in civil engineering programs at the university level (Aamodt 2001). As for economics and business studies, the two-year courses offered at the university colleges gradually came to be regarded as the first part of the four-year degree programs in economics and business administration at the specialized university institutions (Rønhovde 2002). Thus, over time, a flexible student transfer system developed. In a report to the OECD, the Ministry of Education and Research commented on this growing level of integration in the following terms:

The higher education sector is well integrated, with extensive and mandatory recognition of study programmes and degrees across institutional types, and through student mobility between institutions.

(Ministry of Education and Research 2005: 5)

Through the establishment of state university colleges in 1994, based on comprehensive mergers of professional colleges and district colleges in each region and the passing of a common Act on Universities and Colleges in 1995, a formal binary higher education system was created. As a part of this reform, the notion of "Network Norway" was introduced, linking the various institutions within and across the binary divide and sustaining a strong central political steering with the further development of higher education. This concept presupposed that the higher education institutions would be further developed within a national integrated system. Further expansion should go together with specialization so that every state college could set national standards in at least one particular program, which should become a node in a national network. This meant, among other things, that a more clear division of labor between the various institutions was to be developed, while at the same time the cooperation among institutions and across sectors was expected to be further enhanced (Kyvik 2002).

However, the new liberal winds that swept over Western Europe at that time also reached Norway. Some of the colleges soon used the opportunity to tell the political establishment that the Network Norway concept had strong connotations to feudal societies with no possibility for social mobility. Gradually, the term "Network Norway" disappeared in public documents as a political steering concept. Contrary to the intentions of governmental authorities, the establishment of the notion of Network Norway initially devised to sustain the demarcations across the binary system while simultaneously facilitating the coordination between the university and college sectors, led gradually to the dissipation of important structural and cultural differences across the two sectors. With the passing of the common Act on Universities and Colleges in 1995, a process of rule-harmonization (e.g. organization and management principles, funding structures, personnel policies) across the sectors was initiated. The intended division of labor between the universities and colleges was further undermined as a result of the implementation of a common academic career system (Kyvik 2008). At the turn of the millennium, various state colleges started actively to work towards the achievement of university status and the question was raised whether Norway should introduce a unified system of higher education. Finally, the 2003 "Quality Reform" (Michelsen and Aamodt 2006), which aimed at improving academic quality and the efficiency of the sector, as well as adjusting the Norwegian higher education system to the Bologna process, also contributed to the further dissipation of the boundaries between universities and colleges. This process was most pronounced with the introduction of a common two-tier degree structure (as per Bologna) across the boundary divide, not to mention the steps taken to improve student mobility across sectors via the introduction of a European System for Credit Transfers.

From the side of the colleges, upward drift or imitative tendencies (DiMaggio and Powell 1983) towards the traditional university model have, for quite some time, been observed (Kyvik 2008). This phenomenon is most visible in the types of program being offered at the colleges, with the progressive introduction of master's degrees. Moreover, ministerial decisions allowing colleges meeting specific requirements to offer PhD degrees in certain areas has also contributed to the gradual erosion of the traditional binary divide in Norwegian higher education. Concurrently with academic drift in the college sector, there have been clear signs of vocational drift in the university sector, driven by two major processes. First, the transformation of universities from elite institutions to mass higher education institutions has changed governmental opinions on the role and purpose of universities in the production of candidates for the labor market. While continuing their traditional academic programs, universities are also expected to introduce more directly work-oriented courses to serve the needs of society and the demands of new student groups. Secondly, recent studies indicate that about one fourth of all first-year students enrolled at Norwegian universities transfer to university colleges (Hovdhaugen 2008). Because of the increasing competition for students caused by a new funding system, universities have for these two reasons established new work-related courses as well as courses that were originally offered by colleges in order to retain current and attract new students who would opt for a vocationally oriented course.

In the new Act on Universities and Colleges of 2004, the former regulation regarding the designation of individual institutions as universities, specialized university institutions, or state colleges was abolished. It was determined that the issue of institutional designation should no longer be a policy decision but strictly an academic matter. The new Act states that university colleges and specialized university institutions may opt for the preferred status themselves, but have to be accredited by the Norwegian Agency for Quality Assurance in Education (NOKUT), in order to attain the status according to specific criteria. NOKUT must approve a change of status prior to the Ministry granting approval. However, NOKUT's approval does not have to be accepted by the Ministry. On the other hand, the Ministry cannot change the status of a given institution without the institution being formally recognized by NOKUT as having the necessary quality/capacity (Stensaker 2004).

The attainment of full university status by two university colleges in 2005 and 2007 led to a further blurring of the binary divide in higher education. Nowadays many of the remaining colleges want to follow in their footsteps. In order to attain university status according to the new regulations, individual colleges with such ambitions subsequently chose different strategies: (a) to make it on their own, (b) to merge with nearby colleges and create a network university, or (c) to advance to the status of specialized university institution. The government was not comfortable with this development, which might result in the creation of a large number of universities in a country with a population of fewer than five million people, and set up a committee to address this problem. In its recent report, the committee suggests that a possible solution might be to abolish the binary system, leading to the establishment of a unified higher education system (Norges Offentlige Utredninger 2008). According to the committee's recommendations, the traditional notion of what counts as a "university" has been eroded and the crucial point is to clarify "what type of university," rather than sustain the traditional distinction along the binary divide. In reality, the debate on the modern notion of "university" transcends Norwegian boundaries and is becoming an important element of academic and policy debates at the European regional level (Maassen and Olsen 2007). As stated in the committee's report to the Ministry, as more and more colleges obtain the status of "university" and the fundamental differences between universities and colleges are eroded, it becomes even more problematic to maintain the division of labor in teaching and research.

Policy Implications

At this stage it is worth addressing the following question: In what way have the policies pursued by the state authorities with respect to integrating the various arms of its tertiary education sector affected the status and core mission of the various types of institutions, as well as the scope and nature of the relationships across the entire tertiary education sector? The policy of continuing demarcation of institutional boundaries in Norway's tertiary education, combined with the adoption of student transfer mechanisms, led to a set of unintended consequences. Two of the most prevalent effects were changes in curricular structures and a new dynamic characterizing structural relations among institutions.

As demonstrated above, the continuous adaptation of program offers at the vocational schools to the requirements of the universities and colleges led to the academicization of what was supposed to be a more practical-oriented type of instruction. Thus, rather than strengthening the position of vocational institutions, as initially planned, the adoption of student transfer mechanisms and the consequent curriculum adjustments contributed to *weakening* rather than *strengthening* the distinctive function and overall standing of vocational education in the context of the broad tertiary educational sector. This led to both positive and negative reactions at a variety of levels. Students who wanted to transfer into university programs acclaimed this development, while students who had initially chosen vocational education owing to their close links with the labor market were skeptical. Some of the teachers were, in fact, important drivers of this academicization process, while others not only had difficulties in conceiving of themselves as part of the academic profession but, most importantly, did not possess adequate training to engage in theoretically driven instruction. Finally, parts of the labor market dependent on vocational institutions for the proper instruction of their professional members complained about the lack of practical skills among graduates, while other parts acclaimed the increased theoretical knowledge of graduates.

Turning now to the scope and nature of the relationships among the various institutions composing Norway's tertiary educational sector, Neave (1983), a quarter of a century ago, argued that all systems of higher education display a dynamic towards "integration," even if government policy may be aimed at sustaining a binary system. Thus, it could be argued that the harmonization of rules and regulations across the binary divide, together with the process of academicization (at the vocational schools and colleges), has contributed to a closer relationship among the various types of tertiary institutions as their destinies have become more interdependent and their structural arrangements more alike. Seeing these developments from the perspective of organizational/institutional theory, it could be argued that both the state and higher educational institutions exercise considerable institutional pressures which, over time, result in greater levels of homogeneity across the entire sector, or the "organisational field" (DiMaggio and Powell 1983) of tertiary education.

The imitation of university curricula by colleges—a phenomenon known in the institutional literature as "mimetic isomorphism" (DiMaggio and Powell 1983)—contributed to the blurring of the system boundaries between university and non-university institutions. Through a continuous and gradual process of academicization, in part via the adoption of curriculum structures similar to those of universities, the colleges have attempted to improve their system-level posture, market-status and public recognition. This process was achieved at the expense of the sector's unique educational features, namely to provide a viable alternative to long-term, theoretically based higher education at the university level. On the other hand, the isomorphic tendencies observed across colleges and universities have caused new tensions or dilemmas, both *between* and *within* institutions, as these struggle to re-define their unique cultural identities and sense of purpose (Stensaker 2006)—a legitimating social function capable of guaranteeing their future survival and growth.

In terms of future developments, as shown above, ongoing debates on the possibility of further integrating the higher education sector via mergers or network arrangements may exacerbate the current academicization (homogenization) tendencies in Norwegian higher education. It is feasible that the above process, if it is to occur, could affect the dynamics of the vocational school sector as well, assuming that the current policy of student mobility across the entire tertiary sector is to be pursued in years to come. Notwithstanding, it is important to bear in mind the potential impacts brought about by the recently adopted legal framework regulating the vocational sector. At least three scenarios are possible. First, the Act may contribute to a renewed "sense of identity" among vocational schools, resulting in a stronger demarcation of the systemic boundaries between the vocational and the higher education sectors. On the other hand, the legal framework is likely to increase the regulative power of the state (through accreditation), thus potentially decreasing the autonomy of vocational institutions to define the scope and nature of their program offerings. A third scenario originating from the gradual stagnation and decline of the student population after 2015 (Norges Offentlige Utredninger 2008: 34–5) could see the inclusion of various types of post-secondary vocational school courses as part of the program offerings of higher education institutions, particularly the colleges, as a means of attracting additional pools of students. It is worth mentioning, nonetheless, that in the case of the adoption of a future higher education model based on *differentiation* rather than *integration*, it could very well be that a stronger focus will be placed on the traditional distinction between university and non-university education, reversing the current tendencies towards homogenization. This will eventually lead to a renewal of the traditional divide along the lines of a binary system of higher education. If this is to occur—and we can only speculate at this stage— then it *could* also be possible that, as part of their search for a distinctive social mission, the colleges would strengthen their vocational and regional orientation, thus enhancing their potential links with the vocational school sector.

In retrospect, and in light of the aspects covered above, it can be tentatively concluded that policy mechanisms like student transfers and network-type arrangements geared towards a tighter integration of the various sub-sectors composing tertiary education should, as much as possible, take into account potential unintended effects. The Norwegian story shows that deliberate attempts by the state at maintaining a rather fuzzy demarcation between the various institutions, while at the same time developing the conditions for the possibility of bridging the divide between them, resulted, in the long run, in a loss of variety (heterogeneity) owing to isomorphic tendencies at the system level.

References

Aamodt, P.O. 2001. *Studiegjennomføring og studiefrafall*, Oslo: NIFU, Norwegian Institute for Studies in Higher Education.

Aamodt, P. O. and S. Kyvik. 2005. Access to higher education in the Nordic countries. In *Understanding Mass Higher Education: Comparative Perspectives on Access*, eds. T. Tapper and D. Palfreyman, London: RoutledgeFalmer, pp. 121–138.

Bleiklie, I., R. Høstaker and A. Vabø (eds.). 2000. *Policy and Practice in Higher Education: Reforming Norwegian Universities*, London: Jessica Kingsley Publishers.

Brandt, E. 2007. *På vei mot fagskoler? En kartlegging av privatskolemarkedet*, Oslo: Norwegian Institute for Studies in Innovation, Research and Education.

Clark, B.R. 1983. *The Higher Education System: Academic Organization in Cross-National Perspective*, Berkeley: University of California Press.

DiMaggio, P. and W. Powell. 1983. The iron cage revisited: institutional isomorphism and collective rationality in organizational fields, *American Sociological Review*, 48, 147–60.

Furth, D. 1992. Short-cycle higher education: Europe. In *The Encyclopedia of Higher Education*, eds. B.R. Clark and G. Neave, Oxford: Pergamon Press, pp. 1217–25.

Hovdhaugen, E. 2008. Transfer and dropout: different forms of student departure in Norway, *Studies in Higher Education*, 33:6, forthcoming.

Kyvik, S. 1981. *The Norwegian Regional Colleges. A Study of the Establishment and Implementation of a Reform in Higher Education*, Oslo: Institute for Studies in Research and Higher Education.

Kyvik, S. 2002. The merger of non-university colleges in Norway, *Higher Education*, 44, 53–72.

Kyvik, S. 2008. The non-university higher education sector in Norway. In *Non-University Higher Education in Europe*, eds. J.B. Ferreira, M.L. Machado and R. Santiago, Dordrecht: Springer, pp. 169–89.

Maassen, P. and J.P. Olsen. 2007. *University Dynamics and European Integration*, Dordrecht: Springer.

Michelsen, S. and P.O. Aamodt. 2006. *Evaluering av Kvalitetsreformen. Sluttrapport Evaluering av Kvalitetsreformen*, Oslo: Norges forskningsråd.

Ministry of Education and Research. 2005. *OECD Thematic Review of Tertiary Education: Country Background Report for Norway*, Oslo: Ministry of Education and Research.

Neave, G. 1983. The dynamic of integration in non-integrated systems of higher education in Western Europe. In *The Complete University*, eds. H. Hermanns, U. Teichler, and H. Wasser, Cambridge, MA: Schenkman, pp. 263–76.

Norges Offentlige Utredninger. 2000. *Mellom barken og veden: om fagskoleutdanninger*. NOU 2000:5, Oslo: Statens forvaltningstjeneste.

Norges Offentlige Utredninger. 2008. *Sett under ett: Ny struktur i høyere utdanning*. NOU 2008:3, Oslo: Statens forvaltningstjeneste.

OECD (Organisation for Economic Co-operation and Development). 1991. *Alternatives to Universities*, Paris: Organisation for Economic Co-operation and Development.

OECD (Organisation for Economic Co-operation and Development). 1998. *Redefining Tertiary Education*, Paris: Organisation for Economic Co-operation and Development.

OECD (Organisation for Economic Co-operation and Development). 2006. *Thematic Review of Tertiary Education, Norway*, Paris: Organisation for Economic Co-operation and Development.

Powell, W. and P. DiMaggio (eds). 1991. *The New Institutionalism in Organizational Analysis*, Chicago: University of Chicago Press.

Rønhovde, L. 2002. De økonomisk-administrative utdanningene—utviklingstrekk i studiet og kunnskapsmiljøet. In *Faglige forbindelser: Profesjonsutdanning og kunnskapspolitikk etter høgskolereformen*, eds. S. Michelsen and T. Halvorsen, Bergen: Fagbokforlaget, pp. 87–104.

Stensaker, B. 2004. The blurring boundaries between accreditation and audit: the case of Norway. In *Accreditation in the Framework of Evaluation Activities: Current Situation and Dynamics in Europe*, eds. S. Schwarz and D.E. Westerheijden, Dordrecht: Kluwer Academic Publishers, pp. 342–65.

Stensaker, B. 2006. Governmental policy, organisational ideals, and institutional adaptation in Norwegian higher education, *Studies in Higher Education*, 31, 43–56.

5

Australia: The Emergence of Dual Sector Universities

GAVIN MOODIE

Introduction

At the turn of the twenty-first century, five Australian universities started describing themselves as a "dual sector university." This chapter looks at the use of the term in Australia and the characteristics of the universities so described, and speculates why other Australian universities with otherwise similar histories developed as single sector universities. The chapter concludes by considering the potential for the development of new dual sector universities in Australia.

The Term "Dual Sector University"

The first use of the term "dual sector university" that I have been able to find is in a paper published in 2000 that considers how dual sector universities can challenge the binary divide between vocational and higher education (Doughney 2000). Later that year, Wheelahan (2000) reviewed the difficulties faced by dual sector universities in bridging the deep divide between vocational and higher education in Australia. The first reference to "dual sector institution" or its cognates that I have been able to find is in a 1995 conference paper by Cole and Corcoran (1995: 9) describing the early development of Charles Darwin University, a dual sector university then called Northern Territory University. Other early references to dual sector institutions are by Trembath et al. (1996), Patterson (1997: 301), Donleavy (1998: 68), and Sommerlad et al. (1998: xxii).

The Australian institutions that identify themselves and recognize each other as dual sector universities are Charles Darwin University, Swinburne University of Technology, Royal Melbourne Institute of Technology, the University of Ballarat, and Victoria University in Melbourne. These universities share two characteristics that define them as dual sector universities: they have a substantial student load in both vocational education and higher education, and they undertake substantial research and award research doctorates.

Higher Education

Higher education comprises programs that typically require a minimum of three years' full-time study after the final year of secondary schooling, are theoretically based, and either provide access to high-status occupations or prepare students for research in basic disciplines. While many countries have higher education institutions that are not universities, the sector is dominated by universities that are similar throughout the Western world, and the oldest of which trace a continuous history back to the Middle Ages (Moodie 2008). Higher education is therefore readily identified in most jurisdictions, although there are important differences in the sector in each country that should inform international comparisons. Higher education is classified as level 5A by the United Nations Educational, Scientific and Cultural Organisation's (1997) international standard classification of education.

Vocational Education

There is far less international coincidence in the definition of the sector of tertiary education that is called in this chapter vocational education: it is the upper levels of further education colleges in the UK and it is the tertiary education offered by two-year colleges in the US, community colleges in Canada and the US, *Berufsakademien* (vocational academies) and *Fachschulen* (trade and technical schools) in Germany, *instituts universitaires de technologie* (university institutes of technology) and *sections de techniciens supérieurs* (higher technical education units) in France, *hogescholen* (higher vocational colleges) in the Netherlands, vocational education and training providers in Australia, and polytechnics in New Zealand. Vocational education comprises programs that typically require no longer than two years' equivalent full-time study, are practical, and either provide access to middle-status occupations or prepare students for higher education. There is considerable variation between countries in the structure, orientation, and, as we have seen, nomenclature of vocational education. Nonetheless, the United Nations Educational Scientific and Cultural Organisation's (1997) international standard classification of education identifies vocational education as a distinct sector, which it classifies as level 5B. While organized vocational education probably pre-dates higher education, few if any vocational education institutes can trace a continuous history beyond the industrial revolution (Moodie 2008).

Other Instances of Dual Sector Provision

Many Australian universities appear to be dual sector because they offer some vocational education programs. Some offerings are vestiges of history. Thus, the University of Adelaide offers three vocational education diplomas and four certificates in music through the Elder Conservatorium of Music established by a bequest in 1898. Many dual sector offerings are the result of amalgamations with previously single sector institutions. For example, the University of Queensland offers the Queensland certificate of agriculture at its Gatton College, which was formed as a result of the university's amalgamation in 1990 with the Queensland Agricultural College. Curtin University has 320 full time equivalent students, or 1 percent of its total student load, enrolled in vocational education programs at its Kalgoorlie and Esperance campuses, which are more than 500 kilometers from Curtin's main campus in Perth. Edith Cowan University has 400 full time equivalent students, or 3 percent of its student load, enrolled in vocational education programs in music and theatre.

An institution is vertically integrated to the extent that it owns its upstream suppliers and its downstream buyers. Thus, a university is more vertically integrated if it offers vocational education or the final year of compulsory schooling since these programs supply its students. Chipman (2002) argued that higher education may be made more affordable by reducing vertical integration—by having research done by one part of a university system, scholarship and curriculum design by another part, and delivery by yet another part of the system. But the trend seems to be in the opposite direction, towards greater vertical integration of tertiary education, often by pragmatic extensions of existing programs or integration of programs or services that had previously been offered by other organizations.

Thus, the University of Sydney and most other Australian universities offer English language programs that are secondary or vocational education in level and had hitherto been offered by English language institutes. The University of Adelaide offers a certificate in teaching English to speakers of other languages, and Flinders University offers a certificate in disability studies offshore. The Australian Catholic University is a registered training organization and offers vocational education certificates and diplomas in education, exercise science, frontline management, and nursing.

Some Australian universities have vertically integrated programs and services systematically, most often for international students. One of the earliest and most successful vertical integrations was the University of Technology Sydney's offering of secondary and vocational education and other sub-bachelor programs and services through Insearch, which it established as a wholly owned for-profit subsidiary in 1987. At its Sydney center Insearch offers academic pathway programs to the university, a range of English pathway and language programs, and one of the world's largest international English language testing system centers. In China, Insearch has offered diplomas in English and business as well as the university's bachelor of business in partnership with Shanghai University since 1994. Insearch established a center at the University of Essex in 2004, where it offers English language preparation programs and academic and English pathway programs that lead to direct access to Essex University (Insearch 2006a).

Several other Australian universities have followed the University of Technology Sydney's example in offering vocational education and secondary-level programs mainly, although not exclusively, for international students. The University of Wollongong established Wollongong College Australia in 1988 to offer English language, university preparation, and diploma programs to international and domestic students. Monash University established Monash College as a wholly owned for-profit subsidiary in the 1990s, and it now teaches diplomas at the university's Clayton, Caulfield, and Peninsula campuses and also in Singapore, Guangzhou (China), Jakarta, and Colombo (Monash College 2007). Monash University's English language center mounts intensive language programs, and the Monash University foundation year is an equivalent Australian final school year program offered by Taylors College in Australia and other partners in Laos, Jakarta, and Malaysia (Kuala Lumpur and Johor Bahru). The Australian National University (ANU) has established ANU College as a registered training organization that offers a foundation studies program, an ANU access English program, English language instruction for overseas students, extended university English, an advanced secondary studies program, math bridging courses, and group study tours. Charles Sturt University has established CSU Training as a registered training organization to offer programs for its staff, industry, and professionals in niche areas and to embed vocational qualifications within higher education programs.

Most Australian universities' vocational education programs are small in size, confined to one campus (Australian universities have an average of 3.4 campuses[1]), are in one or two disciplines, and many are offered through separate organizational units. They therefore have little if any impact on the university outside their immediate area. Dual sector universities first identified themselves as being distinctive in having to manage dual systems and processes to report to two levels of government since in Australia responsibility for vocational and higher education is split between the state and federal governments. Where vocational education is a small part of a university's operations it can be handled as an exception to the structures, systems, and processes established to handle higher education. But where vocational education is a substantial part of the university's operations a separate system has to be established to handle it. Vocational education must also be a substantial part of the university's student load to affect higher education.

"Substantial"

Dual sector universities have never specified the proportion of load needed in each sector to be considered "substantial." The issue can be put rigorously by asking: how high a proportion of total student load must vocational education be before it is no longer considered an exception and it is generally accepted as a normal part of the institution? The same question arises in different contexts:

how many women do there have to be in an occupation or worksite before they are no longer considered exceptional but are accepted as part of the norm? Conversely, when do women become so large a part of a workforce that it becomes "feminized," its wages and working conditions deteriorate, and men leave it (Pfeffer and Davis-Blake 1987)? A similar dynamic has been observed in the racial segregation of housing in US cities (Grodzins 1958). Another context is the adoption of an innovation, a new technology, a fad, or a new idea: at what point does an innovation pass from the innovators to the early adopters and thence to the early majority (Wilson 2006)?

A number of analytical perspectives have been proposed for these problems: threshold models, bandwagon effects, contagion effects, epidemic theories, and tipping point. As LaFree (1999: 162) points out, while these concepts vary greatly, all of them assume that in the right circumstances social trends may be nonlinear. The phenomenon has also been studied empirically. The phrase "tipping point" was coined by Grodzins, who studied the racial integration of US neighborhoods in the 1950s and 1960s. He discovered that most white families would remain in a neighborhood as long as the number of black families remained comparatively small. But at a certain point, when "one too many" black families arrived, the remaining white families would move out en masse in a process known as white flight. He called that moment the "tipping point" (Grodzins 1958). The threshold or tipping point differs for each social trend, but 20 percent is often observed (Wilson 2006). So for the want of a better alternative one may posit that a university is a dual sector university when at least 20 percent but no more than 80 percent of its load is in vocational education. It will be noted from table 5.1 that from 26 percent to 51 percent of the total student load of Australia's dual sector universities are in vocational education.

Table 5.1 Australian dual sector universities' full time equivalent student load by type of program (2006)

Type of program	Ballarat	Charles Darwin	RMIT	Swinburne	Victoria
Vocational education	3,111	3,562	10,525	12,211	12,285
Higher education coursework	7,563	2,938	29,221	11,384	14,019
Higher education research	142	143	1,102	405	410
Total higher education	7,705	3,081	30,323	11,789	14,429
Total	10,816	6,643	40,848	24,000	26,714
Vocational education as % of total	29	54	26	51	46

Source: DEST (2007) and universities' annual reports

"University"

Australia has many non-university providers that offer both vocational and higher education. Some were established as higher education providers and subsequently added vocational education programs to broaden the range of prospective students from which they could recruit. Others were established as vocational education providers and added higher education programs to follow their students up the educational ladder. Some of these institutions might be accurately described as dual sector institutions, like some "mixed economy" (Higher Education Funding Council for England 1995) further education colleges in the UK and some community colleges in Canada and the US that also offer bachelor degrees.

But arguably dual sector universities are more complex than other dual sector institutions because of the research role of universities. Compare the differences between higher education coursework and research programs with the differences between coursework vocational and higher education programs, which are presented in table 5.2. Coursework vocational and higher education follow a curriculum that is specified in advance while research candidates' curriculum is developed with their research. Coursework students are taught in groups whereas research candidates are supervised individually or in a very small group. Moreover, coursework students have substantial contact hours each week whereas research candidates' formal teaching would typically be a meeting with their supervisor for one or two hours every week or fortnight. On some characteristics, such as student independence, there is a continuum from vocational education to coursework higher education to research higher

Table 5.2 Differences between vocational education, coursework higher education, and research higher education programs

Characteristic	Vocational education	Coursework higher education	Research higher education
Curriculum	Specified in advance	Specified in advance	Developed with the program
Program length	6 months–2 years	2–5 years	3–4 years
Orientation	Employment	Employment/ discipline	Discipline
Class size	Small to medium group	Large groups and some small groups	Mostly individual supervision
Contact hours per week	15–30	10–15	1–2
Student independence	Low	Moderate	High

education. On other characteristics, such as length of program, coursework and research higher education programs are more similar than vocational education and coursework higher education programs.

Overall, the differences between coursework and research higher education programs are at least as big if not bigger than the differences between coursework vocational and higher education programs. Research programs thus add considerably to the complexity of managing an institution. Universities with a substantial institutional research role offer programs that prepare students for occupations and for proceeding to advanced study and research. Sometimes they seek to combine both these functions within one program while on other occasions they offer programs that concentrate on either occupational preparation or research training. Whichever approach is adopted, the curriculum has to be developed and presented and students' performance has to be assessed differently for occupational and research expertise. And universities need policies and processes for students to transfer between occupational and research tracks with minimal loss of progress.

Universities with a substantial research role need to appoint and promote academic staff not only for teaching expertise, but also for research expertise. Some universities aim for all their academic staff to have substantial teaching and research roles; others appoint significant proportions of academic staff to concentrate in either teaching or research, and others seek to systematize staff's different allocations of their effort to teaching and research in proportion to their expertise and inclination and the institution's needs. Whichever approach a university adopts, it needs to have appointment and promotion criteria for research that are different from those for teaching, it needs to establish relativities between appointment and promotion criteria for teaching and research, and it needs a mechanism for allocating staff resources between teaching and research.

Many universities not only differentiate academic staff roles by their engagement in teaching and research, but differentiate academic organizational units by the extent of their teaching and research roles. Thus, while some universities seek to have all their departments, schools, and faculties engaged equally in teaching and research, many more recognize different levels and types of engagement in research by allocating different levels and types of support. Many universities establish specialized research institutes, centers, or schools, and some establish specialized teaching schools and units. These organizational units with different levels of engagement in teaching and research are typically established within the same formal organizational structure, but the more collective decision-making appropriate for teaching is infrequently adopted for research, which typically relies more heavily on the judgments of research leaders. In practice, the organizational dynamics of the two types of units are quite different and have to be managed differently by subordinate staff, the heads of units, and the institution's senior management.

Teaching and research require different types of facilities and resources and different support arrangements and operate on different academic calendars. Universities typically handle this by establishing different central service and support units for teaching and research, multiplying the organizational complexity of central and support units. While a few universities establish research libraries and research computing units dedicated to supporting specialized research function, most ask their libraries and computer centers to support both teaching and research. This seems straightforward from outside those units, but it of course internalizes the complexity of supporting different functions and allocating resources between them.

Because of the different demands of teaching and research, Newman, in his *The Idea of a University*, argued against universities having a research role:

> The nature of the case and the history of philosophy combine to recommend to us this division of intellectual labour between academies and universities. To discover and to teach are distinct functions; they are also distinct gifts, and are not commonly found united in the same person.
>
> (Newman 1853/1959: 10)

Much academic effort has been spent countering Newman's observation by positing a teaching–research nexus. For example, Hattie and Marsh (1996) reviewed fifty-eight studies of the relationship between research and teaching (to find no relationship).

Having a substantial research role therefore adds considerably to the complexity of institutions and therefore justifies dual sector universities distinguishing themselves from other dual sector institutions. But what amounts to a substantial research role? The new US Carnegie classification of institutions of higher education (Carnegie Foundation 2007) defines doctorate-granting universities as institutions that award at least twenty doctoral degrees per year. As will be seen from table 5.3, the University of Ballarat just satisfies this criterion and Charles Darwin University falls somewhat short. Both are located in rural cities without a large urban elite or industrial base to generate local demand for research degrees. Even research students in Australia do not tend to relocate for

Table 5.3 Measures of research intensity of Australian dual sector universities (2006)

Indicator	Ballarat	Charles Darwin	RMIT	Swinburne	Victoria	All unis mean
% research load	1.8	4.6	3.6	3.4	2.8	5.0
PhD graduates	20	17	127	68	67	141
% research fund	2.3	3.8	4.7	3.7	2.8	8.6

Source: DEST (2007)

study, and neither Ballarat nor Charles Darwin University has much money to allocate to research scholarships.

Research adds a significant complexity to an institution, not by its scale but by its size in proportion to the institution's other activities. Research intensity rather than research scale is salient for institutional complexity. The Carnegie Foundation further classifies doctorate-granting universities by research intensity on measures specific to the US. Measures of research intensity commonly used in Australia are the proportion of full-time equivalent students undertaking research degrees and research block grants as a proportion of total revenue. Charles Darwin does reasonably well on these measures because of its strength in tropic and desert knowledge. The University of Ballarat does less well and is generally understood to be one of the least research-intensive of Australian universities. Nonetheless, it (just) meets the Carnegie Foundation's criterion for doctorate-granting universities and it seems reasonable to conclude that both Ballarat and Charles Darwin universities have enough research activity to be classified as research-active universities.

University Groupings

Hirsch (1976) pointed out that some products and services have positional value. Consider a diamond. It has special characteristics that give it objective value, such as extreme hardness, clarity, and luster. These characteristics are not any more special or objectively valuable than other characteristics of other precious and semi-precious stones, yet diamonds are much more valuable than other stones. This value is a result of their scarcity. Diamonds have a positional value—they are a positional good—because their possession indicates a high position in the social hierarchy. Similarly, highly sought real estate, the "best" table in the "best" restaurant, and membership of exclusive clubs are positional goods that are valued far more highly than their objective characteristics warrant because they indicate high social standing.

Education is also a positional good. Possession of a university qualification indicates an academic achievement that makes the graduate a more valuable citizen and employee. When university education was accessible only to the social elite, possession of a university qualification also indicated membership of the elite: it therefore also had considerable positional value. With the mass expansion of higher education following the Second World War, possession of a university degree no longer signals such exclusivity. However, some institutions remain accessible mostly only to members of the social elite. These institutions, normally the oldest, and almost always the universities well established before the mass expansion of higher education, have greater positional value than other, normally younger institutions (Moodie 2008). Examples of these institutions are the members of the Ivy League in the US, Oxbridge in the UK, and the "sandstones" in Australia.

As access to higher education expands, the desire for social differentiation is increasingly sought, not just in the fact of graduating from a university, but in the choice of institution, program, and higher degree study (James 2007: 10). The expansion of participation therefore leads to overtly tiered systems, whatever their official designation by government. This segmentation has been made explicit by the universities with the greatest positional value forming themselves into self-selected clubs. Interestingly, one of the oldest of such groups was formed in the US, the first country to move from elite to mass higher education. In 1900 the fourteen well-established universities offering the PhD formed themselves into the Association of American Universities. This association of "leading research universities" currently comprises sixty-two US and two Canadian universities. In the UK an informal self-selected group of twenty "research-led" institutions formed itself into the Russell Group in 1994. In the same year in Australia the eight "leading" universities with the biggest research expenditure formed itself into the Group of Eight.

Subsequently, other groups of universities with less positional value have formed, some to distinguish themselves from other universities with even less positional value, and others to challenge the older groups' valorization of positional good. Thus, in 1994 many of the UK's "smaller research-intensive universities" formed themselves into the 1994 Group. In 2003 the Australian universities established in the 1960s and 1970s, following to various extents the interdisciplinary example of the University of Sussex in the UK, established themselves as Innovative Research Universities Australia. This group associates with the UK's 1994 Group. In 1997 UK institutions recognized as universities since 1992 formed the Coalition of Modern Universities, later called the CMU —campaigning for mainstream universities—and currently called Million+. A similar group of newly designated universities in Australia formed themselves into the New Generation Universities Network in 2002, but this has since disbanded. The Australian Technological Network was formed in 1999. It is a group that seems to be unique to Australia, formed of universities located in or near capital cities' central business districts that originated as technical colleges. RMIT, formerly known as the Royal Melbourne Institute of Technology, is a member of the Australian Technological Network.

A potentially salient distinguishing characteristic of universities that is different from and to some extent cuts across positional value is cross-sectoral provision. This is significant in Australia in providing opportunities for vocational education students to transfer to higher education. Table 5.4 shows the number of domestic students commencing a bachelor level program or below who were admitted on the basis of a Technical and Further Education (TAFE) qualification. It will be noted that most Australian dual sector universities admit a higher proportion of undergraduate students on the basis of TAFE qualifications than other universities. The University of Ballarat reports admitting a very low proportion of students on the basis of a TAFE qualification even for a single sector university, as will be noted from the table. The university's vice-

Table 5.4 Students admitted on the basis of a TAFE program and all students commencing a bachelor program by university group (2005)

Institution/group	All	TAFE	% TAFE
Swinburne University of Technology	2,893	719	25
RMIT	5,462	1,147	21
Charles Darwin University	2,101	405	19
Victoria University	4,466	619	14
University of Ballarat	1,266	40	3
Average, dual sector universities	16,188	2,930	18
Metro new generation universities	28,291	4,466	16
Rural universities	33,285	4171	13
Australian Technological Network	26,140	2583	10
Innovative Research Universities Australia	34,831	3,053	9
Group of Eight	44,022	1,390	3
All universities	183,329	18,593	10

Source: DEST (2006), table 3.1.11: domestic students commencing a course at bachelor level or below by state, higher education provider and basis for admission to current course, full year 2005

chancellor, Professor David Battersby, reported in a personal communication of April 1, 2008, that the source for this data is students' self-report. Students transferring from a TAFE program offered by the University of Ballarat report that they are admitted on the basis of an award from the university, which they do not consider an award of a TAFE institution. Battersby says that the figure reported by the university is probably of students transferring to the university from other TAFE institutes. He reports that the university's internal data suggest about 15 to 17 percent of its higher education enrolments are students with a TAFE award.

"Metro new generation universities" in table 5.4 are all universities located in a metropolitan area with a population of at least 250,000 that were recognized as universities after the collapse of the binary divide in Australia in 1988, not including Victoria University, which is classified in the table as a dual sector university. "Rural universities" are all universities located outside a metropolitan area with a population of at least 250,000, not including Charles Darwin University and the University of Ballarat, which are classified in the table as dual sector universities. The "Australian Technological Network" are the universities formed from central institutes of technology, except RMIT, which is categorized as a dual sector university. "Innovative Research Universities Australia" is the group that associates with the UK's 1994 Group, and the Group of Eight is the group that associates with the UK's Russell Group.

Why Did Only Some Universities Develop as Duals?

Three of Australia's five dual sector universities are in Victoria and developed from vocational education institutions: RMIT, Swinburne, and Victoria universities. Several other Australian universities also developed from vocational education institutions but discarded their vocational education programs to develop as single sector universities: Curtin University (which was formed from the tertiary programs formerly conducted in the Perth Technical College and which subsequently amalgamated with the Western Australian School of Mines), Deakin University (Gordon Institute of Advanced Education), Queensland University of Technology (Central Technical College), the University of New South Wales (Sydney Technical College), the University of South Australia (South Australia School of Mines and Industries), and the University of Technology, Sydney (which developed from the Sydney Technical College two decades after the University of New South Wales separated from the college).

Other universities in the UK and the US also developed from vocational education institutions but discarded their vocational education programs as they acquired and strengthened their higher education programs. For example, the University of Bath traces its history back to the Bristol Trade School of 1856 and Carnegie Mellon University was established as the Carnegie Technical Schools in 1900. But as they developed their higher education programs and gained university status they relinquished their founding vocational education programs.

The four Australian universities that retained their vocational education programs to become dual sector universities therefore seem anomalous. The following section seeks to explain these apparent anomalies by speculating that three factors contributed to the development of dual sector universities in Victoria and not in other Australian states: geography, the strength of college councils, and politics.

Geography

The large majority of Australian university students—even those at the elite universities—commute to campus from home. One might therefore expect that dual sector institutions and universities would be established in the smaller population centers that could support one dual sector campus but not two tertiary education campuses. However, most dual sector universities emerged from technical colleges that developed strong upper-level programs. They therefore had to be in a population center big enough to generate enough demand for vocational higher education of a type not adequately supplied by the local university. This explains why most of the technical colleges outside Melbourne and Sydney did not develop into dual sector institutions.

College Councils

Many vocational education institutions in Victoria were founded as a result of the financial contributions and political activism of industrialists and philanthropists who formed and occupied positions on the institutions' councils or governing bodies. The philanthropist Francis Ormond was a founder of the Working Men's College, which became RMIT. George Swinburne was a founder of the Eastern Suburbs Technical School, which became the dual sector Swinburne University of Technology, and other powerful figures contributed to the establishment of vocational education institutions in Footscray (which became the dual sector Victoria University) and elsewhere.

These institutions' councils directed the development of their institutions to further the interests of the institutions and the communities they served, which was not always consistent with the policies of government departments.

Vocational education institutions in other states did not have councils or even community advisory bodies until recently, and consequently their development was much more subject to government departments' policies. This restricted and in some cases blocked institutions' aspirations to offer programs outside the scope determined by the relevant government department. The lack of an independent council and a continuity of influential supporters made institutions in other states much more vulnerable to government decisions that disadvantaged the institution, such as splitting vocational and higher education parts into separate institutions. This happened to Sydney Technical College twice. Its higher-level programs were first split off in 1949 to form the New South Wales University of Technology, which became the University of New South Wales in 1958 and a founding member of the elite Group of Eight universities. It happened again to the college two decades later in 1969, when the New South Wales (NSW) government reconstituted the advanced programs of Sydney Technical College as a new institution, the New South Wales Institute of Technology, which became the University of Technology Sydney in 1988.

Conservative Victoria and Labor New South Wales

While the Australian government set the framework for the delineation of tertiary education sectors, until recently institutions' development was determined by state governments. State governments have had very different political histories, and I suggest that this was a factor in the development of dual sector universities in Victoria but not in New South Wales.

The Australian Labor Party was founded in 1891 but did not win office until it formed the federal government for three months in 1904 and then for six months in 1909. The first sustained Labor governments won office in 1910: in NSW for six years, in Western Australia for five years, in South Australia for two years, and federally for three years. As shown in table 5.5, since 1910 Labor has

Table 5.5 Percentage of time since 1910 and 1945 that the Australian states and the Commonwealth have been governed by the Australian Labor Party

Jurisdiction	Since 1910	Since 1945
Victoria	30	36
South Australia	39	44
Commonwealth	41	33
Western Australia	51	43
Queensland	56	56
New South Wales	61	70
Tasmania	66	74

formed the government for 30 percent of the time in Victoria, the lowest of any jurisdiction. In contrast, Labor has held office for 61 percent of the time since 1910 in NSW. The civic institutions in Victoria have therefore been overwhelmingly shaped by conservative governments and the citizens who elected them, while in New South Wales they have been overwhelmingly shaped by Labor governments and voters. The formative period of the tertiary education sectors in Australia has been since 1945, when conservative governments and citizens have again dominated Victoria and Labor governments and voters have dominated New South Wales.

The interaction between institutions' councils and state governments' political orientation is seen in New South Wales and Victoria's handling of proposals to establish technological universities in their states. The New South Wales Labor government was sympathetic to the aspirations of the higher education division of Sydney Technical College to form a technological university. While the college did not have a strong council to advance the aspirations of the college to be made the new university, neither was there a strong council to oppose the splitting of the institution, an outcome opposed by its supporters.

The conservative Victoria government was attracted to the financial savings of forming a technological university out of Melbourne Technical College, the forerunner of RMIT, but this was not sufficient to overcome its view that such a development would be second best and, it feared, second rate. This feeling was reinforced by the advocates for a totally new institution, repeating in Victoria the disparaging appellation of the New South Wales University of Technology as "Kenso Tech." The Melbourne Technical College council promoted its institution's aspirations very vigorously, publicly before government enquiries and in private lobbying, but it was associated with vocational rather than higher education.

Future Developments

Of Australia's five dual sector universities, the University of Ballarat became a dual sector university by the merger of two hitherto single sector institutions. However, while the other dual sector universities have merged with other institutions, most with several, they originated as vocational institutions and became dual sector universities by developing higher-level programs and functions over time. That is, they became dual sector institutions by developing from the bottom up.

The current dual sector universities may follow the other universities that developed from vocational education institutions and subsequently discard their vocational education programs to concentrate on higher-level programs and research. However, that seems unlikely at present because the trend seems to be towards vertical integration, not disintegration. This may be observed in other vocational institutions that are following a similar trajectory as dual sector universities.

From 2005 the Australian government started offering income-contingent loans for students occupying full-fee-paying places in higher education programs in public and private institutions. This has greatly expanded the number of degree places offered by private providers, including providers that had hitherto offered only vocational education programs because of their lower market entry barriers. Some public technical and further education institutes are also offering degrees. The private providers are not required to report complete enrolment figures, and enrolment figures are not published separately for individual TAFE institutes, but it seems that the biggest secular vocational institutions have only 100 or 200 students enrolled in higher education programs. However, this provision is expanding fast and is a potential route for the development of dual sector institutions in the medium term and dual sector universities in the long term.

Another possible development of a dual sector university is from the top down. Several single sector universities have been introducing vocational and secondary education programs while at the same time trying to strengthen their research and higher degrees. We have seen that the University of Technology Sydney, the University of Wollongong, Monash University, and the Australian National University, among others, have established what in the UK would be recognized as further education colleges offering English language, final year of school, and diploma programs mainly to international students but also to domestic students. It is hard to know the size of these developments since they are typically established as separate companies that are not required to report even standard information such as enrolment figures.

However, the most recent annual report of the largest such body, Insearch (2006b), the feeder college of the University of Technology Sydney (UTS), notes that over 1,100 international students had progressed from Insearch

English and academic courses to undergraduate and postgraduate degrees at UTS during 2006. This would be almost 5 percent of UTS's total student load of 23,000 full-time equivalent students, and so the university would have to expand Insearch fourfold to conform to the Australian understanding of a dual sector university. Nonetheless, this is a possible route to the development of a dual sector university: from the top down.

A similar development has been entertained by the vice-chancellor of Central Queensland University. The university is located in a region with an estimated resident population of 190,000. Most Australian university students do not relocate to study, so university planning bodies have proposed that a local population of at least 200,000 people is needed to sustain a university. Since the population of Central Queensland is rather less than that and the population within ready commuting distance of the university's foundation campus at Rockhampton is only 70,000, Central Queensland University could not be sustained as a conventional university. It therefore introduced distance education soon after it was founded, and more recently it has established a network of campuses in Brisbane, the Gold Coast, Sydney, and Melbourne, which enroll mostly international students. A recent downturn in international student numbers has made the university vulnerable and the vice-chancellor has discussed the possibility of ensuring its viability by its becoming a dual sector university (O'Keefe 2007).

Another possible development is that made by several large universities based in capital cities such as Deakin, La Trobe, and Monash universities and the universities of South Australia and Tasmania. These have established or taken over campuses in small regional centers with populations of less than 100,000 and some even in towns of fewer than 50,000 people. These are clearly not sustainable and require substantial and draining cross subsidies from the universities' main campuses. An obvious possibility is to amalgamate the regional university campus with the region's technical and further education institute, which will usually already be well-established and viable. Some regional university campuses are co-located with TAFE campuses, and universities with regional operations propose more effective partnerships with TAFE. But university co-locations and partnerships with TAFE still maintain separate teaching staff, administrations, and facilities, making them less efficient than combined operations. A more efficient and effective option would be a full amalgamation of tertiary education institutions in each region to form a dual sector tertiary institute, university campus, or university college.

Regardless of whether the possibilities canvassed in this section emerge, it seems that dual sector developments are likely to be active in Australia for some time yet.

Note

1. I calculated this average from the data file of 2004 student enrollments compiled by the then Australian Department of Education, Science and Training from enrollment returns submitted by universities.

References

Carnegie Foundation for the Advancement of Teaching. 2007. *Basic classification description*, http://www.carnegiefoundation.org/classifications/index.asp?key=791 (accessed January 3, 2008).

Chipman, L. 2002. Affording universal higher education, *Higher Education Quarterly*, 56:2, 126–42.

Cole, M. and P. Corcoran. 1995. Higher education and TAFE: integration or extermination? Paper presented at *XIX AITEA Conference: Partnerships in Tertiary Education*, Hobart, Tasmania, September 20–22.

Department of Education, Science and Training. 2006. *Students 2005 [full year]: Selected Higher Education Statistics*, Canberra: Department of Education, Science and Training.

Department of Education, Science and Training. 2007. *Students 2006 [full year]: Selected Higher Education Statistics*, Canberra: Department of Education, Science and Training.

Donleavy, G. D. 1998. A faculty building exercise, *Journal of Higher Education Policy and Management*, 20:1, 65–75.

Doughney, L. 2000. Universal tertiary education: how dual-sector universities can challenge the binary divide between TAFE and higher education—the case of Victoria University of Technology, *Journal of Higher Education Policy and Management*, 22, 59–72.

Grodzins, M. 1958. *The Metropolitan Area as a Racial Problem*, Pittsburgh: University of Pittsburgh Press.

Hattie, J. and H. Marsh. 1996. The relationship between research and teaching: a meta analysis, *Review of Educational Research*, 66:4, 507–42.

Higher Education Funding Council for England (HEFCE). 1995. *Higher Education in Further Education Colleges: Funding the Relationship*. Reference M 1/95. Bristol: HEFCE, http://www.hefce.ac.uk/pubs/hefce/1995/m1_95.htm#p1 (accessed February 24, 2008).

Hirsch, F. 1976. *Social Limits to Growth*, London: Routledge and Kegan Paul.

Insearch. 2006a. *Corporate Profile*, http://www.insearch.edu.au/about/corporate (accessed February 24, 2008).

Insearch. 2006b. *Annual Report 2006*, Sydney: Insearch Limited, http://www.web.insearch.edu.au/LIVE/WEB/RESOURCES/DOCUMENTS/INS009_AR2007_FA2.pdf (accessed February 24, 2008).

James, R. 2007. Social equity in a mass, globalised higher education environment: the unresolved issue of widening access to university, *Faculty of Education Dean's Lecture Series 2007*, September 18. http://www.edfac.unimelb.edu.au/news/lectures/pdf/richardjamestranscript.pdf (accessed December 23, 2007).

LaFree, G. 1999. Declining violent crime rates in the 1990s: predicting crime booms and busts, *Annual Review of Sociology*, 25, 145–168.

Monash College. 2007. *Welcome to Monash College*, http://www.monash.edu/monashcollege/ (accessed February 24, 2008).

Moodie, G. F. 2008. *From Vocational to Higher Education: An International Perspective*, Berkshire: McGraw-Hill.

Newman, J. H. 1959. *The Idea of a University* (originally published 1853), New York: Image Books.

O'Keefe, B. 2007. CQU shaken by migrant programs, *The Australian*, June 20, http://www.theaustralian.news.com.au/story/0,20867,21934198–12332,00.html (accessed February 24, 2008).

Patterson, G. 1997. Strategies of alliance: models and modes of post-secondary–university integration, *Tertiary Education and Management*, 3, 299–308.

Pfeffer, J. and A. Davis-Blake. 1987. The effect of the proportion of women on salaries: the case of college administrators, *Administrative Science Quarterly*, 32, 1–24.

Sommerlad, E., Duke, C. and R. McDonald. 1998. *Universities and TAFE Collaboration in the Emerging World of "Universal Higher Education,"* Canberra: Department of Education, Science and Training, http://www.dest.gov.au/NR/rdonlyres/6692C59F-18F6–471C-B95F-30710BA4F87E/3956/98_10.pdf (accessed February 24, 2008).

Trembath, R, C. Robinson and M. Cropley. 1996. *The Cross-Sectoral Experience: An Analysis of Credit Transfer in Victoria's Dual Sector Organisations,* Melbourne: Royal Melbourne Institute of Technology.

United Nations Educational, Scientific and Cultural Organisation (UNESCO). 1997. *International Standard Classification of Education* http://www.unesco.org/education/docs/isced_1997.htm (accessed December 23, 2007).

Wheelahan, L. 2000. *Bridging the Divide: Developing the Institutional Structures That Most Effectively Deliver Cross-Sectoral Education and Training,* Adelaide: National Centre for Vocational Education Research.

Wilson, C. B. 2006. Adoption of new surgical technology, *British Medical Journal,* 332, 112–14.

6

England: Merging to Progress

NEIL GARROD

Introduction

Dual sector institutions evolve or are created via a number of routes (Garrod and Macfarlane 2007). Merger is the most immediate and carries with it the consequential strains of dramatic institutional change. In this chapter the merger of Thames Valley University (TVU) with Reading College and School of Arts & Design (Reading College) is charted. The background and rationale for the merger is documented as are the structural changes that were enacted subsequently. Mergers demand not only structural but also cultural change. The TVU–Reading College merger highlights the importance of cultural change in ensuring the effectiveness of structural change in achieving merger goals.

The Merger

TVU and Reading College merged on January 1, 2004. This represented a significant milestone in the development of post-school education in the United Kingdom in general and in England in particular. It was significant for three primary reasons:

1. It was the first successful further–higher education merger hailed as such and identified as a major strategic choice by both partners.
2. It marked the establishment of a comprehensive post-school institution from an existing higher education institution rather than mission development from a further education college.
3. Following the collapse of the proposed merger of Bradford University with Bradford College, it showed that large-scale, cross-sector mergers could be achieved.

While other universities in the UK have pockets of further education activity, none has such a high proportion as TVU. The University of the Arts, London, formerly the London Institute and an amalgam of six separate art colleges, has a proportion of further education provision that approaches that of TVU, but this is primarily for students on foundation courses for the university's own higher education awards. Similarly, while there are a large number of colleges of further education with higher education provision, the proportion of this provision is insufficient to significantly alter the fundamental character of the institution. Moreover, these so-called "mixed economy" colleges (Department of Education and Skills 2003) do not have a research mission that might be found in a higher education institution.

Reading College was a large, general further education college that offered provision across the full array of further education work, and across a diverse subject base. Combined with the higher education provision at the pre-merger TVU, which covered the full range from access to higher education courses to doctoral study, post-merger TVU offers comprehensive post-school education from Level 1 to Level 8 of the National Qualifications Framework (Qualifications and Curriculum Authority 2008).[1] Levels 1, 2, and 3 pertain to further education level while 4 and above denote a higher education level of achievement.

With over 65,000 student registrations, TVU is one of the largest institutions in the higher education sector in the UK. Its diversity is not limited to just the levels of education offered but is also reflected in its student profile—over 125 nationalities, 45 percent ethnic minorities, 60 percent female, 60 percent part-time students and 50 percent over the age of thirty (Garrod 2005).

This educational and demographic diversity is difficult to capture in a sector of monochrome descriptors such as "research led," "regional," "student focused," "access driven," or "business facing." In the 2004 Strategic Plan, TVU described itself as a tertiary institution. By the end of that year "dual sector institution" was used more extensively. However, this Antipodean term (Doughney 2000) itself is often inadequate to describe the diversity of provision in many post-school institutions. For example, TVU is also one of Europe's largest educators of qualified nurses, midwives, and other health professionals, and as a consequence receives similar levels of funding for education and training from the National Health Service as it does from the Higher Education Funding Council for England (HEFCE) and the Learning and Skills Council (LSC—the current funding body for further education in England).

The Decision to Merge

The origins of mergers are generally complex, diverse and a function of history. The TVU–Reading College merger is no exception. TVU had been put under special measures following a special review carried out by the Quality Assurance Agency for Higher Education in 1998 (Brown 2004). In part this had resulted from an exodus of students in October 1997, which itself had resulted from a serious administrative malfunction that summer. This was exacerbated by a significant under-recruitment in October 1998 that collectively led to student numbers in 1999 being some 30 percent below those of 1997. A major rationalization was undertaken (McCaffery 2004) that precipitated the closure of a number of departments, many academic staff redundancies, and the transfer of some academic staff to other universities. Ironically, these transfer staff were generally those that had performed best in the 1996 Research Assessment Exercise (HERO 1996). The university thereby suffered a blow to its academic substance and reputation as well as to its financial position as a result of the events of the summer of 1997.

Discussions with the Higher Education Funding Council for England (HEFCE) following the imposition of special measures led to a unique agreement for TVU to have fully funded growth back to the value of its 1997 contract at a time when other universities were required to make specific bids for increases in their funded student numbers. Thus the priority for TVU was an improvement in its weak financial position through growth in student numbers.

Reading College, on the other hand, had a very healthy balance sheet and cash balance, resulting largely from substantial growth in its further education student numbers. It was keen to match that growth in its higher education numbers. At that time, higher education qualifications could only be offered by further education colleges on a franchise basis from higher education institutions.

Thus both TVU and Reading College were looking for potential partners to meet their own individual needs and aspirations, as reflected in their common desire to increase higher education student numbers. Both institutions did consider and approach other potential partners to meet their goals. At the time none of those were interested or in a position to proceed, and thus the TVU–Reading College merger rapidly became the only one under consideration.

In the UK, the separation of further from higher education is largely unexplained from an educational or pedagogic perspective (Garrod 2005). The TVU–Reading College merger challenged this separation, and thereby cast itself very much as an experiment and faced all of the challenges and risks that result from operating out of kilter with external, systemic structures. Despite the explicit support offered to the merger from both sectoral funding bodies, the HEFCE and the LSC, the merger did challenge accepted views on sectoral mergers held at that time (see e.g. Department of Education and Skills 2003). Nonetheless, Garrod argued that TVU "is agnostic about the suitability of mergers [across the sector]" (Garrod 2005: 61) and that the decision to merge was a specific response to particular local circumstances.

The Case for Merger

Around 10 percent of TVU's academic offer had historically been at further education level, primarily through its culinary arts programs. Similarly, about 15 percent of provision at Reading College was at higher education level, primarily through its creative arts programs. The two institutions had been close collaborators since 1999, with TVU franchise programs in computing, multimedia, and music operating at Reading College from September 2000.

For both institutions this relationship formed only a part of their respective portfolios of partnerships, with TVU working with a number of other further education colleges and Reading College with other higher education institutions. In both cases the partnerships were designed to provide students with local progression opportunities. However, it was the conclusion of both institutions that these evolving and complex arrangements were unable to support and sustain a stable and coherent planning framework and were considered to have hindered the overall development of clear progression pathways from further to higher education (Thames Valley University and Reading College 2003). It was this desire to develop clearer and more successful progression pathways that was the driving concept behind the merger.

The business case for merger relied heavily on an interpretation of government policy in anticipating an

> increased provision of work-based education and training . . . a strong interface with Further Education, developing new routes of progression . . . to the highest level of applied activity . . . Such work is considered to be a defining and central characteristic of a university that is . . . concerned with the provision of education services for the region that . . . relate to employers' and employees' needs and that are accessible through a full range of prior learning, qualifications and experience.
>
> (Thames Valley University and Reading College and School of Arts & Design 2003: 4).

The unique combination of Further and Higher Education of the enlarged University (approximately 30 percent FE and 70 percent HE[2] creates a clear "cradle to grave" mission. A distinct ladder of progression and "Integrated Awards Framework" with several entry and exit points, will truly connect the FE:HE Interface within the one Institution and for the region as a whole

> (Thames Valley University and Reading College and School of Arts & Design 2003: 9).

Implementing the Merger

TVU had been developing a new strategic plan throughout 2003 but this was put on hold in light of the possible merger. June 2004 was set for publication of the new plan, just six months following the date of formal merger. A decision had to be taken quickly about how integration was to be handled. Should there be a comprehensive integration of services, faculties, and subjects across the full educational range or should there be more of a federal structure maintaining two semi-independent organizations? There was a serious debate at the very highest level of executive management as to which route to take. At the time this decision was not informed by data about the structure of other dual sector institutions, largely owing to a lack of national comparators and the availability of relevant research. It was only later, through research carried out with a group of international duals, that the distinction between what Garrod and Macfarlane (2007) call the "unitary" and the "binary" models, respectively, was established.

The decision about restructuring the merged institution was further complicated by the events of November 2003. Following approval of the merger by all relevant bodies but prior to the merger date of January 1, 2004, Reading College failed an Office for Standards in Education (Ofsted) inspection.[3] Whether this was linked to the significant growth in student numbers achieved over the preceding years and the resultant healthy financial position of the College is difficult to say but the "due diligence" undertaken during the merger process had failed to identify the falling success rates that were also linked to this period of growth. A re-inspection of just the Reading College provision was therefore necessary and was timetabled for November 2005. In addition, Thames Valley University was scheduled for a Quality Assurance Agency's (QAA)[4] Institutional Audit at the same time. Both events meant that immediate movement to a unitary structure would raise additional complexities for the audits.

A strong case was made for a binary structure until such time as Reading College passed re-inspection. This debate was being held in the wake of the demise of the anticipated first major cross-boundary merger between Bradford University and Bradford College (Curtis 2002, 2003) some six months earlier. In that case, despite shared origins in the nineteenth century Bradford Mechanics Institute, continued close collaboration, and the investment of a significant amount of planning time that had projected a clear unitary model, the potential partners finally decided not to proceed. Many factors impacted the decision, but the issue of potential mission drift was very influential. Funding and planning bodies recognized that Bradford faced major educational challenges. It was near the bottom of most league tables for educational performance, and the key need was to improve "14–19" educational opportunities and performance, whereas much of the merger plan focused on growth in higher education.

The experiences at Derby University were also contemporary and influential. A merger between Derby University and High Peak College of Further Education took place in August 1998 and the University had embarked on a unitary structure. However, in the light of operational difficulties—not least the different environments created by different funding bodies, quality regimes, reporting mechanisms, and academic contracts—it reverted to a binary structure in 2003. While High Peak College was much smaller than Derby University (in the TVU–Reading College merger both parties were much closer in size), many at TVU felt that the Derby and Bradford experiences suggested that a unitary structure was too challenging given the clear binary nature of the external environment.

Despite doubts among many within TVU and within the senior management itself, it was decided that to wait two years before implementing any integrative changes would undermine the very rationale for the merger itself. A strategic planning away day was held on March 1, 2004, at which members of the Core Executive of the former Thames Valley University and the Senior Management Team of the former Reading College were present. In summarizing the presentations and discussion at the away day, the Deputy Vice-Chancellor identified five major themes, paraphrased in figure 6.1. These became the value propositions upon which the organizational restructuring and strategic plan were based.

These value propositions highlighted seamlessness between all levels of post-school education and indicated the implicit but clear adoption of the unitary model.

Academic Structure of the University

There was considerable overlap between the subject portfolios of the two former institutions and the academic units had the same span of duties, namely subject and curriculum development. However, their focus was different, as reflected in the titles of their academic heads: Curriculum Manager in the case of Reading College and Subject Head at TVU. The importance of maintaining and developing a coherent set of curriculum and qualification offerings and in bolstering staff development, general levels of scholarship, and the reputation of discipline areas suggested a new structure that recognized explicitly both these dimensions of education.

The proposed structure was adopted by the Academic Board in April 2004 and endorsed by the Board of Governors in May 2004.[5] The parameters of the academic structure were set. The academic building blocks of the University would be subject groups headed by a Head of Subject and further clustered within faculties. Those subject groups would embrace all staff in that subject area at all levels, from further education to doctoral work. Operational aspects of the curriculum would be managed by Directors of Study who would focus on clusters of programs at particular levels. Strategic aspects of curriculum and subject development would be the joint responsibility of Heads of Subject and Directors of Study within plans set by faculties. As well as highlighting the two fundamental dimensions of the comprehensive program portfolio, the revised structure created a group of academic managers—Heads of Subject and Directors of Study—that had identifiable equivalents throughout the University and who were, collectively, responsible for academic policy and standards.

Despite the aspirations for a unitary internal structure, the binary nature of the external environment could not be ignored. External intervention and direction at the further education level required coordination across, as well as within, subject groups. This was not necessary for higher education owing to the greater independence afforded this level of provision (see chapters 3 and 10). The coordination was provided primarily through the Pro Vice-Chancellor, Further Education. He led the development and implementation

1. *We are a university*
The role of a university, inter alia, is to widen horizons and challenge existing paradigms. Thames Valley will pursue these goals with a special focus on widening the
horizons of its students and raising their own confidence to achieve their full potential. The title of the University underscores its commitment to the region within which
its campuses are located whilst reaffirming its responsibility, as a university, to the
wider academic and international community.

2. *Growth through full participation*
Full participation means the attraction and involvement of all students who can
benefit from and contribute to a university education, including those who, historically, would never have participated in tertiary education. To break into this circle of
social underachievement is a major aspiration of the University. The further education offerings of the University provide a special focus on craft and skills training, but
as a university it is incumbent upon us to go beyond skills and vocational training.
Just as with the great professions and original vocational qualifications in law, medicine and theology we are committed to the development of educational pathways
that provide vocational direction whilst also introducing students to the wider
schema offered through more broad based learning and knowledge. Our students
deserve to be empowered in a world of ideas.

3. *Curricula and qualifications in support of full participation*
The single most striking opportunity offered by the merger is the development of a
qualification framework that facilitates and encourages progression across the full
range of tertiary education.

4. *Full participation for staff as well as students*
The changing student profile, resulting from success in achieving full participation,
must lead to a reassessment of the skills required by academic staff and the nature
of their academic practice. The University will create a structured framework of staff
development within which existing staff can enhance their own capabilities.

Research underpins the basic university aspirations of widening horizons and
challenging existing paradigms. In a university that is committed to full participation
and the empowerment of its students within a world of ideas they are critical.

5. *Releasing potential through budgetary processes*
The University will develop its budgetary system so that it rewards success and
provides guidance for increased efficiency in the achievement of its core aspirations. Knowledge is transferred from the education sector into the wider world
through the skills and experience gained by its graduates. It is also transferred
through funded and unfunded research, through consultancy, through interactions
with business and the public services, and through work with schools and the community. An open and transparent budgetary system recognises these alternatives
and enables an informed evaluation of the most appropriate mix of the mechanisms
available, in order to maximise the impact of the University on society.

Figure 6.1 Value propositions of Thames Valley University (2004).

of the action plan established in response to the Ofsted inspection. He also offered more general support for the establishment of further education as an important and integral part of faculty operations. The Further Education College was established and took on equivalent responsibilities to that of Faculty Boards. The College Board was empowered to respond to the changing priorities and funding mechanisms of the LSC, particularly with regard to curriculum decisions, more rapidly than was allowed by the traditional higher education committee timetable of the full Academic Board.

The use of the term "college" was both purposeful and reflective of the issues faced by a comprehensive post-school institution operating in an external environment of structural bifurcation. Many titles were considered, including School, Academy, Unit and Faculty. School was the most favored as it mirrored the Graduate School in the academic structure. It was ultimately rejected because of issues that were foreseen in negotiating with the LSC. First, they fund further education provision wherever it occurs, including schools (i.e. providers of education for five- to sixteen-year-olds) and the higher education usage of the term was felt to be potentially confusing. Secondly, and most compellingly, the LSC was not mandated to fund higher education and, by implication, universities. TVU had already experienced difficulties, owing to university title, in accessing certain LSC funding streams even though they were for the provision of further education. By simply using the collective title "Further Education College" for the further education provision at TVU most, if not all, such issues disappeared—an example of the difficulties that institutions face when challenging the environmental and operational status quo.

As a result of these changes, the basic academic structure was modified to that depicted in figure 6.2.

This structure, still operating in mid-2008, was adopted by the Academic Board in July 2005. This is, of course, a fairly conventional matrix structure. The very word "matrix" led to negative reactions from many staff as it had been the introduction of a different matrix structure that had led to the administrative difficulties in 1997 that precipitated the QAA special review of 1998. There was also a view that the introduction of a matrix muddied reporting lines and responsibilities.

To a large degree the decision to pursue a unitary structure made those muddied, or blurred, reporting lines inevitable. Three funding bodies (HEFCE, LSC, and NHS), two quality regimes, and three different sets of performance measures create managerial complexity. Multiple dimensions almost inevitably lead to a matrix structure of some form. The only way to avoid this is to operate a unitary structure within a bifurcated federal structure—in other words a binary model. To paraphrase Winston Churchill, "It has been said that a matrix structure is the worst form of organization except all the others that have been tried from time to time" (Brainy Quote 2008).

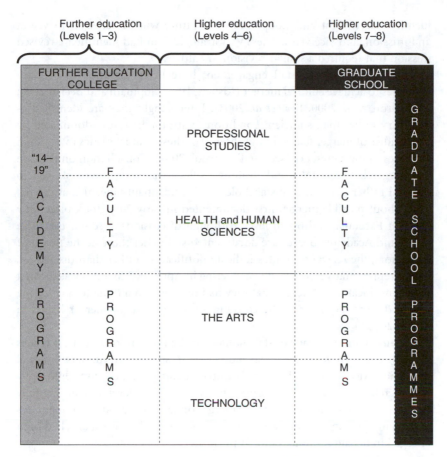

Figure 6.2 Academic structure adopted by the Academic Board (July 2005).

Structure Versus Culture

The structure outlined in figure 6.2 was envisaged by its architects to facilitate the creation of the "Integrated Awards Framework" of the Business Case for Merger. Such an aspiration demands a shared vision and culture (Firstbrook 2007) that pervades all levels of the institution. Significant structural change had been effected in a relatively short space of time. Culture change was less rapid. Changing the structure, in and of itself, had not led to a changed and shared culture. Change is a process, not an event (Fullan 1985).

The importance of organizational culture and its impact on merger success has been recognized for some time in the management literature (see e.g. Kitching 1967; Levinson 1970) and continues to be so (e.g. Lodorfos and Boateng 2006). Organizational culture is concerned with tradition and the nature of shared beliefs and expectations about organizational life (Buono *et al.* 1985) and might be considered the organizational equivalent of an individual's identity (Cartwright and Cooper 1993). Culture will be reflected in vision and mission, and vice versa. The TVU Strategic Plan had identified a revised mission that required a similar revision in culture.

Communication and staff engagement have been identified as primary strategies to achieve cultural merger (Risberg 1997; Gopinath and Becker 2000; Nikandrou *et al.* 2000; Bert *et al.* 2003). Interestingly, they are identified as necessary rather than sufficient conditions, with the literature dominated by case studies of merger failure in the absence of these characteristics rather than successes in their presence (see e.g. Firstbrook 2007). Consultation on the case for merger between TVU and Reading College was very heavily skewed to external rather than internal stakeholders. Confidentiality meant that discussions about possible merger, first documented in early 2002, took place only at Chief Executive and Board level. Although discussions at senior executive teams and Academic Boards are documented soon after those at the Board of Governors, the relevant minutes indicate notification rather than discussion. Union representatives recorded in a meeting in April 2003 that this was the first formal notification of merger that they had received, even though the meeting was to discuss responses to the consultation document for merger issued in March 2003.

When mention is made of stakeholders in the merger documents, it relates almost exclusively to external stakeholders and, specifically, funders. Internal discussion was focused primarily on implementation rather than philosophy and, thereby, offered little or no opportunity for culture development. Thus, by the time of the consummation of the merger on January 1, 2004, staff members of both merging institutions were aware of the merger but few, if any, had been engaged in debate about its value or purpose.

Merged Culture or New Culture?

There is a view in business that there are no mergers, only takeovers (see e.g. Accounting Web 2002). Nonetheless, the shared vision of student progression would support the concept of a merger in the case of TVU and Reading College. However, practical issues militated against this as merger was achieved through the dissolution of the Reading College corporation, the assimilation of Reading College assets by TVU, the maintenance of TVU's former title, and the maintenance by the merged institution of TVU's categorization as a Higher Education Institution (Reading College was categorized as a Further Education College). This approach to merger could be achieved within TVU's existing Articles of Government and so did not require the additional bureaucratic hurdle of Privy Council approval.[6]

Following merger, external consultants were engaged to advise on general branding and the question of the university name. There was a view that a change in title, if even modest, was symbolically important, one proposal being "the University of the Thames Valley." There was an alternative view, particularly among those at TVU that had weathered the difficult times following 1998, that a change in title was something of a betrayal of the enormous advances that had been achieved at TVU over the previous five years. The latter view prevailed and the name remained the same. While this obviated the need for Privy Council approval, yet another opportunity was lost to discuss and develop a new and shared culture. This left both partners with a propensity to dwell on separate pasts rather than a merged future. There was also a widely held view that the new mission, focused as it was on widening access and progression, was sufficiently similar to the existing missions and cultures of the merging institutions that extensive debate on culture and mission was unnecessary.

The lack of broad debate on the very rationale for merger percolated through to discussions on structural change and implementation. As mission emanated directly from the business case for merger, it was seen to have been developed by senior management, almost in isolation from the staff and student body. Thus when discussion of the structure and implementation took place within the university, staff felt legitimized to approach the process from what they knew best—their own culture.

These cultures very much reflected further and higher education stereotypes. Further education is very structured and responsive to direction from the funding council, the LSC. Teaching is the major mission, and with learners as young as fourteen on campus, issues of discipline and control are very important. Higher education is much less concerned with such issues, reflecting a high percentage of mature and part-time students. Academic freedom is reflected through curricula that are jealously guarded against external direction. Equally, explicit recognition of the importance of scholarship to both staff and students underlies staff expectations on workload and curriculum design.

These former two cultures formed the backdrop to discussions on structure and implementation issues using the different further and higher education discourses. A common language is important to comprehensive institutions, and this is difficult to achieve when two different cultures and languages are legitimized. The creation of new, post-merger language was sporadic and often seen to be unnecessary even if encouraged through formal proposals.[7] As a consequence, the focus was very much on merging the two former missions rather than creating a new one for the merged institution. Discussion of a "new" mission that was facilitated by the use of a "new" language might have proved equally contentious but arguably more fruitful and potentially more successful in achieving the merger's fundamental aspiration of increased student progression from further to higher education.

Structure and Culture

Organizational culture is often characterized as "social glue" (Alvesson 2002). This perspective emphasizes shared values, beliefs, understanding, and norms

(Schein 1985; Sathe 1985). Within mergers, however, style differences are often inappropriately labeled as cultural differences:

> Cultural differences do not automatically cause tensions. But when tensions do arise—often due to situational factors such as lack of communication or poor performance—people blame many of the organizational difficulties they encounter on cultural heterogeneity.
>
> (Kanter and Corn 1994: 19)

A more recent perspective on the role of culture in mergers is one that embraces pluralism and ambiguity in organizational culture whereby differences are an everyday feature of organizations (Vaara 1999, 2000). Riad develops this perspective by arguing that "a merger involves a contest of interests even within the same organization, yet cohesive allegiances are drawn upon as temporary locations in dialogic space" (Riad 2007: 27). Her single case study indicates that individuals protect themselves from the uncertainty resulting from merger either by claiming affiliation to the "former" culture or through relational configuration (Davies and Harre 1990). In other words, cultural affinity is a fluid and not static "glue"—a lubricator, not a fixative. Many of the observations documented in Macfarlane *et al.* (2007) support Riad's findings and underscore the importance of the creation of new groupings formed across the merger boundary. Culture as a multifaceted concept can be used as a catalyst for change and not simply seen as an obstacle to change.

The business case for merger was heavily predicated on both the virtue of further education students progressing to higher education and the expectation that merger itself would lead to higher levels of such progression. A mapping of further and higher education qualifications in the newly merged university identified a high level of continuity within the qualification offer, and where gaps existed new programs were developed. Despite this, progression rates remained stubbornly low during the year following merger, and certainly no higher than they had been prior to merger. Faculties produced action plans and progression targets. The following year, progression rates had barely moved. Why was this?

The answer, to some extent, has to be speculation but the following factors likely played a part. Firstly, despite the targets and the action plans, progression was not explicitly included in individual and faculty performance measures. Rather, progression was seen as a collective responsibility with no specific accountability. In a US context Wellman (2002) identifies that accountability structures appeared to be a very important influence on the number of successful transfers between two- and four-year colleges.

Secondly, the lack of an agreed common language and the absence of dialogue on the new mission meant that there were two legitimate and yet diametrically opposed perspectives on progression itself. One view was that progression reflects social justice and is best achieved if the student progresses to the most prestigious university, at both undergraduate and postgraduate levels. TVU is an access-based, post-1992 UK university and does not enjoy the research income or status of many UK institutions. Consequently students benefit more from moving to a more elite university to pursue their higher education or postgraduate studies (Macfarlane *et al.* 2007). In a way such moves legitimize the dual sector institution and thereby benefit all the graduates of that institution. The second view posits that "transfer shock" (Laanan 2007) between further and higher education is such that students are best advised to progress within their own institution. Both views are prevalent at TVU and thus the concept of progression itself does not have an agreed and shared understanding within the university.

Thirdly, there was an implicit perception that the lack of progression was an issue with the students themselves: a lack of finance, home support, or aspiration. These demand, or push, factors were certainly the focus of most of the action plans. However, moving between qualifications is usually a combination of both demand and supply, both push and pull, factors. There was very little consideration given to the supply or pull factors of the higher education programs to which the students might progress. For example, the geographic distance between the principal campuses of TVU acted as a barrier to student mobility. For students living in Reading, the thirty-five-mile journey to Ealing in West London, where many of the higher education programs were based, proved a significant obstacle to internal progression (Macfarlane *et al.* 2007). Even when new higher education programs were offered at the Reading campus, little improvement in progression rates materialized. A criticism of the Reading campus was that it did not have the "feel" of a higher education environment in terms of its social and academic facilities. The absence of a student bar is another symbolic reminder that it was formerly, and still is primarily, a campus catering for students under the age of eighteen (Macfarlane *et al.* 2007).

Finally, it became quite clear in the efforts made to improve progression that the creation of a bridge for progression through articulated program ladders was a necessary but not sufficient condition for success. The students needed more. They needed to be helped across the bridge. They needed to see the link. They needed to be tempted across by "tasters" of what lay on the other side. They needed to feel confident that they would not immediately be disadvantaged in their degree study owing to their choice of entry route. Their confidence and desire needed to be boosted by specific and overt action.

Elsewhere in this book, Wheelahan (chapter 3) makes a similar observation when she argues that while epistemological differences do exist between the sectors, these need not create insurmountable barriers to progression as long as they are explicitly navigated and not ignored. Indeed, she goes on to advocate the need for investment in staff who act as "boundary spanners." These individuals take on a specific and focused role of facilitating and supporting the progression of students from one qualification to another and from one sector to another. Wheelahan argues that with bridges between the sectors at both the systemic and the institutional level being so resource-hungry, the desired outcome of student progression can be better and more cheaply facilitated through these human boundary spanners.

Concluding Remarks

Elsewhere the editors of this book have outlined the different routes that institutions take to become comprehensive post-school or dual sector universities (Garrod and Macfarlane 2007). In this chapter some of the processes and issues raised by gaining dual status through merger have been explored.

Institutional character is a question not simply of structure but also of culture. Significant and rapid structural change was achieved at TVU post merger with a unitary model adopted and advanced very purposefully by executive management. Cultural change, however, did not keep pace, with the result that operational issues often reflected more of a binary model. This disjuncture of cultural and structural change limited the operational gains from merger.

Achieving a shared culture is greatly facilitated through the development of a shared and collective language. In the absence of such a shared language, formal structures, with their history in former languages and cultures, can themselves prove unhelpful to the change process. Informal structures, on the other hand, can play a very important role in bridging the gap from the old to the new. They allow more open discourse that can facilitate the development and embedding of a new culture. Also informal structures can be very illuminating in identifying communication blockages within the organization and rectify any misconceptions on merger processes that may have developed. The identification of progression champions or "boundary spanners" is particularly important in reaping the full potential benefit from merger. These boundary spanners need not simply be individuals but, perhaps more helpfully, may be cross-boundary groups tasked to address specific operational issues.

Educational mergers are no different to other types of merger in that they mark a step change in organizational form. Educational mergers across sectors additionally raise issues of culture that are not necessarily addressed by structural change alone. Recent perspectives on organizational culture as a fluid amalgam of flexible allegiances offer interesting possibilities of developing a new and shared culture while also addressing pressing operational issues. Individual boundary spanners and task groups that are drawn from across the sectoral divide to address specific problems not only focus the full breadth of a dual sector university on a particular operational issue but also offer a contextual base within which to allow relationships to develop that will themselves define the new culture.

The greatest operational successes in the TVU–Reading College merger certainly emanated from such champions and informal but tasked cross-institutional groups. This was even the case when the issue faced was not specifically a "boundary" issue. Indeed, it became increasingly evident that to truly become a unitary dual *all* operational issues need to be addressed as boundary issues, so that the full weight of the new, merged culture and strategy can be brought to bear on their resolution.

Notes

1. The National Qualifications Framework (NQF) sets out the levels against which a qualification can be recognized in England, Wales, and Northern Ireland. Scotland has its own authority, the Scottish Qualifications Authority, and its own twelve-point qualifications framework, but the structure and rationale is very similar to that of the NQF.
2. These percentage figures can vary significantly depending upon whether student head count, student registrations, or student full-time equivalents are used owing to the high percentage of part-time students enrolled.
3. The quality assessors for schools and further education (i.e. all education up to and including Level 3 under the NQF structure).
4. The quality assessors for higher education (i.e. all education above level 3 and funded by the HEFCE).
5. The structure was developed and agreed in a series of meetings, chaired by the Deputy Vice-Chancellor, between the PVC/Deans of the faculties at TVU and the Heads of the four academic faculties of Reading College, along with the Director of Reading Campus, held during February and March of 2004.
6. The Privy Council has a responsibility for approving changes to the Royal Charters of pre-1992 universities and the Instrument of Government and Articles of Government of post-1992 universities.
7. For example, qualification leaders were known as "curriculum managers" at Reading College and "programme leaders" at TVU. A proposal to call qualification leaders at both further and higher education "curriculum leaders" was rejected at the Academic Board meeting of September 2005 and the further/higher education nomenclature difference was formally adopted.

References

Accounting Web. 2002. *Company Reporting: The End of Merger Accounting*, October 2, 2002, http://www.accountingweb.co.uk/cgi-bin/item.cgi?id=92092 (accessed October 10, 2007).

Alvesson, M. 2002. *Understanding Organizational Culture*, London: Sage.

Bert, A., T. MacDonald and T. Herd. 2003. Two merger integration imperatives: urgency and execution, *Strategy and Leadership*, 31, 42–9.

Brainy Quote. 2008. http://www.brainyquote.com/quotes/authors/w/winston_churchill.html, (accessed February 4, 2008).

Brown R. 2004. *Quality Assurance in Higher Education*, London: RoutledgeFalmer.

Buono, A., J. Bowditch and L. Lewis. 1985. When cultures collide: the anatomy of a merger, *Human Relations*, 38:5, 477–500.

Cartwright, S. and C. Cooper. 1993. The role of cultural compatibility in successful organization, *The Academy of Management Executive*, 7:2, 57–69.

Curtis, P. 2002. Bradford Institutes Announce Merger Plans, *Education Guardian*, http://education.guardian.co.uk/universitymergers/story/0,,824353,00.html (accessed November 1, 2002).

Curtis, P. 2003. Bradford merger fails, *Education Guardian*, July 25.

Davies, B. and R. Harre. 1990. Positioning: the discursive production of selves, *Journal for the Theory of Social Behaviour*, 20:1, 43–63.

Department of Education and Skills. 2003. *Models of HE/FE Mixed Economy Provision*, Research Report RR458, http://www.dfes.gov.uk/research/data/uploadfiles/RR458.pdf (accessed October 9, 2007).

Doughney, L. 2000. Universal tertiary education: how dual-sector universities can challenge the binary divide between TAFE and higher education—the case of Victoria University of Technology, *Journal of Higher Education Policy and Management*, 22, 59–72.

Firstbrook, C. 2007. Transnational mergers and acquisitions: how to beat the odds of disaster, *Journal of Business Strategy*, 28:1, 53–6.

Fullan, M. 1985. Change processes and strategies at the local level, *Elementary School Journal*, 85:3, 390–421.

Garrod, N. 2005. The building of a dual sector university, In *The Tertiary Moment: What Road to Inclusive Higher Education?*, ed. C. Duke, Leicester: NIACE, pp. 57–73.

Garrod, N. and B. Macfarlane. 2007. Scoping the duals: the structural challenges of combining further and higher education in post secondary institutions, *Higher Education Quarterly*, 61:4, 578–96.

Gopinath, C. and T.E. Becker. 2000. Communication, procedural justice and employee attitudes: relationships under conditions of divestiture, *Journal of Management*, 26:1, 62–84.

HERO. 1996. *1996 Research Assessment Exercise*, http://www.hero.ac.uk/rae/rae96/ (accessed May 22, 2008).

Kanter, R.M. and R.I. Corn. 1994. Do cultural differences make a business difference?, *Journal of Management Development*, 134:2, 5–23.

Kitching, J. 1967. Why do mergers miscarry?, *Harvard Business Review*, 45, 84–101.

Laanan, F.S. 2007. Studying transfer students: Part II: Dimensions of transfer students' adjustment, Community College, *Journal of Research and Practice*, 31, 35–9.

Levinson, H. 1970. A psychologist diagnoses merger failure, *Harvard Business Review*, 48, 84–101.

Lodorfos, G. and A. Boateng. 2006. The role of culture in the merger and acquisition process, *Management Decision*, 44:10, 1406–21.

McCaffery, P. 2004. *The Higher Education Manager's Handbook: Effective Leadership and Management in Universities and Colleges*, London: RoutledgeFalmer.

Macfarlane, B., O. Filippakou, E. Halford and A. Saraswat. 2007. Managing in the comprehensive university: boundaries, identities and transitions, *SRHE Annual Conference, Reshaping Higher Education*, December 11–13, 2007, Brighton.

Nikandrou, I., N. Papalexandris and D. Bourantas. 2000. Gaining employee trust after acquisition, *Employee Relations*, 22:4, 334–55.

Qualifications and Curriculum Authority. 2008. *National Qualifications Framework*, http://www.qca.org.uk/libraryAssets/media/qca-06–2298-nqf-web.pdf (accessed May 22, 2008).

Riad, S. 2007. Of Mergers and Cultures: What happened to shared values and joint assumptions?, *Journal of Organizational Change Management*, 20:1, 26–43.

Risberg, A. 1997. Ambiguity and communication in cross-cultural acquisitions: towards a conceptual framework, *Leadership and Organization Development Journal*, 18:5, 257–66.

Sathe, V. 1985. *Culture and Related Corporate Realities*, Homewood, IL: Irwin.

Schein, E. H. 1985. *Organizational Culture and Leadership: A Dynamic View*, San Francisco, CA: Jossey-Bass.

Thames Valley University. 2004. *Strategic Plan: 2004 and Beyond*, London: TVU http://www.tvu.ac.uk/theuni/1policy_docs/strategic_plan.doc (accessed November 20, 2007).

Thames Valley University and Reading College and School of Arts and Design. 2003. *Merger of the University and College, Proposal to the Higher Education Funding Council for England and Background Information for the LSC*, London: TVU.

Varra, E. 1999. Cultural differences and post-merger problems: misconceptions and cognitive simplifications, *Nordic Journal of Organizational Studies*, 1:2, 59–88.

Varra, E. 2000. Constructions of cultural differences in post-merger change processes: a sensemaking perspective of Finnish-Swedish cases, *Management*, 3:3, 81–110.

Wellman, J. V. 2002. *State Policy and Community College-Baccalaureate Transfer*, National Center Report #02–6 August, The National Center for Public Policy and Higher Education, Washington D.C., http://www.highereducation.org/reports/transfer/transfer.pdf (accessed January 31, 2008).

7

Canada: What's in a Title?

ROBERT FLEMING AND GORDON R. LEE

Introduction

In their recent study on shifting institutional roles and approaches to post-secondary coordination in Canada over the past ten years, Shanahan and Jones (2007) assert that traditional distinctions between university and non-university post-secondary sub-sectors have become conflated to the point where "hybrid institutions that do not fit neatly into existing classification systems are emerging" (Shanahan and Jones 2007: 38). In fact, "hybrid institutions" emerged much earlier in British Columbia (BC) through the formation of five degree-granting university colleges (formerly community colleges) between 1989 and 1995. The mandate expansion of the university colleges was intended to address degree access inequities across the province. However, as the shift in mandate was not accompanied by legislation clearly delineating the role of these institutions, they were set somewhat adrift in redefining themselves (Dennison 2006).

Levin's (2003a) research on BC's university colleges suggests that mimetic isomorphism has significantly influenced their organizational development. That is, in pursuit of credibility, the university colleges have changed their structures and practices to emulate research-intensive universities. Levin (2003a) further contends that this isomorphic behaviour has created tensions between those seeking to adopt university culture and values and those seeking to re-inscribe college culture and values. Although Levin's assessment is persuasive, the complex array of motivations that underlie the isomorphic behaviour has yet to be examined in adequate detail, and the implications of the cultural confrontation are still unclear. Equally unclear is whether the dynamics of institutional identity are appropriately cast as a binary choice between two traditions.

In an effort to retain their integrity as unique institutions over their fifteen- to twenty-year history, the university colleges have had to establish contiguity with values, traditions, and practices of the university group with whom they seek belonging, and to maintain contiguity with values, traditions, and practices of the colleges from which they are historically constituted. Considering their institutional journey so far and looking to a future promising further institutional mandate and nomenclature change, many intriguing questions emerge. Will legitimation through isomorphism be the dominant force shaping their future? Will "a distinct type of modern university," a dual sector institution that is "characterized by significant provision and commitment for further and higher education" (Garrod and Macfarlane 2007: 579), evolve that combines the cultures and values of both colleges and universities? Is it possible, or even desirable, to garner a "shared vision" that "[creates] harmony between two different organizational cultures" (Macfarlane *et al.* 2007)?

To address these questions, this chapter will focus on understanding these institutions through theory, history, and comparison. First, we examine the concepts of isomorphism and academic drift as they relate to the pursuit of legitimation and identity within dual sector institutions. Second, we represent the historical contexts governing the formation, development, and possible futures of the university colleges. Third, we compare the experiences to date within three of the university colleges in relation to mission and mandate, degree program development, faculty research and scholarship, and current legislation and governance.

Institutional Legitimation and Identity

A large body of literature within the field of institutional theory (Scott 1987, 1995; Scott and Meyer 1991, 1994; DiMaggio and Powell 1983, 1992; Dobbin 1994) defines isomorphism as a constitutive behaviour of organizations seeking "legitimacy by adopting recognizable forms" (Pedersen and Dobbin 2006: 898). More specifically, the literature identifies three interrelated aspects of organizational isomorphism: mimetic, coercive, and normative. Mimetic isomorphism speaks to the tendency of organizations to recreate the "forms and norms of recognized organizations in their field to gain legitimacy" (Rusch and Wilbur 2007: 303). Coercive isomorphism refers to the exertion of pressure on or within organizations under threat of de-legitimization. Normative isomorphism arises in response to the mimetic and the coercive through the application of professional expectations and practices within any given organizational sector.

Morphew and Huisman (2002) utilize institutional theory and a three-pronged framework incorporating coercive, mimetic, and normative isomorphism as a basis for speculation as to why higher education institutions seem to grow more similar over time. To describe this phenomenon, the authors employ the phrase "academic drift," as defined by Berdahl (1985: 303): "the tendency of institutions, absent any restraint, to copy the role and mission of the prestige universities" and generally draw upon a body of research extending from Riesman (1956) in the United States (US) and Neave (1979) in Europe. Neave (1979) builds on existing academic drift research on United Kingdom (UK) polytechnics by Pratt and Burgess (1974). He further expounds academic drift as a departure from publicly stated objectives and mission.

Academic drift, measurable in Neave's (1979) study through the proliferation of degree-level programs, is one aspect of institutional drift, which he describes as the realignment of mission and objectives toward university structures. Both academic and institutional drift are exacerbated by policy drift, understood as ambiguous central policy.

Notwithstanding the utility of research and theory on isomorphism and academic drift within further and higher education institutions, these theories alone seem limited in their capacity to conceptualize the complex dynamic within dual sector institutions. By their constitution and mission, these institutions around the English-speaking world span increasingly blurred boundaries between further and higher education. Regardless of whether they have been created by merger, re-designation, or program development, a distinguishing feature is their commitment to both further and higher education, and opportunities for seamless, two-way movement between programs along an educational continuum (Garrod and Macfarlane 2007). Existing outside of and across the traditional binary typology, duals pose challenges to the bureaucratic systems that frame them. Not surprisingly, duals are as actively engaged in preserving their unique institutional identities as they are in seeking legitimation through emulation of university-centric professional practice norms.

Considering the dilemma of institutional legitimation and identity as a composite of external and internal forces, Pedersen and Dobbin (2006) argue that neo-institutional and organizational culture theories together describe a recursive isomorphic–polymorphic tension within organizations amid change: "organizations create legitimacy by adopting recognizable forms and create identity by touting their uniqueness" (p. 898). In examining the process of organizational culture change initiated within an American college seeking university status and legitimation for its business school through accreditation, Rusch and Wilbur (2007) demonstrate that external expectations exert considerable influence on the working out of legitimate new internal practices of promotion and tenure. Similarly, Locke's (2007) study of the merger of two specialist higher education institutions in the UK foregrounds an understanding of organizational culture as "continually recreating and revising . . . phenomena" that must be understood at the level of underlying values, espoused principles, and observable artefacts in order for meaningful organizational change to occur (p. 85).

Recognizing the reality of increasingly blurred boundaries between further and higher education sub-sectors in England, Burns (2007) notes that institutions are faced with cultural, status, and identity changes that necessitate continual efforts to re-establish boundaries that are shifting and contextual to an institution. Garrod and Macfarlane (2007) extend study on the effects of blurred boundaries within dual sector institutions to English-speaking countries around the world, taking specific note of the unitary and/or binary approaches in the academic management of the further and higher education components. With respect to the bifurcation of faculty roles, disparate institutional histories, and integrated programming in Thames Valley University, Macfarlane *et al.*'s (2007) research reveals extensive areas of challenge—cultural differences, geography and communication, student experiences, and institutional identity—that pose threats to the institution's mission to offer an educational continuum.

Arguably, the very notion of what constitutes a university is contested today as never before. Duke (2004) asserts that Australian universities are amid a crisis of identity as traditional affiliation with nation-building and the idea of a community of scholars has been largely supplanted. In its place has arisen a system focus on a range of institutions responsive to market needs and expectations. Increasingly focused on market responsiveness rather than its modernist compact with the state to build nations and national culture, the university must assume different forms to address diverse and competing frameworks of knowledge and value. Still, a fundamental question remains for universities, and would-be universities: what framing boundaries should remain both to confer legitimation and to facilitate greater heterogeneity of university mission?

British Columbia's University Colleges

Levin (2003a) presumes that the BC university colleges represent a unique form of university—constituted through a paradigm shift that bridges the gap between the mission and role afforded by their community college history and that by research-intensive universities. Specifically, the university colleges represent an attempt to provide degree-level education and training to a marketplace and within communities requiring that level of preparation to participate effectively in a global economy. The university colleges legitimately engage in isomorphic behavior—emulating aspects of traditional university programming, faculty workload, and governance—to ensure their recognition and credibility as degree-granting institutions and in deference to professional practice norms supportive of quality programs. They also maintain firm links to their college roots through non-degree programs and commitment to open access. These distinguishing features provide appropriate focal points for those who will compare the historic and future practices of BC's university colleges and who will critically assess the path of their institutional development. Further, an understanding of the BC post-secondary historical context is integral to any such critical assessment.

At no point previous to or since confederation has post-secondary education in Canada been governed nationally. Federal involvement in post-secondary has been limited to transfer payments to the provinces, subsidies for vocational training facilities and programs, and distribution of research grants. The absence of federal jurisdiction has meant that "the ten provinces and three territories, [although sharing] many common values," have developed unique post-secondary models in response to the "different historical, religious and linguistic traditions" they embody (Dennison 2006: 108).

For more than fifty years BC's higher education system was one public university, the University of British Columbia (UBC). A change to a binary model began in 1958 when an amendment to the *Public Schools Act* permitted school boards to create two-year colleges. The clear legislative purpose was to widen access to degree studies throughout the province. In his landmark report, John B. Macdonald (1962), then president of UBC, described a model for colleges—autonomous, teaching-focused, and locally responsive institutions that would offer primarily academic courses, which would facilitate student access and transfer to UBC after two years of study.

Although no school boards acted upon the 1958 legislation, Vancouver City College came into being in 1965 through the merger of a vocational institute, a school of art, and a continuing education centre. Over the next ten years, thirteen other colleges were created as a result of local plebiscites. Many of these were merged with existing vocational institutes by the provincial government, resulting in mandates to provide both academic and vocational programming. Far from being the autonomous institutions imagined by Macdonald (1962), the colleges were subject to a provincial academic board controlled by members drawn from university senates. University faculty had authority to define curricula, set transfer credit criteria, and determine the academic quality of the college courses. This preserved university autonomy over academic policies, but severely limited professionalism of college instructors (Dennison 2002). The new colleges lacked institutional legitimation in part because college faculty work was focused upon classroom instruction at the lower levels, and college faculty were not expected to do research, have specialist skills, or possess significant theoretical knowledge (Dennison 1984). As the BC college system expanded, organizational structures and values continued to develop differently. In addition to more restrictive legislative control by the province, colleges were distinct in their authority to grant diplomas and certificates; integration of developmental, vocational, technical, and academic programs; and open admission mandate.

By the mid-1980s an expanding BC population and access constraints created a situation in which thousands of potential students could not enroll in programs (Levin 2003b). This reality, and BC's low university participation rate, led the provincial government to commission a Provincial Access Committee, which identified the key system bottleneck as access to baccalaureate degree programs and recommended "the establishment of university colleges that would provide university degree programs through an upper level university college component" (Levin 2003b: 61). The government responded in 1989 with an "Access for All" policy and created three university colleges from existing colleges. Two more were designated between 1990 and 1995.

As Skolnik (2006: 6) acknowledges, "the transformation of some community colleges into university colleges" represented "the first major deviation from the binary design in North America." Predictably perhaps, the creation of the university colleges without engaging in thorough deliberation on their role within the post-secondary system resulted in a certain ambiguity of purpose and identity within the institutions and their communities:

> The general opinion was that the introduction of university level programs would inevitably undermine the essential values of the community college, such as comprehensiveness of curriculum ... open access, a focus on teaching rather than research, and a strong community orientation.
>
> (Dennison 2006: 110)

At the outset, the university colleges found themselves moving between traditions and practices. Perhaps most representative of the disjunction was the initial parochial relationship developed in relation to faculty hiring practices. Because degree-granting authority was initially contingent on a supervisory relationship with the three research-intensive universities, university representatives played a primary role in conducting faculty searches. Needless to say, different perspectives emerged on the roles of faculty. In the university tradition, faculty were expected to be researchers and teachers, and in the college tradition faculty were expected to be teachers rather than researchers. The question of what was good practice was seldom at the forefront of debate.

Over the years, the university colleges became more autonomous, offering a range of baccalaureate and master's degrees under their own authority since 1995. However, in the absence of a clear and formal mandate bridging the college and university traditions,[1] the university colleges continue to face the amorphous challenge of reinterpreting and reintegrating institutional missions, traditions, and practices in a manner that invites external legitimation within the university community and affirms internal identity in a manner consistent with their college history.

In 1998, the five university college presidents retained Howard Petch, former president of University of Victoria, to review university college performance. Petch concluded that "the degree programs currently offered are academically strong and meet accepted Canadian university standards" (Church 2002: 2). Petch (1998) also discussed expanding the mandate of university colleges to include research and graduate studies as well as the enactment of university college legislation that would create a senate-like governance structure. Later that year, the university college presidents formed a consortium—University Colleges of British Columbia (UCBC)—to represent the interests of these institutions, effectively creating a tripartite public post-secondary system. The new UCBC consortium developed common positions on issues such as legislation, funding and research, and in April 2001 circulated a "draft position paper calling for university colleges to become regional

comprehensive universities with a mandate including research, graduate programs and new legislation" (Church 2002: 3).

Notwithstanding the fact that the institutions have responded to program
demand in their communities, Levin suggests the university colleges have
attempted to "resemble universities with their new emphasis upon research
and scholarship, academic rank, and application for membership in a national
association for universities" (Levin 2003a: 454–5). In keeping with Levin
(2003a), Dennison and Schuetze (2004) further suggest that by elevating the
status of these five university colleges, the BC provincial government stimulated dormant academic drift among community colleges, which generally
aspired to degree-granting status. Although evidence of isomorphic behavior
in dual sector institutions seems clear, the university colleges' motivation
to respond to community programming needs in a manner that research-
intensive universities had not must be considered. Further, the motivation to
emulate academic structures prevalent in the universities is doubly reinforced
by internal commitment to ensure high quality, sustainable programs, and
external expectations that these programs and their faculty closely resemble
those within research-intensive universities—whose faculty and administrators
bring the most influence to bear on the adjudication of programming by provincial quality assurance authorities.

Comparing Three University Colleges

In comparing BC's university colleges, the central issue we consider is how and
to what extent these institutions have been able to avoid mission drift while
expanding their university mission. The three institutions we have chosen to
focus on share common histories as community colleges and university colleges
with a range of programs from trades through graduate degrees, but their current status is distinct. In 2004, Okanagan University College (OUC) was divided
into Okanagan College (OC), comprising trades, vocational, and academic
transfer programs, and the University of British Columbia, Okanagan (UBCO),
a branch campus of BC's most highly acclaimed research-intensive university.
At the same time, University College of the Cariboo (UCC) became Thompson
Rivers University (TRU), a dual sector university with the designated special
purpose to offer distance education. Kwantlen University College (KUC),
together with two other university colleges and two further tertiary institutions,
was re-designated a university by the provincial government in April 2008 on
the basis of consultant Geoff Plant's recommendation in his 2007 report on the
future of post-secondary in BC, *Campus 2020: Thinking Ahead* (Plant 2007).[2]
Plant recommended that "the three remaining university colleges . . . together
with Thompson Rivers University, become statutorily designated as regional
universities" (p. 66). In doing so, he accepted the argument put forward by the
university colleges that "the [university college] label has failed" and these
institutions should be recognized as "regional universities" (p. 66).[3]

Change has occurred in a number of ways in the three university colleges studied. For example, the mission statements of the three institutions have been revised over the past five years: KUC in 2003, OUC in 2004, and TRU in 2007. These statements were modified through consultative processes and approved by governance bodies. KUC's mission statement changed the least. KUC's statements focus on serving learners and do not reference an institutional commitment to scholarship (KUC 2003b). TRU's mission also changed very little. A focus on the region was modified to a focus on "regional, national and international learners and their communities" (TRU 2007a: 7). Both the early mission statement and the revised one include education, training, and scholarship. In contrast, the OUC mission changed from a focus on serving learners in the region to serving the region, the province, and the world through comprehensive programming, research and scholarship, and strategic partnerships (OUC 2004b). Despite different emphases, all the statements do reflect the dual sector nature of the institutions and their programming.

In addition to reviewing mission statements, we looked at institutional values. UCC's/TRU's value statements have changed very little over the past ten years. Besides the change in name, TRU's stated values are the same (TRU 2007a; UCC 1997). In its 2003 *Strategic Plan* (KUC 2003b), KUC sorted the values contained in its 1997 *Strategic Plan* (KUC 1997) into three categories and then modified the value statements again in 2007 (KUC 2007b). The revisions include a shift from a focus on learning, quality, and community to include "a commitment to excellence in teaching, scholarship, professionalism, creative artistry, skilled trades, and . . . services" (KUC 2007b: 4). OUC's value statements reflected greater changes. These included explicit references to teaching, research and service, serving the province and the nation, scholarly/research/professional activities, and collegial governance (OUC 1994, 2004b). These references indicate mimetic isomorphism toward a more university-like discourse. Still, the 2004 values spoke about creating "more opportunities for transition, laddering, continuous and lifelong learning, reskilling, upgrading and higher levels of credentials" (OUC 2004b: 7) which could be a sign of differentiation from traditional universities. Overall, our review suggests that the university colleges have attempted to bridge "incompatible institutional values: the egalitarian nature of community colleges and the meritocratic system of universities" (Levin 2003a: 450).

Let us now consider the issue of mandate as set out in the *College and Institute Act* (Province of British Columbia 2006). The Act delineates the objects of university colleges, including programming, the role of faculty in governance, and the power of the minister and the government to control the institutions' operations, finances, and governance. This authority includes the power to replace the board. Any change that the university colleges wish to see requires either a revision of the Act or new legislation.

A common measure of isomorphism relates to institutions offering more degree programs, specifically degree programs that are similar to those of more prestigious universities. Often, this is accomplished and funded by reducing or eliminating lower-level programming. Significant research on isomorphism focuses on this phenomenon (Becher and Kogan 1992; Morphew and Huisman 2002), but does not explore complex contributing factors. Although our research suggests the three university colleges do exhibit some program isomorphism, there is no one story that explains their behavior. Certainly, the initial degree programs offered by UCC (UCC 1997) and OUC (OUC 1994) were modeled on degree programs from the established universities. This is not surprising as degree development for the original university colleges was undertaken by UBC, Simon Fraser University, and the University of Victoria (UVic), and the degrees, until 1995, were conferred in their names. However, when these degree programs were patriated, their structure, courses, and prerequisites stayed more or less the same (OUC 2000; TRU 2007b; UCC 2003).

OUC's business degree was an exception (OUC 2000). Built on its two-year diplomas, the degree program encompassed third- and fourth-year liberal education courses that university students often take in their first and second years and advanced business courses that focused on integration rather than specialization. So, a student originally enrolled in a diploma program could take two more years of courses and earn a degree. This supported the seamless movement of business students from further education to higher education. Typically, business diploma graduates could expect to receive one year of course credits at the research universities. Indeed, BC universities were often criticized for this. The perceived difference in legitimacy between the OUC business degree and the traditional university business degrees was demonstrated in 2004 when UBC took over all of OUC's degree programs except the business degree, despite its success and popularity with students. UBC decided instead to develop its own more traditional business degree.

KUC's history of degree development was different. It did not have a mentor university and its initial degrees were in professional areas (design, nursing, business, and computing). These degree programs were built on existing two-year diplomas and were designed intentionally to improve access to degree completion for diploma students. In contrast, when KUC developed its baccalaureate programs in humanities and social sciences, it modeled these degrees on undergraduate degrees at BC research universities. This was done to meet student demand and facilitate acceptance of KUC graduates in graduate programs across Canada. More recently, in response to program review and accreditation expectations and in order to enhance student mobility to graduate schools, many of the professional degrees in design, nursing, business, and computing have morphed into four-year programs. Still, the laddered diploma pathways remain.

Programming and Practice Within the University Colleges

Despite evidence that both isomorphism and polymorphism have informed degree program development within the university colleges, future practice is hardly certain. In becoming two institutions in 2004—UBCO and OC—the former OUC has separated its programming along quite traditional lines. UBCO has focused on traditional degree programs and structures while OC has focused on traditional college programming and a few applied degrees. It will be interesting to see how TRU and KUC behave in the future. Their vision documents and strategic plans suggest a mix of more traditional degrees and differentiated niche programs focused on direct access to careers (KUC 2007b; OUC 2003a; TRU 2007a).

Considering the course of program development within the university colleges to date, the question of whether or not they have strayed from their mandate as defined in the *College and Institute Act*—to offer both degree and non-degree programs—is perhaps not as easily answered as it may be in other jurisdictions where institutional mandates are more differentiated. Regardless of this, on the whole our research suggests that the university colleges—at least up until the reconfiguration of UC as UBCO and OC—have not strayed but have grown to inhabit an evolving mandate in response to regional needs. A review of the programs they offered over a ten-year period demonstrates growth in degree programming in jurisdictions where degree programs were not easily accessible, as well as expansion in non-degree programming. For example, UCC/TRU had twenty degree programs in 1997, growing to thirty-six in 2007. However, it also expanded its associate degree/diploma programs from 61 to 86 (TRU 2007b; UCC 1997, 2003). This includes a number of transfer programs that provide students with the prerequisite courses required to enter professional programs such as law and veterinary medicine. Similarly, although OUC had eighteen degree programs in 1995, increasing to twenty-seven in 2003, its associate degree/diploma programs grew from thirty-eight to forty-eight and its continuing education programs expanded from thirty-three to fifty-four (OUC 1994, 2000, 2002). Finally, KUC showed the largest growth in degree offerings, probably because it became a university college six years later. In 1998, Kwantlen offered four degrees and in 2007 it offered seventeen. Its associate degree/diploma offerings increased from sixty-seven to eighty-nine (KUC 1999, 2003a, 2007c).

For all three institutions, the number of trades and apprenticeship programs and adult basic education programs remained stable. The data demonstrate that although there has been growth in the number of degree programs, this expansion has not been achieved by eliminating college programs. Moreover, enrolment reports demonstrate that enrolments in trades, adult basic education, vocational, and career programs have remained stable or increased (KUC 1998, 2007a; OUC 1999, 2004a; TRU 2008; UCC 1998). Based on our review of the data, the university colleges have continued to fulfill their legislated college role.

In research and scholarship, the three institutions have followed similar paths. Although research is not included in the university college mandate within the *College and Institute Act*, these institutions, recognizing their responsibilities to their university programs, have implemented research plans (KUC 2002; OUC 2003b; TRU 2006), applied for and received grants for research chairs and institutes from national funding agencies, supported faculty research through reassignment from teaching duties, and funded internal and external research projects. All institutions focused on thematic clusters and promotion of interdisciplinary research. However, based on our review there are some differences concerning definitions of scholarly activity. OUC's definition emphasized discovery research and to some extent applied research, whereas TRU includes discovery, integration and application, and artistic work for faculty teaching across the institution. KUC's definition is the broadest of the three, adding creative artistry to Boyer's definition (Boyer 1990). KUC also is explicit in its support for the scholarship of teaching and learning.

Now under its own legislation, the *Thompson Rivers University Act* (TRUA) (Province of British Columbia 2005), TRU has a mandate for research and scholarly activities. According to the TRUA, research and scholarly activity at the institution is undertaken to support not just undergraduate and graduate education but also post-secondary and adult basic education and training. Based on our review of the institutions' research plans and of the legislation under which they operate, we see indications of both isomorphism and polymorphism. Isomorphism seems to have been dominant at OUC; however, differentiation is evident at both TRU and KUC through their inclusive definitions of research.

One notable example of mission drift at OUC resulted in its demise. In the late 1990s and continuing into the early years of the new millennium, OUC, in its discourse and actions (specifically a new faculty collective agreement), did stray from its mandate (OUC and OUC Faculty Association 2001). This new discourse promoted an institution with a growing number of graduate programs including master's degrees in arts, business, health, and education and a concomitant expansion in research so that OUC is the "pre-eminent research institution in British Columbia's south-central interior" (OUC 2003a: 10). In Spring 2001, OUC's Board accepted "a committee report that says new legislation should give Okanagan full university status, including an unrestricted instructional and research mandate and a faculty-majority Senate" (Church 2002: 3). This would have provided OUC with the autonomy found at BC research universities. Not surprisingly, to government bureaucrats these statements were clear signs of mission drift, if not a declaration of independence from legislated mandates.

Coupled with its new vision, in 2001 OUC signed a new collective agreement with degree program faculty (OUC and OUC Faculty Association 2001). The degree program faculty agreement provided for ranks, differential salary scales, reduced teaching loads for research active faculty, a tenure and promotion system, and research as an explicit component of faculty work. These provisions, commonplace in university agreements and consistent with a merit-based system and discourse, were foreign to BC university colleges and colleges in which all faculty were considered to be equal, regardless of credentials or differentiated work (Levin 2003a). To be fair to OUC, this agreement contained clauses that reflected the dual sector nature of the institution and its college roots. For example, non-instructional faculty such as librarians, counsellors, and educational technology coordinators had parallel ranks to teaching faculty, were expected to be research-active, and would earn the same salaries as their teaching colleagues. Moreover, OUC, unlike UCC or KUC had two faculty union agreements and its collective agreement with vocational faculty continued to follow the college labor relations mandate (OUC and British Columbia Government and Service Employees' Union 2001). However, in July 2001, after the election of a new government, the Ministry dismissed "the Board of Okanagan University College for exceeding its jurisdiction in signing the contract that created a university-style pay system for faculty and [told] the new Board that it must not implement the contract" (Church 2002: 3).

TRU signed a similar agreement with its faculty union in 2007. This agreement provides for differential titles, tenure and promotion, salaries, and work definitions. The tripartite track encompasses teaching, research and service, and the bipartite teaching and service alone. Different academic titles are used in the tripartite track (Assistant Professor, Associate Professor, Professor) than are deployed in the bipartite track (Lecturer, Senior Lecturer, Principal Lecturer) (TRU and the TRU Faculty Association 2007: 60–2). Unlike OUC agreements, there is not a separate agreement or even different provisions for faculty teaching in trades, adult basic education, vocational, or other college-level programs. Theoretically, a trades faculty member could become a full professor and access a work model that supports research-active academics. Clearly, the TRU collective agreement is more university-like. However, it reflects the dual sector nature of the institution by synthesizing university and college values, operations, and discourse.

The term of this collective agreement is April 1, 2004, to March 31, 2010. However, it took from 2004 to 2007 for it to be finalized. During this time extensive institution-wide discussions on the transition from university college to university were held. A review of the TRU Faculty Association newsletters provides evidence that the faculty association, as well as participating in institutional transition consultations, ran its own comprehensive parallel consultations with its members (TRU Faculty Association 2005; UCC Faculty Association 2004). This suggests that the issues of transition were challenging to address. They also point to the important role of faculty in defining the extent to which an institution follows the path of isomorphism or the road of differentiation.

KUC's faculty collective agreement has not seen as many changes to more university-like provisions (KUC and Kwantlen Faculty Association 2007). It includes only one article acknowledging research and scholarship as a component of faculty work, no faculty ranks, no system for tenure and promotion, and no explicit provision for scholarship in faculty workloads. In 2006, in response to Kwantlen's campaign to become a regional university and the launch of transition consultations, the Kwantlen Faculty Association (2006) developed a set of principles to guide its negotiations and discussions with the institution on university transition. These principles strongly advocate for the dual sector nature of the institution and equitable treatment of faculty.

While the BC university college experiences will no doubt remain distinctive, it certainly seems likely that, as has been observed by Harman (1977) and Clark (1983) in Australia and the UK, the academic faculty will continue to exert significant pressure for change in support of academic drift toward more university-like practices. Still, although faculty will influence the development of dual sector universities, and this influence will help to define the extent to which each university college becomes more university-like or chooses a distinctive way forward, they are not the only force in play. Notwithstanding the powerful forces of regional community needs and globalization, each of which exerts considerably more pressure on all post-secondary institutions to remain more directly relevant than in previous eras, the events we have described in relation to three of BC's university colleges provide clear evidence that the BC government has significant power to reign in academic drift by the university colleges. A challenge for the university colleges, now newly designated as universities, will be to modify this power relationship.

Conclusions

Like many faculty and administrators, we seek both legitimation and differentiation for the university colleges, but complex and often competing forces affiliated with each unquestionably affect our planning and decision-making. As well, the dynamics of power within our university college and at the other university colleges shape our institutional evolution. At KUC, for example, the faculty union has been a conservative force resisting change to more university-like forms and structures, whereas, many faculty—in particular, research-active and degree-program faculty—would like to see such changes happen now.

Our research findings suggest that the power of the government over institutional mandates has worked to control, and in one case to stop, mission drift in the university colleges. If government policy makers wish to maintain and support the expansion of dual sector universities, restricting mandates and keeping some level of control over these institutions seems an effective strategy. Similar findings are offered by Garrod and Macfarlane (2007), who note the impact of the regulatory environment, and by Clark (1983), who argues that "tightly administered systems" can maintain "differentiation of sectors" (Clark 1983: 222).

Arguably, the most dramatic outcomes to date demonstrating both academic drift and shifting power relationships with the provincial government has been the conversion of two university colleges into universities in 2004. OUC, without community support for a dual sector university, was partitioned into UBCO and OC—re-establishing a binary divide between institutional types. UCC successfully organized strong community support for a change in name and mandate and achieved university status with new legislation that reflects this status. Of critical importance to TRU and its future are the unique legislative parameters it has been given under the TRUA, which embeds its university college mandate in a manner consistent with the institution's intent to continue its dual sector focus: "Thompson Rivers University will continue to deliver a complete range of university and college programs" (Province of British Columbia 2005: 1).

The redesignation of KUC as a university, in common with the other former BC university colleges, does not resolve the tenuous balance between legitimation and identity for each institution. In considering the possible future for university colleges as regional universities, Dennison (2006) offers a unique vision for the university colleges as "new" institutions in which "neither the university nor the community college component is predominant" (p. 111). Neither traditional universities nor traditional colleges, they are dual sector institutions whose diverse range of "programs collectively contribute . . . to [their] unique culture" (p. 111). Regardless of nomenclature, three factors influencing the future of each institution will be their legislative mandate, the commitment of academic staff to standards of practice both unique to the institution and legitimate in the view of peer institutions, and the support of the external community for a reconceptualized institution.

Acknowledgement

The documents we studied include institutional strategic plans, faculty collective agreements, academic calendars, student enrolment reports, and institutional submissions to government. Much of this information is web accessible. David Cram and Dr. Heather Banham were very helpful in locating some of the more important Okanagan College documents and in directing us to OUC's internet archives.

Notes

1. Despite their status as degree-granting institutions, the university colleges have never been defined by unique legislation. Rather, they are acknowledged as a subset within the *College and Institute Act*, and are not mentioned within the *University Act*. With the formation of TRU in 2004, the *Thompson Rivers University Act* (TRUA) was created to reflect the institution's unique mandate,

bicameral governance, and integrated teaching and research. University college representatives perceive the *TRUA* as appropriate legislation for their institutions.

2. In April 2008, Kwantlen University College was designated as Kwantlen Polytechnic University by the provincial government.

3. In its submission to *Campus 2020*, Kwantlen argued that "the term 'university college' creates confusion. Some people think we are a subordinated component of a research university and others think we are primarily a two-year institution" (KUC 2006: 5).

References

Becher, T. and M. Kogan. 1992. *Process and structure in higher education*, 2nd ed., London: Routledge.

Berdahl, R.O. 1985. Strategy and government: U.S. state systems and institutional role and mission, *International Journal of Institutional Management in Higher Education*, 9, 301–7.

Boyer, E. L. 1990. *Scholarship Reconsidered: Priorities for the Professoriate*, San Francisco: Jossey-Bass.

Burns, D. 2007. Conceptualising and interpreting organizational boundaries between further and higher education in "dual sector" institutions: where are they and what do they do?, *International Conference on Researching Transitions in Lifelong Learning*, June 22–24, University of Stirling.

Church, R. 2002. *A Brief History of the University College Mandate Issue*, http://www.mala.ca/EducationalPlanning/KeyDocuments/HistoryUniversityColleges/ABriefHistoryUniversityCollegeMandate.pdf#search='A%20Brief%20History%20of%20' (accessed October 19, 2007).

Clark, B. R. 1983. *The Higher Education System: Academic Organization in Cross-National Perspective*, Berkeley, California: University of California Press.

Dennison, J. D. 1984. The Canadian community college in the 1980s: strategies for survival, *Canadian Journal of Education*, 9:2, 139–53.

Dennison, J. D. 2002. *Significant Factors in the Development of Transfer and Articulation Policies Among Post-secondary Institutions in British Columbia*, Vancouver: British Columbia Council on Admissions and Transfer.

Dennison, J.D. 2006. From community college to university: a personal commentary on the evolution of an institution, *Canadian Journal of Higher Education*, 36:2, 107–24.

Dennison, J. D. and H.G. Schuetze. 2004. Extending access, choice, and the reign of the market: higher education reforms in British Columbia, 1989–2004, *The Canadian Journal of Higher Education*, 34:3, 13–38.

DiMaggio, P.J., and W.W. Powell. 1983. The iron cage revisted: institutional isomorphism and collective rationality in organizational fields, *American Sociological Review*, 48, 147–60.

DiMaggio, P.J. and W.W. Powell. 1992. Introduction. In *The New Institutionalism in Organization Analysis*, eds. W.W. Powell and P. DiMaggio, Chicago: University of Chicago Press, pp. 1–40.

Dobbin, F. 1994. Cultural models of organizations: the social construction of rational organizing principles. In *Sociology of Culture: Emerging Theoretical Perspective*, ed. D, Crane, Oxford: Basil Blackwell, pp. 117–41.

Duke, C. 2004. Is there an Australian idea of a university?, *Journal of Higher Education Policy and Management*, 26:3, 297–312.

Garrod, N. and B. Macfarlane. 2007. Scoping the duals: the structural challenges of combining further and higher education in post-compulsory institutions, *Higher Education Quarterly*, 61:4, 578–96.

Harman, G. 1977. Academic staff and academic drift in Australian Colleges of Advanced Education, *Higher Education*, 6, 313–35.

Kwantlen Faculty Association. 2006. *Principles for Kwantlen*, February 23, 2006, http://www.kfa.bc.ca/principles.html (accessed October 30, 2007).

Kwantlen University College (KUC). 1997. *Strategic Framework, Spring 1997*, Surrey, BC Canada: Kwantlen University College.

Kwantlen University College (KUC). 1998. *Audited 1997–1998 FTE Enrolment Report*, Surrey, BC Canada: Kwantlen University College.

Kwantlen University College (KUC). 1999. *Kwantlen University College Calendar 1999–2000*, Surrey, BC Canada: Kwantlen University College.
Kwantlen University College (KUC). 2002. *Strategic Research Plan*, Surrey, BC Canada: Kwantlen University College.
Kwantlen University College (KUC). 2003a. *Kwantlen University College Calendar 2003–2004*, Surrey, BC Canada: Kwantlen University College.
Kwantlen University College (KUC). 2003b. *Strategic Implementation Plan*, Surrey, BC Canada: Kwantlen University College.
Kwantlen University College (KUC). 2006. *Campus 2020, Submission by Kwantlen University College*, October 2006, Surrey, BC Canada: Kwantlen University College.
Kwantlen University College (KUC). 2007a. *Audited 2006–2007 FTE Enrolment Report*, Surrey, BC Canada: Kwantlen University College.
Kwantlen University College (KUC). 2007b. *Creating Our Future*, Surrey, BC Canada: Kwantlen University College.
Kwantlen University College (KUC). 2007c. *Kwantlen University College Calendar 2007–2008*, Surrey, BC Canada: Kwantlen University College.
Kwantlen University College and Kwantlen Faculty Association. 2007. *Collective Agreement between Kwantlen University College and Kwantlen Faculty Association, April 1, 2007—March 31, 2010*, Surrey, BC Canada: Kwantlen University College.
Levin, J. S. 2003a. Organizational paradigm shift and the university colleges of British Columbia, *Higher Education*, 46, 447–67.
Levin, J. S. 2003b. Two British Columbia university colleges and the process of economic globalization, *The Canadian Journal of Higher Education*, 33:1, 59–86.
Locke, W. 2007. Higher education mergers: integrating organizational cultures and developing appropriate management styles, *Higher Education Quarterly*, 61:1, 83–102.
Macdonald, J. B. 1962. *Higher Education in British Columbia and a Plan for the Future*, Vancouver: University of British Columbia.
Macfarlane, B., O. Filippakou, E. Halford and A. Saraswat. 2007. Managing in the comprehensive university: boundaries, identities and transitions, *SRHE Annual Conference, Reshaping Higher Education*, December 11–13, 2007, Brighton. Available online at http://www.srhe.ac.uk/conference2007/list.search.results.asp?search=macfarlane (accessed May 24, 2008).
Morphew, C. C., and J. Huisman. 2002. Using institutional theory to reframe research on academic drift, *Higher Education in Europe*, 27:4, 492–506.
Neave, G. 1979. Academic drift: some views from Europe, *Studies in Higher Education*, 4:2, 143–59.
Okanagan University College (OUC). 1994. *Okanagan University College Calendar 1994–1995*, Kelowna, BC, Canada: Okanagan University College.
Okanagan University College (OUC). 1999. *1998/1999 Full Time Equivalent Student Enrolment*, The Office of Institutional Research, Okanagan University College.
Okanagan University College (OUC). 2000. *Okanagan University College Calendar 2000–2001*, Kelowna, BC Canada: Okanagan University College.
Okanagan University College (OUC). 2002. *Okanagan University College Calendar 2002/03*, Kelowna, BC Canada: Okanagan University College.
Okanagan University College (OUC). 2003a. *2013 Looking Ahead Ten Years, Program, Research and Infrastructure Vision for Okanagan University College for the coming 10 years*, Kelowna, BC Canada: Okanagan University College.
Okanagan University College (OUC). 2003b. *OUC Strategic Research Plan*, Kelowna, BC Canada: Okanagan University College.
Okanagan University College (OUC). 2004a. *Audited 2003–2004 Actual Program FTE Enrolment Report*, Kelowna, BC Canada: Okanagan University College.
Okanagan University College (OUC). 2004b. *OUC Draft Business Plan, Building Access and Opportunity*, Kelowna, BC Canada: Okanagan University College.
Okanagan University College and British Columbia Government and Service Employees' Union. 2001. *Collective Agreement—Vocational Instructors*. Kelowna, BC Canada: Okanagan University College.
Okanagan University College and Okanagan University College Faculty Association. 2001. *Collective Agreement April 1, 2001, to March 31, 2004*, Kelowna, BC Canada: Okanagan University College.

Pedersen, J.S. and F. Dobbin. 2006. In search of identity and legitimation: bridging organizational culture and neoinstitutionalism, *American Behavioral Scientist*, 49:7, 897–907.

Petch, H.E. 1998. *Degree Programs at the University Colleges: A British Columbia Success Story*, Prepared for the Presidents of the University Colleges of BC: Victoria, BC.

Plant, G. P. 2007. *Campus 2020: Thinking Ahead: The Report*, Province of British Columbia: Ministry of Advanced Education.

Pratt, J., and T. Burgess. 1974. *Polytechnics: A Report*, London: Pitmans.

Province of British Columbia. 2005. *Thompson Rivers University Act*, Province of British Columbia, Victoria: Queen's Printer, http://www.qp.gov.bc.ca/statreg/stat/T/05017_01.htm (accessed October 29, 2007).

Province of British Columbia. 2006. *College and Institute Act*, http://www.qp.gov.bc.ca/statreg/stat/C/96052_01.htm, (accessed October 30, 2007).

Riesman, D. 1956. *Constraint and Variety in American Education*, Lincoln: University of Nebraska Press.

Rusch, E.A. and C. Wilbur. 2007. Shaping institutional environments: the process of becoming legitimate, *The Review of Higher Education*, 30:3, 301–18.

Scott, W.R. 1987. *Organizations: Rational, Natural, and Open Systems*, 2nd ed., Englewood Cliffs, NJ: Prentice-Hall.

Scott, W.R. 1995. *Institutions and Organizations*, London: Sage.

Scott, W.R. and J.W. Meyer. 1991. The organization of societal sectors. In *The New Institutionalism in Organization Analysis*, eds. W.W. Powell and P. DiMaggio, Chicago: University of Chicago Press, pp. 108–40.

Scott, W.R. and J.W. Meyer (eds.). 1994. *Institutional Environments and Organizations: Structural Complexity and Individualism*, Thousand Oaks, CA: Sage.

Shanahan, T. and G.A. Jones. 2007. Shifting roles and approaches: government coordination of post-secondary education in Canada, 1995–2006, *Higher Education Research and Development*, 26:1, 31–43.

Skolnik, M.L. 2006. *Postsecondary Design and Governance: A Think-Piece*, Prepared for the British Columbia Ministry of Advanced Education Campus 2020 Project regarding the future of British Columbia's postsecondary system. http://www.campus2020.ca/EN/416/ (accessed October 26, 2006).

Thompson Rivers University (TRU). 2005. *The university college of the Cariboo (UCC) is now Thompson Rivers University (TRU)*, http://www.truworld.ca/news.htm (accessed November 4, 2006).

Thompson Rivers University (TRU). 2006. *Strategic Research Plan*, Kamloops, BC: Thompson Rivers University.

Thompson Rivers University (TRU). 2007a. *Institutional Accountability Plan and Report 2007/08 to 2009/10*, Kamloops, BC Canada: Thompson Rivers University.

Thompson Rivers University (TRU). 2007b. *Thompson Rivers University 2007–2008 Calendar*, Kamloops, BC Canada: Thompson Rivers University.

Thompson Rivers University (TRU). 2008. *Enrolments by Division*, http://www.tru.ca/assets/ipa/docs/Exelcius/html/Division.html (accessed February 13, 2008).

Thompson Rivers University and Thompson Rivers University Faculty Association. 2007. *Collective Agreement between Thompson Rivers University and the Thompson Rivers University Faculty Association*, Kamloops, BC Canada: Thompson Rivers University.

Thompson Rivers University Faculty Association. 2005. *The Newsletter of the Thompson Rivers University Faculty Association*. Kamloops, BC Canada: Thompson Rivers University Faculty Association.

University College of the Cariboo (UCC). 1997. *The University College of the Cariboo 1997–1998 Calendar*, Kamloops, BC Canada: The University College of the Cariboo.

University College of the Cariboo (UCC). 1998. *Audited 1997–1998 FTE Enrolment Report*, Kamloops, BC Canada: University College of the Cariboo.

University College of the Cariboo (UCC). 2003. *The University College of the Cariboo 2003–2004 Calendar*, Kamloops, BC Canada: The University College of the Cariboo.

University College of the Cariboo Faculty Association. 2004. *The Newsletter of the University College of the Cariboo Faculty Association*, Kamloops, BC Canada: University College of the Cariboo Faculty Association.

8
New Zealand: The Impact of the Market

JOHN WEBSTER

Introduction

In all developing countries over the past 200 years, citizens without significant knowledge and skills have progressively become less well-equipped to participate in the workforce. While on-the-job training remains important, increasing workplace complexity and worker mobility have made tertiary education, once restricted to a small, elite group, almost a prerequisite for career advancement. In New Zealand, as elsewhere, participation rates in tertiary education have risen sharply, and students have been required to carry an increasing proportion of the total cost of their education. Governments facing increased financial demands, and seeking to justify the costs by enhancing business innovation and workforce productivity, have based their investments in tertiary education ever more closely on economic priorities, and demanded increasing levels of institutional responsiveness and accountability.

Background

Between 1990 and 2006, New Zealand, consciously or otherwise, conducted a radical experiment in market-driven tertiary education. In 1989, a new Education Act had brought all tertiary education in New Zealand under a single legislative framework. The Act identified four categories of public tertiary education providers, namely universities, polytechnics, colleges of education (basically concerned with teacher training), and *wananga* (conceived as delivering education and training in and through Maori traditions, customs, and language). The Act also defined the processes and criteria by which private education organizations could be recognized, and funded on the same basis as public providers, and established a New Zealand Qualifications Authority (NZQA) to exercise quality assurance across the entire sector. Shortly afterwards, to address an impending collapse of the apprenticeship system after privatization and deregulation had led to the disappearance of most large public sector agencies, which had traditionally trained a majority of apprentices, the government introduced an Industry Training Act. This Act established a system of Industry Training Organisations, each responsible for defining the competencies required at trades and technical level within an industry cluster, accrediting providers to deliver training and assessment and, often more controversially, purchasing training and assessment to meet industry needs.

New Zealand currently has eight universities, twenty polytechnics (one of which, Unitec New Zealand, delivers a high proportion of university-level studies, and attracts significant levels of research income), and three *wananga*. There were originally four colleges of education, but all have now merged with the nearest universities. In addition, more than 800 private tertiary establishments offer a wide range of academic programs, and a few have been authorized to deliver degrees. In fact, public and private providers can, in principle, deliver academic programs at any level, within a National Qualifications Framework extending from trades and technical certificates to doctorates. However, all programs at bachelor degree level and above are subject to a statutory requirement that they be delivered mainly by persons active in research. The interpretation of that requirement has led to some controversy, with the Minister for Tertiary Education suggesting at one point that the provision be abandoned, or replaced by a more realistic requirement that the teachers be active in research or in advancing practice. However, the provision remains, largely because of pressure from the universities.

The funding system introduced in 1989 was simple, at least in principle. The basis was that teaching students was the essential service for which the government was prepared to pay. Since education was both a private and a public good, the students would pay tuition fees to cover part of the cost of the programs in which they were enrolled and would have access to low-interest loans, with income-contingent repayment via the tax system. The government would meet the balance of the cost. Students could choose what particular kind of teaching they wished to receive, and all providers would be paid on a consistent basis for the actual services they delivered. Initially, students paid a low, fixed fee, covering about 10 percent of the average program costs. The government did, however, accept that some programs are more expensive to deliver than others, and that this fact should be reflected in their own contribution. Reliable information on teaching costs was (and is) hard to obtain, and the approach appears to have borrowed heavily from the relative funding model developed in Australia between 1988 and 1990 to support the emerging unified national system of higher education. The origins of that model were discussed by Taylor (1991).

In both cases, funding was allocated to courses (subjects) rather than programs. These courses were assigned to categories, each covering one or more fields of study and academic levels. To help the providers sustain research activity, a research quantum was added to the funding rates for courses contributing to programs at and above bachelor degree level (researchers could also apply for contestable grants to fund specific projects). The research quantum was set at between 5 percent and 50 percent, depending on the academic level of the courses in question.

When the system was introduced, the arrangement was that each provider would be funded for equivalent full-time students (EFTS) up to a maximum level negotiated in advance with the Ministry of Education. The internal distribution of EFTS between course categories was expected to be broadly in line with the stated mission of the provider. However, a major goal was to increase overall participation from what had been rather low levels by the standards of the developed world. As a result, these controls were progressively relaxed, and EFTS-based competition between providers became intense. The impact was particularly acute in small regional centers, where private providers delivering only profitable programs undercut local polytechnics, which had to subsidize expensive, but socially important, services while suffering from decreasing levels of funding for the training and assessment commissioned by industry training organizations. Regional polytechnics began to experience serious financial difficulties, with several being restructured or merged with larger institutions.

The new government elected in 1999 wanted to establish a more structured and collaborative system, reflecting national priorities rather than unrestricted student choice. Many in the tertiary education sector supported their proposals for *charters*, to define the overall roles of providers, *profiles*, to provide an agreed three-year funding framework, and an independent *intermediary body* to coordinate and represent sector interests.

The government then began a protracted consultative process, in which university interests gradually assumed a dominant role. In 2002, the Education Act was amended to establish a Tertiary Education Commission (TEC) and give that body overall responsibility for system-wide funding and strategic coordination, covering public and private providers as well as industry training organizations.

In practice, the TEC had much less independence from government than had initially been promised, and was burdened with a range of operational functions, many of them relevant only to the lower levels of tertiary education. Meanwhile, senior officials from the Ministry of Education persuaded the Minister that they should retain the primary responsibility for giving policy advice to the government. This division of responsibility led to significant confusion.

While the process was under way, the government made major concessions to students. Loans became interest-free, initially while the students were enrolled in tertiary education, and later while they remained in NZ after graduating. Predictably, the numbers of loans being taken out increased sharply. A one-year freeze on tuition fees was extended for two further years before being replaced by a complex capping regime, which reduced the capacity of providers to offset shortfalls in government funding by increasing tuition fees.

The government also decided that increasing funding for curiosity-driven research would provide the most effective driver for economic transformation, and therefore that the funding for research should be detached from that for teaching. Between 2004 and 2007, the research quantum was progressively removed from EFTS funding rates to support the introduction of performance-based research funding.

In consequence, significant resources were transferred from polytechnics to universities, and particularly to the two universities with medical schools. A separate, closely targeted fund was introduced to mitigate the impact of the transfer on polytechnics, but the capacity of the smaller regional institutions to maintain the applied research and scholarship required to sustain professional teaching at degree level was seriously undermined.

During the extended period of uncertainty that preceded and followed the establishment of the TEC, competition intensified as providers sought to optimize their positions prior to any real controls being applied. The writing was on the wall for non-university providers, which had to find alternative sources of funding that might enable them to survive and prosper within the new order. Unfortunately, this period coincided with a significant downturn in international student numbers, driven by changes in the policies of overseas governments, international events such as terrorism and the SARS epidemic, and adverse trends in exchange rates.

Some providers found and exploited loopholes in an EFTS-based funding system that had been designed for a less competitive environment. Political pressure relating to a few well-publicized excesses led the TEC to place tight controls on adult and continuing education programs and on entry-level programs generally. The controls applied to the innocent with at least as much force as to the guilty, and the outcome was further to reduce the capacity of non-university providers to respond to the demonstrated needs of their stakeholders.

Tertiary Reform

In late 2005, the Labour government that had been elected in 1999 was re-elected for a third term, and the Deputy Prime Minister and Minister of Finance had Tertiary Education added to his portfolio. He immediately announced that his first priority would be to implement a more strategic approach to government investment in tertiary education. He considered that the tertiary education system should value quality and relevance; learning programs should have clear educational and vocational outcomes; all teaching and research should be benchmarked against international standards; there should be an increased focus on quality of teaching; students should have access to a clear set of educational choices; students should be able to progress seamlessly between levels as their needs evolved; government and providers should be able to plan with confidence; and tertiary education should become a collaborative, rather than competitive, activity.

Many in the sector supported those views. Both the government and the providers wanted a rational and predictable funding system that reflected the real value of tertiary education to students, communities, industry, and business. They also agreed in principle that the resources available must be sufficient to provide all students with learning experiences of a high and sustainable quality although, inevitably, they had different views as to the adequacy of the existing funding allocations.

The original EFTS funding system had been simple, and reasonably easily understood, with modest compliance costs. The downsides were a high level of uncertainty for providers and government alike, and an undue reliance on process-based quality assurance mechanisms to avoid inappropriate allocation of resources. However, the version of the system that was in place by 2005, distorted by the host of ad hoc government funding decisions taken since 1999, had lost most of the positive aspects of the original model.

The events of the period from 1999 to 2005 had demonstrated the inherent difficulties of a completely, or almost completely, deregulated system, with split policy responsibilities, in which the funded student numbers for each provider were potentially unlimited. Intense competition and expensive marketing became more or less inevitable, and the government was faced by high and unpredictable demands on scarce resources, often being generated by services that were seen as having a low educational and economic priority. Mechanisms for rationing funded places had to be introduced, since government funds were not unlimited, and there was an urgent need to increase the level of per capita funding provided to institutions.

The specific policy responses decided upon in 2006 are summarized in table 8.1.

Table 8.1 Summary of New Zealand government funding policy (2006)

- Public and most private providers will be funded through three-year investment plans
- These plans will include overall domestic EFTS targets and an indicative portfolio of provision
- The total government funding available to a public provider will comprise: a student achievement component, allocated on a similar basis to Equivalent Full-Time Students (EFTS) funding; and a tertiary education organization component, supporting other government priorities
- SAC (Student Achievement Component) funding will be constant provided the actual enrolled EFTS are within 3 percent of the target
- No additional SAC funding will be available if the actual EFTS exceed the agreed target
- TEO (Tertiary Education Organisation) funding will mainly be project-based and dependent on achieving defined goals
- Most existing competitive funding schemes will be subsumed in the TEO funding. In general terms, the TEO component will not be available to private providers

---

The initial announcements indicated that the TEO component would account for 30 percent of the total student-related TEC funding across each sub-sector, but that proportion was, for practical purposes, reduced to 10 percent as investment plan negotiations unfolded. While investment plans were approved for the period from 2008 to 2010, the new funding system will not become fully operational until the 2011 to 2013 period, and further evolution can be expected. The official position remains that the TEO component will ultimately approach the 30 percent level. However, that might require open interference in the internal operations of institutions, and would risk upsetting the current broad consensus in favor of the reforms.

The government clearly wishes to encourage mission differentiation, between and within the various categories of provider, in order to reduce competition and encourage collaboration across the broader tertiary education sector. However, the extent to which that intention will translate into solid policy commitments is yet to become clear.

For example, there is a fairly general view in New Zealand that the country is too small to have more than one, or perhaps two, research-led universities funded on a basis comparable to that applicable to major universities in other OECD member countries. The other universities would, on that basis, have to build their reputations in a more focused subset of disciplines, and address more explicitly the needs of the regions in which they are located. For the present, however, the government has maintained the polite fiction that all universities are created equal. Mission differentiation has been pursued only in relation to polytechnics, and even there the main objective has been to strengthen their regional focus.

Much policy work remains to be completed, and the government has yet to come fully to terms with the continuum of missions undertaken by public and private providers. A useful step was taken in late 2006, when the Minister issued a revised Tertiary Education Strategy and Statement of Tertiary Education Priorities. This did at least recognize the need for a comprehensive system of professional and vocational education, integrating the contributions of a range of public and private providers, complementing the established university system, and delivering qualifications up to and including doctoral level.

Achieving that goal will require that the system of categories, and access to protected terms, set out in the Education Act be updated to reflect current realities, including the emergence of one university of technology and the demise of colleges of education. By late 2007, a private bill that would introduce a separate university of technology category had, with government support, been referred to the Select Committee on Education and Science. In addition, private providers will need to be integrated more completely into the tertiary education system, and incentives provided for them to develop close relationships with appropriate public providers. New modes of operation will need to be devised for industry training organizations, and better arrangements made for them to collaborate with polytechnics and universities of technology.

Higher Education: General

The government has decided to reduce the influence of student choice on tertiary education strategy, and to find mechanisms for emphasizing what government considers are, or should be, national priorities for education and skills development. To date, however, few concrete proposals have emerged as to how this is to be achieved. While the first round of investment plan negotiations with public providers has been completed, the underlying priorities have been addressed only in the broadest terms.

Clearly, in time, some universities will become more "research-intensive" while others will develop more "research-extensive" missions, and seek to build their reputations upon good teaching informed by applied research and practice, but the TEC has appeared reluctant to accelerate this process. At the same time, while the TEC has been anxious to see polytechnics place less emphasis on entry-level programs and offer a broader range of diplomas and applied degrees, students and employers have been offered few incentives to participate in that process, and thereby address critical skills shortages. While the concept of strategic direction at discipline (or industry) level can certainly be justified by pointing to the more perverse outcomes of an entirely market-driven system, there are obvious risks involved in attempting to substitute the judgment of public servants and politicians for that of the students, their employers and institutions.

All funding systems that incorporate a measure of direct ministerial involvement, and particularly those in which discretion can be exercised in relation to the activities of individual institutions, are vulnerable to accusations that political interference has taken place, and has been motivated by considerations other than the educational merits of the situation. Tertiary education is inherently longer term in nature, and can be seriously destabilized by such accusations, whether or not they are justified.

Higher Education: Teaching

In general terms, most of the initial investment planning negotiations appear to have been undertaken in a relatively benign climate, with institutions having been allocated sufficient EFTS to deal with their core domestic demand. The EFTS quotas do not apply at program level, and institutions are free to distribute their funded places across academic disciplines and levels, consistent with their investment plans. Over time, the research-led universities might logically be expected to allocate a higher proportion of their available EFTS to research-based postgraduate degrees and a lower proportion to undergraduate programs, particularly those offering a less direct pipeline to postgraduate programs.

One of the critical issues that should be addressed by government is how best to recognize and fund the added value generated by tertiary study. From a philosophical perspective, any government that chooses to fund tertiary education on the basis that such education creates a public, as well as a private, good must be concerned to assess the level of public good being generated per unit of investment. While success and retention at course level may have a role to play in that assessment, assuming that the learning outcomes in question are well-defined and relate to broader educational and vocational priorities, completion of formal programs is a much less certain measure of public benefit (although the resulting qualifications usually represent a private benefit).

Within a traditional university setting, there is a tendency to see completion of a standard qualification, constructed and defined primarily by the university, as the primary objective. That may have some justification in the case of school leavers, where one aim is to provide a framework within which educational and social maturation can occur, but adult learners may have different goals. Concern has often been expressed at the capacity for students who have completed lower-level programs to become lost in the system, with no opportunity to have their work credited towards more advanced, and vocationally relevant, programs. This, of course, constitutes a strong argument for establishing dual sector universities of technology, committed to ensuring that all students have opportunities for seamless progression. These universities can normally offer an embedded series of qualifications, each with specific vocational outcomes, allowing students to learn as and when their personal and/or career aspirations dictate. The process becomes more difficult when students have to move between institutions in different categories, and with very different educational approaches and goals.

Higher Education: Research

The government has clearly decided that, as a matter of strategic policy, expenditure on pure research and research training should be concentrated in fewer institutions, and governed by considerations of excellence. The system has much in common with the Research Assessment Exercise that has operated in the United Kingdom for more than a decade. On the basis of the evidence of the unintended consequences from that scheme, one wonders whether the New Zealand research-led universities will be able or willing to meet demand for equity and access at degree level and above, or to undertake research activities that do not contribute directly to their official research rating. The Performance-Based Research Fund (PBRF) places a premium upon selectivity and proven track records. If the statutory requirement that most teaching at bachelor degree level and above be undertaken by persons active in research is to be given effect, mechanisms will be needed to distribute at least some research funding more widely than is possible via the PBRF, and to hold institutions accountable for spending those funds specifically to inform teaching and learning.

The statutory requirement does mean that institutions delivering degree programs are under pressure to allocate funds sufficient to maintain a reasonable level of scholarship, and to generate an expectation that staff members teaching at degree level will undertake relevant research. There is a danger that moving away from what, given the broad statutory definition of research, is not an unduly onerous requirement could be used as a justification for further reducing the funding allocated to undergraduate education, which remains the foundation of academic and professional development for most students.

The government has already made some tentative moves to address the risk that teaching and technology transfer may be devalued in comparison with curiosity-driven research, notably by establishing a national center for research into tertiary teaching and recognizing the excellence of individual teachers. These are useful steps, but more work will be needed if the intention is both to foster improved teaching quality and to moderate the trend towards a one-dimensional league table of providers, based on research performance alone.

Vocational Education and Training

The key driving factors behind the more recent developments in vocational education and training in most developed countries have been the same. The extensive privatization of what were once seen as natural monopoly services, to be delivered by large government agencies, and the consequent focus on shorter-term business competitiveness have led to the demise of traditional apprenticeship models. These models tended to equate time spent in work under supervision directly with skill acquisition, which is not always true, but also had an inherent tendency to expose students to a range of experiences and workplace environments. The usual assumption was that apprentices would, in parallel with their workplace exposure, engage in structured educational programs delivered by public providers.

The traditional apprenticeship model has been largely replaced by systems based on the incremental assessment of modular competencies, expressed in the form of unit standards that have been defined and often assessed by industry-based organizations. The natural result has been a reduction both in the time taken to train people for workplace roles and in the range of the capacities that they are required to demonstrate prior to assuming those roles. There is an increasing body of evidence suggesting that the trade skills possessed by people trained in New Zealand are falling behind those possessed by their counterparts in other developed economies (Department of Labour 2007).

The stresses associated with these developments have found expression in the overlaps that have arisen between formal educational programs delivered by tertiary providers (mainly polytechnics and private providers) and other training and assessment services delivered by, or under contract with, industry training organizations. The current efforts being made to address these overlaps are bringing some of the underlying conflicts to the surface, and emphasizing the need for significant policy interventions.

Of course, apprenticeship is not the only context in which students pursuing educational qualifications must spend time in an industrial and/or professional environment in order to develop a comprehensive and balanced range of skills. Examples in higher education would include clinical studies in medicine and nursing, cooperative education in business, computing, engineering, architecture, and design, and teaching practicum. In practice, industry training organizations control much trade training, and professional bodies have considerable influence on professional education delivered at degree level and above. However, these professional bodies do not usually receive public funds to support their efforts in developing curriculum or in designing, implementing, and obtaining international recognition for the accreditation processes by which they influence tertiary providers. Nor are they funded to deliver educational services themselves, occasionally in direct competition with the very providers they are responsible for accrediting.

There is growing concern in New Zealand that, by securing training at the lowest price, and targeted at the lowest common denominator, the industry training organizations are failing to meet the needs of more capable students and more committed and innovative employers.

The mechanisms by which employers are funded to deliver training need to be rationalized. Industry training organizations may well remain the most appropriate agencies to develop competency standards and accredit providers to deliver relevant training, and to assess students against those standards. However, there is no need for those organizations to hold a monopoly over apprenticeship training, and to be funded to secure the necessary professional services. For example, a cooperative education paradigm might be adopted, with government funding for apprentices engaged in tertiary education being directed through accredited public or private providers, on the basis that at least a specified minimum proportion of that funding would be applied to providing supervision and assessment in a workplace environment. A similar approach has already, in effect, been adopted in several fields of higher education, where employers contract with education providers to deliver on-the-job supervision and training, and the model could readily be extended to the field of vocational education and training.

Dual Sector Universities in NZ

Reference has already been made to the essential role that dual sector universities play in a modern tertiary education system. In the mid-1990s, it seemed likely that NZ would have two such universities, both located in Auckland. In 1992, the Councils of the Auckland Institute of Technology (AIT) and Unitec Institute of Technology resolved independently to develop as dual sector universities of technology. Both institutions applied for university status in 1996 but agreed to suspend processing while the New Zealand Qualifications Authority (NZQA) established guidelines to govern their assessment. AIT renewed their application in 1998, and, in 1999 Unitec explicitly applied to be designated as a university of technology. The then Minister of Education advised that there was no separate category, but that the guidelines were intended to be broad enough to accommodate a dual sector profile. In October 1999 he designated AIT as a university, under the title Auckland University of Technology (AUT).

A change of government took place in November 1999. The incoming Minister claimed to have an open mind on the matter, and both Unitec and NZQA invested considerable effort in preparing for an assessment against the same guidelines that had been applied in the case of AIT. However, in May 2000, two weeks before an international panel was scheduled to visit Unitec, the Minister introduced the Eight Universities Bill to prevent the assessment from proceeding. Unitec and its stakeholders made strong submissions to the Select Committee, and the Minister asked the committee to defer its report. The Eight Universities Bill was eventually abandoned in May 2003.

At the same time, within the broader tertiary review process referred to earlier in the chapter, Unitec promoted a separate "university of technology" category, with an essentially dual sector mission. However, the final report in March 2001 concluded that there was no need for such a category, since the NZQA guidelines could accommodate a dual sector profile, and cited the AUT assessment as an example. Later in 2001, Unitec was elected as a member of the International Association of Universities.

Unitec continued to press the Minister and NZQA to resume processing its application, but was subjected to threats, interference, and administrative delays. At one point, the Minister tried to withhold funding on the basis that research did not form part of the normal activities of a polytechnic, but was persuaded to reverse that decision. In May 2004, the TEC published a paper on the *Distinctive Contributions of Tertiary Education Organisations* (TEC 2004) that would, if translated into government policy, have prevented Unitec from continuing to pursue a dual sector mission. The Unitec Council decided that it would, if necessary, initiate legal action to progress its application. In September 2004, the government introduced an *Establishment of Universities Bill* including retrospective clauses designed to stop the application being considered. In January 2005, very reluctantly, Unitec initiated legal action against the Minister. The action later succeeded in the High Court. In March 2005, the Select Committee recommended that retrospective elements be removed from the *Establishment of Universities Bill*. The bill has yet to have its second reading.

Processing of the application then resumed, and an international panel visited Unitec in May 2005. Unfortunately, contrary to precedent, the NZQA had instructed the panel that, in New Zealand, either the whole institution operated as a university or it did not. On that basis, the application could not succeed, although Unitec was, by any measure, far in advance of the developmental stage AIT had reached in 1999. Despite serious concerns with the decision, and the misleading terms in which it was announced, Unitec decided not to seek a judicial review. A successful outcome to such a review would simply have resulted in the matter being considered again by those who had taken the original decision.

Meanwhile, AUT was subjected to intense government and university pressure to conform more closely to established university norms. In response, AUT progressively withdrew from sub-degree provision, increased enrolments in research-based postgraduate programs, and focused on school leavers, rather than adult learners.

Meanwhile, Unitec continued to pursue, and attracted an increasing measure of financial and political support for its distinctive dual sector mission which addressed, and often informed, key priorities identified for the tertiary reforms introduced from 2006 onwards. Curiously, despite this differentiation in mission, the relative performance of AUT and Unitec in attracting PBRF funding has not changed as much as might have been expected.

The Way Ahead

Unitec is committed to dual sector education, transforming lives through outstanding career-focused education, and seeks to achieve the interconnected goals summarized in table 8.2.

Above all, Unitec aims to educate people for work, in work, and through work. This principle mandates vocational and professional outcomes for all programs, regular interaction with industry, professional and community groups to shape content, curricula and delivery modes, and a commitment to applied research that informs, and is informed by, practice.

Unitec seeks to ensure that students can learn, grow, and succeed within a consistent and supportive environment. To that end, clear mechanisms for articulation are vital. The aim is to deliver academic education intertwined

Table 8.2 Unitec values

- Be teaching-led and research-informed
- Focus on professional and vocational education
- Be student-centered in all its services and activities
- Put the concept of real world learning fully into practice
- Make the quality of teaching and learning its fundamental priority
- Foster research valued by its stakeholders and the academic community
- Ensure that the principles of te noho kotahitanga inform all its activities
- Understand and respond effectively to the needs of pacific peoples
- Demonstrate a continuing commitment to access and equity

---

with vocational education so that students can access the benefits of both environments, and move seamlessly across traditional systemic barriers.

Special attention is paid to adult learners, many already in the workforce, who aim to change or enhance their careers, and all students are offered access to credit-bearing, work-based educational opportunities wherever practicable. Unitec works closely with schools to ensure that, wherever appropriate, school leavers are equipped and motivated to pursue professional and vocational education.

Several of the problems faced by the tertiary education sector in New Zealand can be traced back to discontinuities created within a system formed more by pressures for definition and control than by student, community, and employer needs. Failure to offer genuine pathways through these discontinuities will create major problems for students seeking to proceed to higher levels of education within an increasingly differentiated system.

As the only institution in New Zealand currently dedicated to developing as a dual sector university of technology, Unitec accepts responsibility for serving as a regional facilitator and a national resource, and thus helping to ensure that the broader professional and vocational education sector can develop and maintain a capacity to deliver advanced and specialized programs to meet the emerging needs of communities, professions and industries.

Concluding Thoughts

The world is becoming a small and highly interconnected place, with skills shortages emerging in similar disciplines in every developed economy. In such circumstances, immigration cannot provide anything more than a temporary palliative. Retraining, and persuading groups within society who have traditionally been denied, or have avoided seeking, access to tertiary education to engage with the opportunities that such education generates, are the only obvious remedies. Extensive process automation and the introduction of components and materials requiring lower levels of skill have failed to achieve any major or lasting impact. Despite high expectations, pure distance education, even when extensively mediated by ICT, has yet to penetrate significantly beyond its traditional target markets, and remains dominated by adult professionals, based in the major urban centers, who are seeking to upgrade their skills.

The concentration of government research funding in a diminishing number of universities has enhanced the already high prestige of the institutions concerned, but has also increased the extent to which the relevance of the teaching–research nexus is questioned by government and others (particularly given the need for an increasing proportion of tertiary education to be, in some sense, practice-led). The strategy is also coming under increasing pressure from those who argue that concentrating the funding in research-only institutions would be significantly more cost-effective, and allow universities to concentrate more on their core business. In general terms, the normal policy response to these trends has been to encourage increased mission differentiation (sometimes successfully), to restrict competition (less successfully), and to increase the extent to which institutions are expected to engage with stakeholders.

The original free market model of tertiary education in NZ was conceived by people who had a somewhat optimistic view of market disciplines and the power of accreditation mechanisms to moderate market excesses, and implemented by people who held very traditional views on tertiary education in general and university education in particular.

For the most part, the experiment was quite successful in increasing participation rates, especially in Auckland, the only really large urban center in the country. Where population density was sufficient to allow providers to identify and pursue discrete market niches, and to allow students to exercise some genuine choice, the market model operated quite effectively, and the overhead costs in terms of marketing and program duplication remained modest. Furthermore, compliance costs were notably low.

Elsewhere, however, the outcomes were very different. Earlier in this chapter, reference was made to the difficulties that arose in the regional centers where polytechnics, burdened with a range of largely unfunded responsibilities and expectations, were unable to compete with private providers that could and did focus on a limited range of profitable offerings.

A more pervasive, although initially less obvious, issue arose from the failure of policy makers to take a coherent view of technical and vocational education. The polytechnics had traditionally delivered integrated teaching and learning experiences that, in combination with industry-based training, gave students a reasonably comprehensive basis for the continuing development and deployment of theoretical know-how and practical skills.

By 1990, however, privatization and deregulation had seriously damaged the traditional apprenticeship system. Efforts were made to devise other training paradigms that aligned with a highly competitive, just-in-time workplace. Competency-based assessment was embraced with almost religious fervor, not least because such assessment was inexpensive and could be carried out with minimal disruption to company operations. The value of sound teaching and learning, backed by diverse industry experience gained over an extended period, was discounted, and attention focused on defined, measurable outcomes.

The results were predictable. In many areas, the range and depth of technical skills acquired by the average NZ apprentice has dropped well below that expected in comparable developed countries. The public image of vocational education has suffered, and fewer parents and students see such education as a desirable option, despite extensive government-funded advertising, increasing salaries and better working conditions.

NZ now faces major challenges in rebuilding its professional and vocational education system, while dealing with the powerful vested interests that have become established since the *Industry Training Act* was passed into law. Tentative steps towards that end were initiated at the end of 2007, but the process will be neither easy nor rapid.

However, there are now grounds for hope. After a long period in which government seemed to be looking backward to a period in which tertiary education faced less complex demands, and when the boundaries between the worlds of university education and of professional and vocational education were more clearly delineated, there appears to be a greater measure of understanding that these worlds are parallel and interdependent, and that each of them must provide opportunities for, and encourage, the highest levels of educational achievement.

How best to achieve that goal is still work in progress. The bill now before Parliament would allow the government to establish, over time, either a small cluster of regional dual sector universities, or a single national dual sector university. The latter option might involve either a unitary institution with multiple campuses or a federated network of institutions. Such flexibility seems highly desirable, given the uncertainties associated with future tertiary education needs and responses.

While there are, of course, variations arising from history and economic circumstances, it would seem fair to conclude that the tertiary education sector in most developed countries is facing remarkably similar challenges as workplace complexity grows and students, employers, and communities place ever-increasing expectations on institutions to deliver education offering both the broad capacities to learn and adapt that have traditionally been associated with the graduate, and the specific knowledge and skills needed for a graduate to succeed in a profession or vocation. Dual sector universities of technology will have a key role to play in responding to these challenges.

References

Department of Labour. 2007. *Survey of Employers who have Recently Advertised*, Wellington: Department of Labour. Available at http://www.dol.govt.nz/PDFs/jvm-shortage2007.pdf

Taylor, Robert L. 1991. *Institutional Funding of Higher Education in Australia*, AIR Annual Forum, San Francisco, USA.

Tertiary Education Commission (TEC). 2004. *Distinctive Contributions of Tertiary Education Organisations*, Wellington: Tertiary Education Commission.

9

South Africa: (re)Forming A Sector

MARTIN OOSTHUIZEN

Introduction

Within the government-coordinated restructuring of the South African higher education system, the creation of comprehensive universities constitutes a key policy initiative for offering a mix of vocational, sub-degree and general-formative degree level programs within one institution. However, this chapter argues that the challenge of comprehensiveness, in the sense of institutions that offer a spectrum of sub-degree and degree-level qualifications extends beyond the comprehensive universities.

To place this challenge in context, the broad transformational imperatives on the South African higher education system are sketched out in the opening part of the chapter. In the section that follows, the restructuring of the higher education system that has led to the creation of comprehensive universities as a particular institutional type is discussed. It is then argued that the notion of comprehensiveness extends beyond comprehensive universities to include, at least, the newly classified universities of technology. The various challenges that the new South African Higher Education Qualifications Framework poses for academic planning within the comprehensive universities and the sector in general are discussed in the following section. The particular response of the Nelson Mandela Metropolitan University, as one of the newly constituted comprehensive universities, to the academic planning challenges posed by system-level restructuring and the Higher Education Qualifications Framework (HEQF) is then outlined, and this is followed by a consideration of the possibility of greater collaboration between the further and higher education sectors.

A System in Transition

Since the early 1990s the South African higher education system, as well as the education system in general, has witnessed an intense period of policy development that addresses the legacy of fragmentation, inequality, and inefficiency under the previous dispensation. The system of separate development (*apartheid*) split the provision of higher education along racial lines, with institutions for white, African, colored, and Indian students falling under

different legislative bodies, while some institutions resided under the jurisdiction of the four so-called independent homelands (Bunting 2002: 58–86).
Since the election of the first democratic government in 1994, key reports and
policy documents such as the National Commission on Higher Education
(NCHE 1996), the Education White Paper 3 (Department of Education 1997)
and the National Plan for Higher Education (NPHE) (Ministry of Education
2001) have developed a range of goals and policies linked to various government initiatives aimed at creating a single nationally coordinated system that
is equitable, responsive, and efficient. Understandably, the goals of access and
equity have enjoyed considerable prominence as mechanisms for addressing
the legacy of inequality, though there have been shifts in the policy environment to a greater focus on efficiency and economic responsiveness (Cloete
2002: 87–108; Badat 2004: 1–50).

In conjunction with the specific challenges of social and economic redress,
the reform of the higher education system is also being driven by the wider
international trends relating to the importance of lifelong learning within a
knowledge society (Salmi 2001: 105–25; United Nations Educational, Scientific
and Cultural Organisation 2005). The development of the new nationally
coordinated system is grounded upon a program-based approach that will
allow for meaningful program differentiation within the higher education system. An appropriately coordinated and differentiated system should provide
learners with optimal opportunities for articulation and progression to higher
levels of study, as well as for continuing education (Badat 2004: 29). The
latter matter is particularly important as by far the majority of enrollments
within the South African further and higher education system fall in the age
groups between eighteen and thirty-four years (Department of Education and
Department of Labour 2001: 26–7; Kraak 2004: 44–5).

In order to achieve the goal of program differentiation, the South African
government has implemented a comprehensive restructuring of the higher
education system, leading to the dissolution of the binary divide as well as the
creation of two new institutional types, namely comprehensive universities and
universities of technology. Concurrently with the reform of the higher education system, the Education White Paper 4 (Department of Education 1998) has
provided the basis for the creation of a differentiated but coordinated further
education and training (FET) sector. Between 1998 and 2002, a fractured
environment consisting of 152 technical colleges, colleges of education, and
training centers has been restructured into a public FET sector consisting of
fifty new colleges, many of which are multi-campus institutions, distributed
throughout South Africa (Department of Education 2002; Fisher *et al.* 2003;
Akojee *et al.* 2005). These reforms have largely occurred in parallel with each
other, and there has been little systematic attempt to create a coherent framework for collaboration between the higher and further education sectors in
terms of articulation and program provision. In South Africa, therefore, the

creation of comprehensive universities constitutes a particular form of restructuring at the tertiary level, distinct from that provided by dual sector universities as they exist in countries such as the UK and Australia.

Comprehensive Universities

The South African higher education system previously consisted of thirty-six institutions: twenty-one universities and fifteen technikons, with the University of South Africa and the Technikon South Africa functioning as dedicated distance education institutions in the university and technikon sectors respectively. In line with trends in countries such as Germany, the Netherlands, the UK, and Australia since the 1960s and 1970s to address the growing demand for higher education through the creation of a non-university sector (Scott 1995; Neave 2000; Huisman and Kaiser 2001; Codling and Meek 2006: 32–3), four Colleges of Advanced Technical Education were created in 1967 from the technical college sector, while a further two were formed by 1969 (Fisher *et al.* 2003: 329; Kraak 2006: 137). In 1979 the name of these six institutions was changed to "technikon." The mission of the technikons was to provide vocational and technical education as well as to conduct applied research. Nine additional technikons were constituted in the 1980s and 1990s in order to ensure opportunities for this type of education at racially segregated institutions (Winberg 2005: 191–2; Kraak 2006: 13).

Various characteristics of the binary system in South Africa indicate that it had a purer or stricter nature than that of the UK, which Trow (1987) describes as an elite binary system, and that it was perhaps more akin to the systems in countries such as the Netherlands or Germany, with a clearer demarcation between the university and non-university sector. However, the particular ideological apparatus of *apartheid* under the nationalist government led to certain idiosyncratic tendencies. In particular, there was a fundamental assumption that it was possible, or perhaps desirable, to draw a neat distinction in essence between university education and technikon education in terms of missions that focused on *science* and *technology* respectively. Universities were to focus on the development of knowledge and fundamental science, and technikons on applied knowledge (Bunting 2002: 62–3). Separate national policies regulated parallel structures for university and technikon qualifications. The technikons therefore offered a range of undergraduate and postgraduate diplomas up to doctoral level, which were regarded as separate from but equivalent to university qualifications at the same level. Minimum admission requirements for technikon study were lower than those for universities, though both institutional types could set higher entrance requirements for study in specific fields.

Approximately 75 percent of enrollments in the technikons were in the three-year undergraduate national diploma, so named because its curriculum was to a large extent nationally determined. The diploma had a strong vocational or career-oriented focus and often included a substantial work-integrated learning component. After 1993, the technikons were allowed to offer degrees at the bachelor's, master's and doctoral level, but the parallel qualification structure continued, with all technikon degrees retaining the term "technology" as part of their distinctive nomenclature. Thus, regardless of the field of study, technikon degrees were referred to as a Bachelor, Master or Doctor of Technology in a certain field. Approximately 10 percent of students who completed the national diploma enrolled for the Bachelor of Technology (B Tech), which allowed them to receive a bachelor's degree after one further year of full-time study. The model is an "extended track model" (Gibbon 2004: 30–1) rather than an articulation pathway. Students who complete the national diploma are not required to articulate into a separate degree program but are provided with a customized pathway that is designed to provide a sufficient theoretical orientation to allow them to reach degree-level status. While the B Tech provides the basis for postgraduate studies, few technikon students pursue or complete studies at master's or doctoral level (Subotzky 2003: 368).

When the eight-level National Qualifications Framework (NQF) was introduced in 1995 by the South African Qualifications Authority Act (Republic of South Africa 1995), technikons and universities continued to operate parallel qualification structures within the higher education and training band (levels 5–8) of the NQF.

However, the phenomenon of academic and vocational drift, as described by Codling and Meek (2006: 35) ensured that there was an increasing overlap between the program offerings of universities and technikons. Gibbon's depiction of the variety of program types, identifying a continuum between technical/vocational technikon programs and the general-formative focus of those found in universities, provides a helpful basis for understanding academic and vocational drift in South African higher education.

Within the former binary system, technikons increasingly became involved in career-oriented programs at the degree level, introduced a stronger theoretical focus into their programs, and were more involved in the provision of programs in the humanities and social sciences. At the same time universities increased their activities in career-oriented diploma programs, leading to a blurring of the boundaries between the two sectors (Ministry of Education 2001: 56–7; Centre for Higher Education Transformation 2004: 9–11; Winberg 2005: 194). In the interests of system-level differentiation, the NPHE emphasized that the purpose of the technikons was to offer career-oriented programs at the diploma level, although it did provide for a "loosening of the boundaries" by permitting limited provision of career-oriented undergraduate and postgraduate degree programs by technikons, as well as some provision of undergraduate diplomas by universities (Ministry of Education 2001: 56–7).

The Ministry of Education tasked the Council on Higher Education (CHE) to develop recommendations on the size and shape of the HE system. The CHE's report, which was released in June 2000, recommended that there should be a unitary, but differentiated, HE system based on three distinct institutional types with different mandates. "Bedrock" institutions would focus on undergraduate programs with limited postgraduate provision up to master's level, and research related to the curriculum, teaching, and learning. In addition to undergraduate programs, a second set of institutions would offer an extensive range of taught and research master's programs with a limited range of doctoral programs and select areas of research, while a third group would provide a range of programs up to the doctoral level, as well as engaging in extensive research. In addition, the CHE report argued for institutional combinations as an important mechanism for improving system coherence (Council on Higher Education 2000). This hierarchical scheme met with considerable resistance, and in the NPHE two approaches were identified to system level restructuring, namely program and infrastructural collaboration as well as institutional mergers (Ministry of Education 2001).

A National Working Group (NWG) was tasked to take these proposals forward, and its report to the Minister recommended that the HE system should be reconfigured from thirty-six to twenty-one institutions, based on an analysis of the quality, sustainability, and equity of provision within each province or region in South Africa. Key recommendations of the NWG report were the creation of comprehensive universities, as well as the maintenance of the binary divide (National Working Group 2001). In its final restructuring decisions, announced in December 2002, the Ministry substantially endorsed the recommendations of the NWG, albeit with some modifications (Ministry of Education 2002). The restructured system would consist of twenty-four institutions, consisting of eleven universities, six comprehensive universities, five technikons, and two higher education institutes in provinces without a higher education institution (Council on Higher Education 2004: 39–58). Four of the comprehensive universities would be created through merging a university with one or more technikons into one institution offering both university and technikon qualifications, while in the other case two universities would be required to expand their existing university qualifications to include technikon qualifications. The Ministry emphasized that the mergers should follow a unitary rather than a binary model, and also that they would be mandatory.

A significant further development is that while the NPHE envisaged that the binary system would remain in place for at least a further five years, lobbying by the technikons as reflected in the 2001 position paper by the Committee of Technikon Principals (Committee of Technikon Principals 2001) led to the announcement in 2003 that technikons would be re-designated as universities of technology. As a result, South Africa now has a unitary but formally segmented HE system, which implies that the various institutional types should be able to achieve meaningful differentiation in terms of their program profiles. The two levers by means of which the Ministry will coordinate program differentiation are the approved program and qualification mixes (PQMs) and enrollment plans of each institution.

The six comprehensive universities constitute the most idiosyncratic feature of the new system, as they bring together university and technikon qualifications within one institution. The rationale for their creation includes improved opportunities for access, especially to career-focused programs, improved articulation between career-focused and general-academic programs, enhanced responsiveness to regional social and economic needs, a more efficient use of resources and capacity, and opportunities for synergy in research through an appropriate mix of basic, strategic, and applied research (Ministry of Education 2002: 24). Significantly, the ministerial announcement stressed that a primary purpose behind the creation of comprehensive universities was "to strengthen the provision of technikon programmes through ensuring that technikon programmes are available throughout the country, in particular, in rural areas, which are currently inadequately serviced in terms of technikon provision" (p. 24). However, neither the NWG report, nor the subsequent restructuring announcement by the Ministry, went beyond such generalities to consider the plausibility of the underlying academic model by means of which the comprehensive universities may achieve their intended objectives.

The Challenge of Comprehensiveness

A number of position papers and discussion documents have been produced with respect to the nature and role of the universities of technology (Committee of Technikon Principals 2004; Du Pré 2004; Reddy 2006). These documents refer to characteristics such as the vocational and career-focused nature of qualifications, program responsiveness through close links to industry and business, flexible learning models, and opportunities for work-integrated and service learning, as well as applied research, technology transfer, and innovation. Yet, they have still to develop a clear sense of how the bestowal of university status will impact on their academic mission. In terms of their enrollment profile, it is clear that a key characteristic of these institutions must be a certain proportion of enrollments in the field of science, engineering, and technology, as well as in business and management. Furthermore, as Kraak (2006: 150) argues, in order to develop as fully fledged universities of technology, these institutions will need to develop a stronger proportion of enrollments at the degree and postgraduate level, alongside other traditional university attributes.

The comprehensive universities have widely divergent backgrounds and academic profiles, and operate within quite different contexts, ranging from more urban or metropolitan to more rural target groups or a combination of both. Table 9.1, which is based on the Department of Education's management

Table 9.1 Headcount (to nearest 1,000) enrollment profile of comprehensive universities in the South African higher education sector in 2006

Head count enrollments	University of South Africa	University of Johannesburg	Nelson Mandela Metropolitan University	Walter Sisulu University of Technology	University of Venda	University of Zululand	TOTAL
Undergraduates certificates and diplomas	62,000	17,000	11,000	16,000	1,000	1,000	108,000
Undergraduate degrees: three and four year bachelors and B Techs	128,000	19,000	10,000	7,000	9,000	7,000	179,000
Sub-degree % of total undergraduates	33	48	53	70	14	10	38
Degree % of total undergraduates	67	52	47	30	86	90	62
Undergraduate as % of total enrollments	83	83	84	95	93	78	84
Total undergraduate	189,000	36,000	20,000	23,000	10,000	8,000	287,000
Total enrollments	228,000	43,000	24,000	24,000	11,000	11,000	341,000

Source: Based on Department of Education data

information database, illustrates the quite different headcount enrollment profiles of the six comprehensive universities.

The Universities of Zululand and Venda, the two comprehensive universities that are tasked with developing a more comprehensive program profile from the basis of their traditional university qualifications, are both historically disadvantaged institutions that serve a black student population with a significant concentration of enrollments at the undergraduate degree levels. The key challenge for these institutions is to develop a suitable range of undergraduate certificate and diploma qualifications that will address the needs of the large groups of learners from educationally disadvantaged backgrounds in their immediate, more rural, catchment areas. Within the group of four comprehensive universities that were formed on the basis of mergers, the University of South Africa has by far the highest proportion of degree to sub-degree headcount enrollments. As a dedicated distance education institution that serves more than 200,000 students throughout South Africa, as well as the rest of Africa and even further afield, it faces unique challenges in determining the enrollment balance and academic qualifications structure and program profile that will best serve the needs of its learners. Among the remaining three so-called "contact" comprehensive universities, the balance of enrollments at the two urban universities, Johannesburg and Nelson Mandela Metropolitan University, is fairly similar, while the Walter Sisulu University of Technology, which draws its students from a mix of urban and rural settings, has a much stronger weighting in favor of undergraduate diplomas and a very small proportion of postgraduate degrees. All of the comprehensive universities have relatively small percentages of postgraduate enrollments.

The current enrollment profiles of the merged comprehensive universities reflect a situation that has been inherited through a government-mandated merger process. For all six comprehensive universities, it is now critical to develop consolidated PQMs that eliminate duplication between different qualification types, and that are appropriate in terms of their learner profiles and the education and training needs within their context. Therefore, while the program profile of comprehensive universities should reflect an appropriate mix of programs at the sub-degree and degree level, each institution will need to be provided with considerable latitude in negotiating an educational mission and enrollment profile that is suitable to its situation.

Both the universities of technology and the comprehensive universities are involved in a developmental trajectory that requires them to reshape their existing PQMs and enrollment profiles. In particular, both institutional types share the challenge of building learning pathways that employ appropriate articulation routes that traverse the boundaries between sub-degree programs of a more vocational and career-oriented nature, and degree-level study. The key difference between these types of institution is that comprehensive universities, at least in the case of those that were formed through mergers, have developed qualification structures that provide a basis for curriculum alignment and articulation between more vocational and career-focused sub-degree study and study at degree level.

However, as both the universities of technology and the comprehensive universities begin to define their academic missions more coherently, it is plausible that the boundaries between these types of institutions will become increasingly fuzzy, and that both institutional types will be marked by greater or lesser degrees of comprehensiveness. Whether some of the traditional universities will also choose or be permitted by government to develop more comprehensive academic profiles in the sense referred to in this discussion remains to be seen. Be that as it may, the main thrust of this argument is that in South African higher education the challenge of crossing the boundary between what are currently still referred to as university and technikon programs is shared by both comprehensive universities and universities of technology. In the longer run, therefore, it will become increasingly problematic to base program differentiation on a formal distinction between these two institutional types. Instead, it would be more appropriate for them to collaborate in developing meaningful approaches to the provision of education and training at sub-degree and degree level.

The Higher Education Qualifications Framework

A remarkable aspect of government policy is that the creation of a unitary system, and in particular the comprehensive universities, has occurred in the absence of an integrated higher education qualifications framework. As already indicated, the mapping of technikon and university qualifications onto the NQF maintained the parallel qualification structure. As a result the status and equivalence of different qualifications on the NQF, and therefore of the articulation possibilities that should be provided to students, has been an area of considerable contestation among academic staff from universities and the former technikons (now the universities of technology). This debate is particularly problematic in comprehensive universities that need to develop consolidated qualification structures and program mixes on the basis of their inherited, and still current, university and technikon qualification structures.

The most controversial issue concerns the status of the characteristic vocational and career-oriented qualifications offered by the former technikons, namely the three-year national diploma and the B Tech degree. In the absence of an integrated higher education qualifications framework, the formal duration of specific qualifications, rather than the complexity of learning that is required in different qualification types, has frequently served as a basis for judgments concerning levels of achievement on the NQF. Thus the three-year national diploma and the three-year bachelor's degree were formally placed on the same level (NQF level 6), while the B Tech degree was placed on the same level as an honors degree or a four-year bachelor's degree (NQF level 7). In practice, however, judgments on articulation and the equivalence of different qualification types have largely been made in an ad hoc manner within specific academic fields and disciplines. In some cases, especially where specific qualifications are linked to requirements for professional registration or occupational categories, more principled analyses have helped to place decisions on articulation on a firmer conceptual base.

The design of the new six-level Higher Education Qualifications Framework (HEQF) that will replace the parallel university and university of technology qualification streams with one integrated structure has taken several years to complete. Its promulgation in October 2007 introduces a principled but contested framework for articulation (Ministry of Education 2007). The NQF now consists of ten levels, with the higher education and training band distributed across levels 5 to 10. In turn, the HEQF incorporates nine qualification types, five at the undergraduate and four at the postgraduate level (three- and four-year bachelor degrees are regarded as one qualification type: Ministry of Education 2007: 11).

The Ministry of Education has yet to announce a formal date by which existing qualifications must conform to the requirements of the HEQF. The key question concerns the relationship between vocational, career-focused, professional, and general-formative qualifications. The proposed structure mirrors that of a discussion document, *New Academic Policy* (NAP), produced by the CHE in 2002, in which higher education qualifications are accommodated within an integrated framework consisting of two distinctive learning pathways, namely a general and a career-focused track, extending through all qualification levels. Horizontal and diagonal articulation between the two learning pathways would be achieved by means of an articulation column consisting of various qualification types (Council on Higher Education 2002).

While the new HEQF eschews a formal two-track approach, it recognizes the different nature of various qualification types, especially at the undergraduate level. In particular, the framework provides for a range of undergraduate certificates and diplomas with a more career-focused or vocational purpose, alongside three and four-year bachelor degrees with either a general-formative or a professional purpose. In one sense, therefore, the new framework retains two learning pathways at the undergraduate level. Concomitantly, it acknowledges that degree-level study accommodates a subtler interrelationship between general-educative and career-focused elements. The new qualification framework and its relationship to the other components of the NQF is presented diagrammatically in table 9.2.

For comprehensive universities and universities of technology, the most problematic aspect of the new HEQF relates to the vertical progression opportunities afforded to students who enter higher education by means of certificate or diploma study. The three-year diploma, whose curriculum will no longer be nationally prescribed, will be placed at one level lower than

Table 9.2 South African Higher Education Qualifications Framework (HEQF)

Education sectors	Levels		New NQF (HEQF: levels 5–10)			
Higher education and training band	10	P O	Doctoral			
	9	S T	Master's (coursework and research)			
		G R	**Vocational/Career-focused**		**Professional/General-formative**	
	8	A D		Postgraduate Diploma	Honors	4 yr+ Bachelor's degree
	7	U N		Advanced Diploma (1 yr)	3 yr Bachelor's degree	
	6	D E R G	Advanced Certificate (2 yr)	3 yr Diploma		
	5	R A D	Higher Certificate (1 yr)			
Further education and training	2–4		National Senior Certificate or National Certificate (Vocational): replaces current Senior Certificate			
General education and training	1		General Education and Training Certificate			

three-year bachelor degrees—NQF levels 6 and 7 respectively. Furthermore, provision is no longer made for an extended program track in the form of the current B Tech degree.

The position set forward in the draft versions of the HEQF is that diploma students should progress through articulation into three- or four-year bachelor's degrees. Advanced diplomas that lie at the same level as a three-year bachelor's degree are not viewed as qualifications that typically lead to postgraduate study, as their purpose is to provide for specialization in a specialist area. Furthermore, the HEQF stipulated that pending the development of a system-level credit and accumulation transfer scheme, only half the credits of a completed qualification such as a diploma could be transferred into a qualification such as a three- or four-year bachelor's degree (Ministry of Education 2007: 9). In the final version of the HEQF, this position has been qualified to an extent as advanced diplomas now provide for progression to postgraduate diplomas, which in turn meet the minimum requirements for study at master's level.

The question, of course, is whether study by means of an advanced postgraduate diploma route will prepare students for master's study in the same manner as, for example, a four-year professional bachelor's degree or a three-year bachelor's degree followed by an honors degree. Faced with the difficulties relating to vertical progression from undergraduate sub-degree programs, at least some comprehensive universities and universities of technology may find it attractive to progressively move away from offering certificates and diplomas in favor of degree programs.

The complexity of vertical progression within the qualifications framework must form part of a wider nexus of considerations that inform the program-based coordination of the HE system. From an institutional academic planning perspective, reference has been made to the need for both comprehensive universities and the universities of technology to develop program and qualification mixes and enrollment profiles commensurate with their situational realities, in terms of their learner profiles, inherited program capacities and strengths, and local and regional contexts. One critical consideration in this regard is that the majority of students who wish to enter higher education come from educationally disadvantaged backgrounds, so that despite their potential to succeed at degree-level study they do not necessarily meet the requisite admission requirements for study at this level. For such students, appropriate provision at the sub-degree level constitutes a critical access route into degree study. Thus, purely in terms of their internal academic planning processes, the comprehensive universities and universities of technology need to pay careful attention to the question of access in considering the balance between sub-degree and degree level provision.

From a government steering perspective, it is important to note that the South African further and higher education systems continue to be characterized by an inverted triangle/pyramid. Enrollments at universities have historically been much higher than those at the universities of technology as have the number of university qualifications compared to those offered at further education and training colleges (Department of Education and Department of Labour 2001: 29–30). Though enrollments at the former technikons grew at a rate of 77 percent compared to a growth rate of 44 percent for universities for the period between 1993 and 2003, technikons had a headcount enrollment of 230,000 in 2003 compared to 488,000 at universities (Council on Higher Education 2004; also Subotzky 2003: 362). While headcount enrollments in the public FET colleges have grown exponentially from 76,435 in 1991 to 377,584 in 2005, it is important to note that many of these students are not enrolled on a full-time basis, so that the headcount numbers reflect an inflated view of learner volume at the colleges (Department of Education and Department of Labour 2001: 30; Akojee et al. 2005: 105; Department of Education 2005). While the imbalance has improved, the key point is that South Africa faces a critical shortage of medium-level skills, and that its human resource development strategy must provide for substantial expansion in vocational, technological and career-focused education and training at the sub-degree level (Kraak 2004: 65–87).

How, then, may the academic planning imperatives of the comprehensive universities and universities of technology, the systemic challenges of educational disadvantage, and national human resource development needs be brought into a meaningful interrelationship? A plausible approach would be to relate program-based coordination to the wider context of the post-secondary system rather than the more confined framework of the HE sector alone. As Badat (2004: 5) remarks, "a program-based definition of higher education rather then a purely institutional definition means that further education institutions may also offer higher education programmes." The next section includes a brief discussion of how one comprehensive university, the Nelson Mandela Metropolitan University, is approaching these academic challenges.

Academic Planning at the Nelson Mandela Metropolitan University

The Nelson Mandela Metropolitan University (NMMU) was created at the start of 2005 from the merger of the former University of Port Elizabeth (UPE) and the Port Elizabeth Technikon (PET). Prior to the merger, UPE had incorporated the Port Elizabeth campus of the former Vista University, a multi-campus institution that provided contact and distance education to black students throughout South Africa. Owing to the imperatives of the merger process, the NMMU is only at the initial stages of defining its academic mission and addressing the curricular challenges that it faces as a comprehensive university. The discussion that follows presents work in progress rather than an official position that has been adopted by the university.

In a report prepared for the Centre for Education Policy Development in the Department of Education, Muller (2008) contends that at a strategic level comprehensive universities should decide whether they wish to define their academic mission in terms of an overarching model of conceptual or of contextual relevance. He relates these two forms of relevance to four qualification routes that lead to the world of productive labor. At one end of the spectrum, there are general-formative qualifications where coherence is defined in a predominantly conceptual sense. At the other end, relevance assumes a strongly contextual nature in terms of the ability to perform clearly prescribed occupational roles. Between lie more general career-oriented and professional qualifications combining a mix of contextually and conceptually determined relevance. In effect, Muller's model places the spectrum of qualification types identified by Gibbon (2004) within a theoretical framework.

This model does present a heuristic device by means of which the NMMU can make informed strategic decisions about its academic mission, based on its inherited program profile, areas of program strength, staff capital, and the constraints and opportunities of its regional context. The university's head-count enrollments (see table 9.1) indicate that it has a strong presence in the qualification types that Muller places in the middle two streams of the qualification spectrum. Thus, 50 percent of the bachelor's degrees that the NMMU offers have a professional nature, while the additional 1180 enrollments in B Tech degrees would lift this ratio to 56 percent. Furthermore, the three-year national diploma accounts for 60 percent of all enrollments at the sub-degree level. The majority of the other undergraduate certificates and diplomas lie in the field of teacher education. In terms of its undergraduate enrollment profile, it would be consistent for the NMMU to focus its program offerings on career-oriented and professional qualifications while also taking account of the human resource needs of the region—which is an industrial hub with a strong presence of the automotive industry.

The Kolb-Biglan classificatory scheme, as discussed by Becher and Trowler (2001), provides a useful reference point to address the curricular and peda-gogical problems facing the NMMU. The fourfold classification of disciplinary groupings in terms of their epistemological properties—hard-pure, soft-pure, hard-applied and soft-applied—provides a basis for making substantiated decisions with respect to access, retention, articulation, and curriculum design within the context of the new higher education qualifications framework. As Muller (2008: 20) observes, it should be acknowledged that there is no precise correlation between disciplinary structure and the design of the curriculum. However, where disciplines have a more clearly defined core knowledge struc-ture (hard), the design of the curriculum will normally require a progressive sequencing of learning components in a vertical structure. Where disciplines have a more loosely defined knowledge-base, the design of the curriculum may assume a more segmental nature. What is more, especially in disciplines with a more applied nature, the contextual requirements of specific occupational roles will determine the weight that should be assigned to specific learning com-ponents within the structuring of the curriculum. The practical point is that judgments on articulation and vertical progression need to be based on the knowledge properties of specific academic fields and disciplines, as well as con-textually determined occupational requirements. In order to make informed judgments on the curricular and pedagogical issues that need to be addressed in bringing sub-degree and degree qualifications into an appropriate relation-ship, it is therefore necessary to conduct an analysis finer grained than the more overarching stipulations of the HEQF in its current format.

The NMMU is conducting projects in a variety of its academic disciplines and fields to develop such finer analyses, and the field of architecture serves as an illustrative example. The professional requirements of the field require that students who wish to register as professional architects should follow a curriculum with a strong design core with initial study in either a four-year bachelor's degree or a three-year bachelor's degree followed by an honors degree. Students who wish to become architectural technologists normally enter higher education through the diploma route, and follow a curriculum with a strong focus on applied building science, complemented by a less intense mastery of design components. Learning pathways should be developed that allow for articulation between both qualification routes. Within the technology-focused pathway, it seems appropriate to allow a student who completes a three-year diploma at NQF level 6 to articulate seamlessly into a four-year professional bachelor's degree with a focus on architectural technology, and in this case there is no warrant for the restrictions that the HEQF currently places on credit transfer. However, should a student wish to articulate from the technology-focused to the design-focused route, the different nature of the curricula will require substantial bridging work at appropriate levels on the NQF. In the interests of consistency, there is an urgent need for more extensive system-level analyses that will develop appropriate learning pathways and articulation frameworks across a range of academic disciplines.

Possible Linkages Between the Further and Higher Education Sectors

As discussed at the beginning of this chapter, the creation of the South African FET sector is a recent phenomenon, and much remains to be done to achieve meaningful sectoral coordination as well as articulation with the HE sector. The FET colleges offer qualifications at both the secondary level (N1–N3) and the post-secondary level (N4–N6), in six broad vocational fields, with nearly half the enrollments at the post-secondary level (Department of Education 2002; Fisher *et al.* 2003: 337–8). However, enrollments at the colleges fall overwhelmingly in the fields of business studies and engineering (Department of Education 2002: 20). Enrollments in the other subject areas should increase substantially if the FET colleges are to realize their potential in addressing national human resource development needs within the post-secondary sector.

Despite the importance that the Education White Paper 4 (Department of Education 1998) accords to articulation between the FET and HE sectors, progress in this regard has been slow. Until recently, it has been left to individual higher education institutions to develop articulation arrangements with specific FET colleges (Fisher *et al.* 2003: 340). At the NMMU, for instance, institutional protocols have been developed that provide for admission into either diploma or degree-level study for students with FET qualifications, as well as for the recognition of course credits in qualifications in engineering, business management and to a lesser extent the creative arts.

The most important development in terms of articulation between the FET and HE sectors is the implementation of the new curriculum framework for the National Certificate (Vocational—NCV) since the start of 2007. These vocational qualifications will provide an alternative entry route to HE alongside the revised National Senior Certificate. However, at the post-secondary level the FET colleges will continue to offer qualifications where there is no clarity as to how, if at all, these qualifications will be mapped onto the new HEQF. Much still needs to be done to develop meaningful linkages between the FET and HE sectors.

Conclusion

The chapter has described the extensive restructuring process that is underway within the South African post-secondary sector. Much has been achieved in terms of policy frameworks and sectoral consolidation in both the higher education and further education and training sectors, but the critical work of coordinated system-level and institutional academic planning is still at an early stage. Both comprehensive universities and universities of technology face complex challenges as they develop coherent approaches to the problem of comprehensiveness within the context of the Higher Education Qualifications Framework. More widely, the challenge of forging meaningful linkages between sub-degree and degree-level provision in order to address national human resource development needs will require a far more coordinated approach to the development of the post-secondary system.

References

Akojee, S. A. Gewer and S. McGrath. 2005. South Africa: Skills development as a tool for social and economic development. In *Vocational Education and Training in Southern Africa: A Comparative Study*, eds. S. Akojee, A. Gewer and S. McGrath, Pretoria: Human Sciences Research Council, pp. 99–117.

Badat, S. 2004. Transforming South African higher education 1990–2003: Goals, policy initiatives and critical challenges and issues. In *National Policy and Regional Response in South African Higher Education*, eds N. Cloete, P. Pillay, S. Badat and T. Moja, Cape Town: David Philip, pp. 1–50.

Becher, T. and P. Trowler. 2001. *Academic Tribes and Territories: Intellectual Enquiry and the Cultures of Disciplines*, 2nd ed., Buckingham: Society for Research into Higher Education/ Open University Press.

Bunting, I. 2002. The higher education landscape under apartheid. In *Transformation in Higher Education: Global Pressures and Local Realities in South Africa*, eds. N. Cloete, R. Fehnel, P. Maassen, T. Moja, H. Perold, and T. Gibbon, Cape Town: Juta, pp. 58–86.

Centre for Higher Education Transformation (CHET). 2004. *Organising the Curriculum in the New Comprehensive Universities*, Cape Town: University of Cape Town Press.

Cloete, N. 2002. Policy expectations. In *Transformation in Higher Education: Global Pressures and Local Realities in South Africa*, eds. N. Cloete, R. Fehnel, P. Maassen, T. Moja, H. Perold, and T. Gibbon, Cape Town: Juta, pp. 87–108.

Codling, A. and L. Meek. 2006. Twelve propositions on diversity in higher education, *Higher Education Management and Policy*, 18:3, 31–54.

Committee of Technikon Principals. 2001. *Report of the CTP Task Team on "Universities OF Technology,"* Pretoria: Committee of Technikon Principals.

Committee of Technikon Principals. 2004. *Position, Role and Function of Universities of Technology in South Africa*, Pretoria: Committee of Technikon Principals.

Council on Higher Education. 2000. *Towards a New Higher Education Landscape: Meeting the Equity, Quality and Social Development Imperatives of South Africa in the 21st Century*, Pretoria: Council on Higher Education.

Council on Higher Education. 2002. *A New Academic Policy for Programmes and Qualifications in Higher Education (Discussion Document)*, Pretoria: Department of Education.

Council on Higher Education. 2004. *South African Higher Education in the First Decade of Democracy*, Pretoria: Council on Higher Education.

Department of Education. 1997. *Education White Paper 3: A Programme for the Transformation of Higher Education*, Pretoria: Government Printers (Government Gazette Notice 18207).

Department of Education. 1998. *Education White Paper 4: Preparing for the Twenty-First Century Through Education, Training and Work*, Pretoria: Government Printers (Government Gazette Notice 19281).

Department of Education. 2002. *Quantitative Overview of the Further Education and Training College Sector: The New Landscape,* Pretoria: Department of Education.

Department of Education. 2005. *Education Statistics in South Africa at a Glance in 2005,* Pretoria: Department of Education.

Department of Education and Department of Labour. 2001. *Human Resource Development Strategy for South Africa: A Nation at Work for a Better Life for All,* Pretoria: Department of Education/Department of Labour.

Du Pré, R.H. 2004. The philosophy of a university of technology in South Africa: an introduction, *Sediba sa Thuto,* 1, 9–37.

Fisher, G., R. Jaff, L. Powell and G. Hall. 2003. Public further education and training colleges. In *Human Resources Development Review 2003: Education, Employment and Skills in South Africa,* eds. A. Kraak and H. Perold, Cape Town and East Lansing: Human Sciences Research Council and Michigan State University Press, pp. 327–51.

Gibbon, T. 2004. *Creating Comprehensive Universities in South Africa: A Concept Document,* Pretoria: Department of Education.

Huisman, J. and F. Kaiser (eds.). 2001. *Fixed and Fuzzy Boundaries in Higher Education: A Comparative Study of (Binary) Structures in Nine Countries,* Den Haag: Adviesraad voor het Wetenschaps- en Technologiebeleid.

Kraak A. 2004. *An Overview of South African Human Resources Development,* Cape Town: Human Sciences Research Council.

Kraak A. 2006. "Academic drift" in South African universities of technology: Beneficial or detrimental?, *Perspectives in Education* 24:3, 135–52.

Ministry of Education. 2001. *National Plan for Higher Education,* Pretoria: Ministry of Education.

Ministry of Education. 2002. *Transformation and Restructuring: A New Institutional Landscape for Higher Education,* Pretoria: Government Printers (Government Gazette Notice 23549).

Ministry of Education. 2007. *The Higher Education Qualifications Framework,* Pretoria: Government Printers (Government Gazette Notice 30353).

Muller, J. 2008. *In Search of Coherence: A Conceptual Guide to Curriculum Planning for Comprehensive Universities,* Commissioned report prepared for the Centre for Education Policy Development, Pretoria: Department of Education.

National Commission on Higher Education. 1996. *A Framework for Transformation,* Pretoria: Government Printers.

National Working Group. 2001. *The Restructuring of the Higher Education System in South Africa: Report of the National Working Group to the Minister of Education,* Pretoria: Government Printers (Government Gazette Notice 23549).

Neave, G. 2000. Diversity, differentiation and the market: The debate we never had but which we ought to have done, *Higher Education Policy* 13:1, 7–22.

Reddy, J. 2006. The reclassification of technikons to universities of technology. In *Universities of Technology,* Pretoria: Council on Higher Education, pp. 24–49.

Republic of South Africa. 1995. *South African Qualifications Authority Act No.58 of 1995,* Pretoria: Government Printers (Government Gazette Notice 1521).

Salmi, J. 2001. Tertiary education in the 21st century: challenges and opportunities. *Higher Education Management,* 13:2, 105–25.

Scott, P. 1995. *The Meanings of Mass Higher Education,* Buckingham: Society for Research into Higher Education/Open University Press.

Subotzky, G. 2003. Public Higher Education, in *Human Resources Development Review 2003: Education, Employment and Skills in South Africa,* Cape Town and East Lansing: Human Sciences Research Council and Michigan State University Press.

Trow, M. 1987. Academic standards and mass higher education, *Higher Education Quarterly,* 41:3, 268–92.

United Nations Educational, Scientific and Cultural Organisation. 2005. *Towards Knowledge Societies,* Paris: UNESCO

Winberg, C. 2005. Continuities and discontinuities in the journey from technikon to university of technology, *South African Journal of Higher Education,* 19:2, 189–200.

III

Operational Responses

10
Governance

ROGER BARNSLEY AND JOHN SPARKS

Introduction

With the growth in the number of comprehensive post-secondary institutions in recent years, the subject of governance at these types of institutions is becoming an increasingly relevant and important subject. While the majority of these institutions in the English-speaking world apparently share the same basic governance structure, with a corporate board and a single academic board or senate (Garrod and Macfarlane 2007), there are many ways in which the governance at these institutions can vary.

In this chapter we consider how post-secondary institutions may be governed by a source external to the university, that is, by government. The level of autonomy that universities have from government is one of the most fundamental aspects of how universities function, and their autonomy is an important criterion that separates universities from other post-secondary institutions. We then shift from looking at governance from an external perspective to a consideration of internal governance structures in a comprehensive university. In this discussion we draw on examples from Thompson Rivers University (TRU), which is a comprehensive university that until 2005 was a university college in British Columbia, Canada (we explain below what university colleges in British Columbia are).

In looking at governance from an external source, we focus on the level of autonomy appropriate for comprehensive universities. Inasmuch as universities generally have more autonomy than do technical or vocational schools, a question arises as to how much autonomy should be accorded to comprehensive, post-secondary educational institutions that incorporate both higher and further education components. In British Columbia, when TRU was being established in 2004/05 as a comprehensive university, there was concern about the governance model that would be provided for the institution and the level of autonomy that it would allow.

Post-secondary Education in British Columbia

Canada is a confederation in which legislative authority over education is given to the provinces. Accordingly, each of the ten provinces in Canada has its own regime governing post-secondary education. Against this background, the province of British Columbia has developed governance models for post-secondary institutions to meet the distinctive needs of the province.

Prior to 1995, British Columbia's post-secondary education system consisted of both higher (universities) and further (community colleges) educational institutions. In 1995, British Columbia created, through legislation, university colleges from five former community colleges that, in addition to their existing community college programs, were authorized to award baccalaureate degrees (both academic and applied) and applied master's degrees.

In 2005, the British Columbia government amalgamated the University College of the Cariboo and the British Columbia Open University into Thompson Rivers University. TRU is a comprehensive university that maintains all the programs previously offered by the two amalgamated institutions and was given the authority to awards master's degrees generally and to engage in research. TRU is seen as being distinct from the established British Columbia universities that are considered to be research intensive. TRU has approximately 10,000 students studying in a face-to-face format and another 15,000 students studying at a distance through its Open Learning Division. Given its uniqueness, TRU was provided its own legislative Act and its own governance model.

Governance Models Prior to 2005

Looking more closely at the post-secondary education system in British Columbia, it can be seen that until 2005 there were two basic governance models for post-secondary education institutions. These governance models are embedded in two separate Acts of legislation adopted by the government of British Columbia. The *University Act* (Province of British Columbia 1996a, c. 468) governs degree-granting institutions that have no technical or vocational component (we refer to these institutions as "pure higher education universities"). The *College and Institute Act* (Province of British Columbia 2006, c. 52) governs most of the other public post-secondary institutions, including community colleges and university colleges. In this chapter we generally refer to universities that have both further and higher education components as being comprehensive. However, as will be seen below, we believe that there is an important distinction between a dual sector university and a comprehensive university.

The *University Act* applies to the institutions of pure higher education in British Columbia. It establishes a governance model with a convocation, a chancellor, a board of governors, and a senate. It creates a system of bi-cameral governance in which the "management, administration and control of the property, revenue, business and affairs of the university" are vested in the board (section 27) and in which "the academic governance of the university is vested in the senate" (section 37). The senate advises the board with regard to the establishment or discontinuance of faculties and courses of instruction.

The *College and Institute Act* sets out what, on the surface at least, appears to be a similar model. It creates a system of bi-cameral governance with a board and an education council. In wording that is remarkably similar to that used in the *University Act*, boards are given the responsibility to "manage, administer and control the property, revenue, expenditures and business and affairs of the institution" (section 19). The education councils, though not given all the powers of a senate under the *University Act*, are given powers that include the exclusive right to control curriculum content at the institution. As with a senate under the *University Act*, the education council plays an advisory role to the board with regard to the establishment or discontinuance of courses of instruction at the institution and it is important to note that the board is required to seek advice from the education council before making a decision in this area.

The membership of a senate under the *University Act* includes a majority of faculty members with equal representation from all faculties and the balance including academic administrators and students. The membership of an education council is half faculty members elected by faculty members (but there is no requirement that there be equal representation from all faculties), and the balance is composed of students, educational administrators, and support staff.

The seeming similarity between the governance structures under the *University Act* and the *College and Institute Act* belies the fact that governance under the two structures is conducted in significantly different manners. This difference is related to one of the most fundamental features of governance in post-secondary education, that is, the level of autonomy that an institution is accorded from government. The provisions under the *University Act* and the *College and Institute Act* differ significantly with regard to the level of autonomy they accord the institutions they respectively govern. This is analyzed in the following section.

In addition to the governance models outlined above, there is another model encompassed in the *Royal Roads University Act* (Province of British Columbia 1996b). However, in the unique circumstances of Royal Roads University, the board is given all the powers of the board and senate under the *University Act* except for powers given to the president of Royal Roads University. There is a body referred to as an "academic council" but it functions in an advisory capacity only.

Governance from External Sources: Autonomy from Government

It is generally accepted in Canada that public universities have greater autonomy from the provincial governments that establish them than community colleges (Dennison 2006; Shanahan and Jones 2007). In British Columbia, this difference is clearly set out in the provisions of the *University Act* and the *College and Institute Act*.

The *University Act* provides (section 48) that the provincial government may not interfere with a university with regard to the adoption of academic policies or in the appointment of staff. Conversely, the College and Institute Act provides broad powers for the government to intervene in the affairs of public, post-secondary institutions other than universities. These powers include: (i) the right of government to establish policy or directives for post-secondary education in British Columbia with which institutions must comply (section 2); and (ii) the power of government to assume control of an institution at any time by dismissing all of the members of the board and the education council of the institution and appointing an administrator to replace them (section 41). It is worth noting that this latter power has been exercised on one recent occasion in British Columbia when, during a period of transition for the Okanagan University College, the government appointed an administrator to take control of its affairs in 2004; this serves as a real reminder to the governing bodies of these institutions that they remain in office at the pleasure of the provincial government.

It is true that the provincial government provides a large part of the funding to both universities under the *University Act* and institutions under the *College and Institute Act*, and it cannot be denied that government is able to exercise some measure of control over these organizations through that funding function. However, to the extent that government cannot exert its will over public, post-secondary education organizations through the funding function, it may be able, in the case of institutions under the *College and Institute Act*, to exert its will through the mechanisms referred to above; the government does not have those mechanisms open to it with respect to universities. Consequently, the organizational culture with regard to autonomy is markedly different at the universities governed by the *University Act* than it is at institutions governed by the *College and Institute Act*.

Of course, the legislation does not provide an explanation of the reason(s) that universities are accorded greater autonomy than colleges, though common sense would suggest that it is likely related to the foundational principle of academic freedom (i.e. the freedom to study and teach without external control), which is generally considered to be central to institutions of higher education and of lesser importance to institutions of further education.

We do not attempt here to examine in any significant detail why universities should have autonomy while technical or vocational schools do not. Indeed, the reason(s) for this may be understood differently from one jurisdiction to another. In considering this issue in the British Columbia context, one senior commentator put it this way with reference to the university colleges that exist under the *College and Institute Act*:

[I]t is evident that university colleges do not enjoy the same level of autonomy as the universities and it is difficult to argue that they deserve the title of university. Even the legislated roles of faculty members in the two institutions are not comparable. The University Act acknowledges the responsibilities of faculty in the area of research. The College and Institute Act is silent on this task for faculty.

(Dennison 2006: 121)

Accordingly, it appears that Dennison considers that there should be a link between autonomy and the mandate of a university to engage in research and not just teach. We generally agree with that view, as research seems to be a core attribute of what constitutes a university.

In fact, there is strong support for this view in British Columbia in the legislative regime governing public, post-secondary institutions. Looking at the regime established by the government in British Columbia, it is clear that the government is more frugal in bestowing autonomy on public, post-secondary education institutions than it is in bestowing other attributes that are characteristic of a university. These other attributes can include the ability to offer degree programs, bi-cameral governance, and the use of the word "university" in the institution's title. Surveying the distribution of these attributes across the twenty-five public, post-secondary education institutions in British Columbia, the following can be seen. All twenty-five of these institutions have the capacity to offer degree programs, although community colleges are restricted to applied baccalaureate degrees and university colleges to applied master's degrees at the graduate level. Also, twenty-four of the twenty-five have bi-cameral governance with a senate or education council responsible for academic governance and a board responsible for the other affairs of the institution. Nine of the twenty-five use the word "university" in their title, though three of those are university colleges with the further education governance model as legislated by the *College and Institute Act*. However, only six of the twenty-five have autonomy from government and these are the same six that have a legislated mandate for research; these are also the same six that are "universities."

Thus, in British Columbia, though there is no express statement from the government articulating that autonomy should be granted to institutions with a research mandate, it seems clear that that is the approach the provincial government has taken. Other jurisdictions may, of course, take different approaches. There may well be characteristics of a university in addition to its having a research mandate that justify its being given autonomy from government. In any event, it seems clear that whatever characteristics of a university may justify its having autonomy, those characteristics may also be present in a comprehensive institution that has the characteristics of both pure higher and further education institutions. That being the case, there is no apparent reason why a comprehensive institution should be accorded any less autonomy than a pure higher education university. The inclusion of a technical or vocational component in a comprehensive university should not disentitle it to the autonomy it deserves for its pure higher education component. Such was the challenge in creating the legislation for TRU.

The *Thompson Rivers University Act*

As noted above, prior to 2005 Thompson Rivers University existed as a university college under the *College and Institute Act*.

As their names suggest, university colleges in British Columbia share characteristics of both universities and colleges. Dennison (2006: 107) refers to them as "a unique experiment in higher education" and further describes them as follows:

> In many respects an innovation, the university college attempted to integrate two distinctly different cultures, those of the comprehensive community college and the traditional values of the conventional university
>
> (p. 107)

Levin (2003: 449) says that they "can be viewed as hybrid institutions combining characteristics of community colleges and universities or four-year colleges."

It is important to note that while university colleges may be hybrid institutions in many respects, in matters of governance, they are not; they use exactly the same model as colleges under the *College and Institute Act* and they have no more, or less, autonomy from government than colleges have.

When the *Thompson Rivers University Act* (Province of British Columbia 2005, c. 17) was brought into force on March 31, 2005, a new governance model for public post-secondary institutions in British Columbia came into being to reflect the transition of TRU from a university college.

At that point in time there was concern that the provincial government would adopt a "halfway house" approach in legislation, in which TRU would be given autonomy at a level less than the full autonomy given to universities under the *University Act* but greater than the relative lack of autonomy shown to institutions under the *College and Institute Act*. Fortunately, the provincial government did not take that approach and TRU was given the full autonomy of a university in a context where it remained a comprehensive institution.

Looking at the *Thompson Rivers University Act*, it can be seen that it provides a governance structure that was designed for the institution in the knowledge that it would remain a comprehensive university. In this respect, the Act defines the purposes of the university to include: (a) offering baccalaureate and master's degree programs, (b) offering post-secondary and adult basic education and training, and (c) undertaking research and scholarship in support of the previous two purposes. These purposes are considerably broader than those of a university college, which are limited to offering only applied master's programs and which do not include any mandate for research.

This mandate had the following consequences: (a) it restricted TRU from offering doctoral degrees; (b) it guaranteed that TRU would remain comprehensive and continue to provide further education programs; and (c) it tied research and scholarship to the teaching function to differentiate TRU from research-intensive universities.

Surprisingly, beyond the description of its purposes, there is very little in the *Thompson Rivers University Act* that is based on the fact that it is a comprehensive institution. In fact, the approach used in the Act is to draw heavily from the *University Act* and to depart from that model primarily with regard to the composition and powers of the academic governance body.[1]

Consequently, the *Thompson Rivers University Act* incorporates by reference most of the provisions of the *University Act*. Specifically, the *Thompson Rivers University Act* incorporates 61 of the 74 sections of the *University Act* that existed in early 2005 when the *Thompson Rivers University Act* was enacted.

As may be expected, the *Thompson Rivers University Act* provides a framework with a newly constituted board of governors, and with a new academic governance body (referred to as a "university council") replacing the education council that previously had been responsible for academic matters at the institution. As noted above, the departures in the *Thompson Rivers University Act* from the *University Act* relate primarily to the composition of the university council and its powers. With regard to the composition of the university council, the provisions in the *Thompson Rivers University Act*, while somewhat different than those of the *University Act*, are not designed to create a significantly different type of body; the TRU university council parallels a senate rather than an education council. Therefore, TRU's university council includes the chancellor, the president/vice-chancellor, the vice-president academic, the deans of faculties, the chief librarian, and student representatives, and a majority of its seats are held by faculty members (with equal representation from all faculties). With regard to the legislated powers of the university council, they are somewhat broader than the powers of an education council under the *College and Institute Act* and somewhat narrower than those of a senate under the *University Act*, in that it is given more powers than an education council but there is no statement in the *Thompson Rivers University Act* that "academic governance of the university is vested in" the university council as there is for senates under the *University Act*. In any event, from a practical point of view the university council at TRU simply handles academic governance. A more detailed description of the academic governance structure is set out below.

A critical characteristic of the *Thompson Rivers University Act* is the absence of the types of provisions found in the *College and Institute Act* that allow the provincial government to intervene in the affairs of the institution. Consequently, government no longer has the right to set policy directives for TRU; nor does it have the power to dismiss all the members of the board and academic governance body and replace those members with an administrator, which powers government does continue to hold with regard to university colleges, as noted above. In fact, the section of the *University Act* that prohibits government from interfering in the adoption of academic policies and the appointment of staff (section 48) is incorporated by reference into the *Thompson Rivers University Act* and applies to TRU. Thus, TRU was given a level of autonomy that is the same as that accorded to universities under the *University Act*. To have done otherwise would have penalized TRU for the comprehensiveness of its programming. Indeed, to accord any comprehensive university less autonomy than a pure higher education university would amount to penalizing the institution for its comprehensiveness. This would send a signal that if a university wishes to be autonomous from government, it should eschew comprehensiveness.

Assuming that comprehensiveness is a characteristic of post-secondary institutions that governments seek to encourage, then from a policy perspective they would do well to avoid utilizing a halfway house approach to governance.

Impacts of the "Campus 2020 Report"

There have been other, more recent developments in the British Columbia context that provide further information in considering the subject of university autonomy.

In April 2007 the government of British Columbia released a wide-ranging report concerning the future of the post-secondary education system in the province entitled *Campus 2020: Thinking Ahead: The Report*. It was prepared by a former Attorney General of the province, Geoff Plant QC, and the report is sometimes referred to as the "Plant Report" (Plant 2007).

That report recommended that the remaining university colleges in British Columbia be converted to what it refers to as "regional universities" (i.e. teaching-intensive universities that would serve their respective regions of the province) and that those new universities should adopt the TRU governance structure.

The Campus 2020 Report does not spell out the governance structure it proposes for the regional universities, other than to recommend that they adopt "the Thompson Rivers University governance structure." Consequently, it is not clear from this whether "governance structure" refers only to structures within the universities or whether it could include matters external to the university. However, it does not seem reasonable to seek to meaningfully emulate the structures in place at TRU unless the other university colleges are given the same level of autonomy that has been accorded to TRU under the *Thompson Rivers University Act* since the autonomy accorded to an institution is at the core of its governance structure. Accordingly, any new legislation enacted to convert the three existing university colleges to university status should, if it is to follow the recommendation of the Campus 2020 Report, entail the elimination of the government's rights currently found in the *College and*

Institute Act to set academic policy for the institutions as well as the ability of government to dismiss the institutions' boards and academic governance bodies. Such a result would be consistent with the governance structure found in the *Thompson Rivers University Act.*

At this point it is worthwhile to return to the correlation in legislation in British Columbia between an institution being given a legislated research function and its being given autonomy from government. Interestingly, the Campus 2020 Report makes research a focus of its discussion when recommending that the existing university colleges be transformed into universities. It makes the following recommendation in this respect:

> In this regard, I should observe that the existing legislative mandate for institutes, colleges and university colleges, found in the *College and Institute Act,* makes no reference to research. . . . I suggest adopting a statutory mandate for regional universities along the following lines: . . . (3) A regional university may undertake and maintain research and scholarly activity for the purposes of supporting teaching.
>
> (Plant 2007: 67)

It is worth noting that the wording proposed in the Campus 2020 Report is permissive in that it proposes that a regional university "may" undertake research and scholarly activity to support teaching. This is different from the wording in the *TRU Act,* which indicates that it is a purpose of TRU to undertake research for the purpose of offering higher education programs and offering further education. Accordingly, TRU has a requirement to conduct research, which the province would have some obligation to fund, whereas the new regional universities have no requirement to conduct research so the provincial government would have no obligation to fund any research. Notwithstanding the fact that the recommendation in the Campus 2020 Report is permissive in nature, it is clear that the intent of the recommendation is that the regional universities would be involved in conducting research.

In any event, if the government of British Columbia elects to implement the recommendation to convert the remaining university colleges to regional universities, it will be instructive to see whether the linkage between a research mandate and autonomy that is clearly present in the existing legislative regime is continued for these new universities.

Internal Governance Structures

At this point we shift from discussing governance from external sources to look at internal governance structures and focus on academic governance.

With regard to academic governance in comprehensive institutions, there are, in theory at least, two approaches that can be used. The first is to have a unified academic governance structure in which both higher education and further education representatives work side by side. The alternative is to have a bifurcated governance system in which higher education matters are dealt with primarily by representatives of the higher education component of the institution, and further education matters are dealt with primarily by representatives of the further education component of the institution. Garrod and Macfarlane (2007) refer to these organizational structures as "unitary" and "binary" respectively. They also note (correctly in our view) that the distinction between unitary and binary structures is stark and that these characteristics represent extreme ends of a continuum. They found that of nineteen institutions surveyed that identified themselves as duals (i.e. institutions with both further education and higher education components), seventeen had a single academic board or senate.

Like most other comprehensive universities, TRU has adopted a unified approach. The academic governance body at TRU, the university council, includes representation from all academic divisions of the university. There are ten faculties, schools, or divisions at TRU, and each of those academic divisions has equal representation on the university council. Each academic division elects two faculty members to the university council, and the Dean of each academic division sits on the university council. Together these representatives account for thirty of the forty-seven members on the TRU university council.

Of the ten academic divisions at TRU, three are predominantly in the further education sector and seven are predominantly in higher education. However, it is important to note that it is not really possible to draw clear lines between further and higher education within academic divisions at TRU. For example, of the ten academic divisions, all but one offer both four-year degree programs as well as shorter certificate or diploma programs that would generally be considered further education. Some examples of this include the School of Education offering a two-year Diploma in Early Childhood Education, or the Faculty of Science offering a two-year Diploma in Horticulture and Management.

TRU distinguishes itself on the unification, articulation, and integration of the further and higher education components of its programs. This program structure allows students to ladder up programs or bridge across programs with the maximum credit transfer. TRU has, for example, a Bachelor of Leadership in Trades and Technology program that allows students with a background in trades or technology to learn management skills and acquire a bachelor's degree. It is believed that the unitary academic governance model facilitates and sustains this integrated arrangement by having governance structures aligned with an integrated educational structure. It is because of this blending of further and higher education at TRU that it prefers to view itself as a "comprehensive" university as opposed to a "dual" sector university. This blending, where almost every academic division has both a higher and further education component, also means that there is a community of interest among members of the university council on many, if not most, matters.

In his 2003 article, Levin (2003) refers to tensions among and between employee groups as a result of the fact that university colleges were a hybrid institution combining characteristics of community colleges and of universities. To the extent that this tension may have existed at TRU in the past, it is greatly mitigated by the current blending of the further and higher education functions within each academic division.

Accordingly, members on university council are not identified as to whether they represent a higher education or a further education component of the university. Nor is there any expectation that, when university council makes decisions, members of an academic division that is predominantly from one sector would defer to members of divisions from the other sector when the decision relates to that other sector.

It is worth pointing out that, though the *Thompson Rivers University Act* refers to the academic governance body at TRU as the "university council", this body has adopted a bylaw to refer to itself internally as the "senate"; this decision is largely intended to underscore that academic governance at TRU is conducted in the same way as at other universities in British Columbia.

As with other universities, much of the work of academic governance at TRU is referred to committees of the academic governance body. There are fourteen such committees at TRU, each with its own Terms of Reference defining its membership and responsibilities. In establishing these committees the university council has made a concerted effort to ensure that there is wide representation on each committee from across the university's academic divisions. A common provision in the terms of reference for these committees is that, among their members, the committee will "normally" have one member from each of the ten academic divisions (faculties) at the university, reflecting the diversity of disciplines at the university. Thus far, the system seems to be functioning satisfactorily and it is our sense that the new governance structure has led to enhanced collegiality across disciplines.

Conclusion

Models available for governance in post-secondary education are becoming increasingly sophisticated. Perhaps the single most important aspect of governance is the extent to which an institution is free to manage its own affairs with autonomy from government. Universities generally have full autonomy from government whereas other public, post-secondary institutions have much less autonomy. Comprehensive universities have components of both higher education and of further education. Consequently, it might be argued that comprehensive institutions should have a level of autonomy greater than that of vocational or technical schools but less than that of universities. The government of British Columbia has recently had to contend with this issue when it enacted the *Thompson Rivers University Act*. When it did this, it acted consistently with the legislated regime in British Columbia where public, post-secondary institutions with a research mandate are given autonomy from government. This seems to be a reasonable approach that recognizes that a comprehensive university should not be deprived of autonomy simply because it has a technical or vocational component.

With regard to internal governance structures, the transition to the new governance structures within TRU that were adapted to accommodate its new autonomy have led to greater involvement from the university community in its academic governance. The experience at TRU shows that the comprehensiveness of an institution may have very little impact as it moves from a college style governance model to an autonomous university style governance model, though the new governance model has produced enhanced collegiality across disciplines.

Postscript

On April 29, 2008, subsequent to this chapter being written, the government of British Columbia tabled legislation that, when enacted, will allow the conversion of the three remaining university colleges (and two other institutions) in British Columbia into universities. This will be accomplished by amendments to the *University Act* that will create a new form of university that will be referred to as a "special purpose, teaching university." TRU will remain incorporated under the *Thompson Rivers University Act* and will not be impacted by the new legislation other than to have its academic governance body formally referred to as a "Senate." The new special purpose teaching universities are given a mandate to undertake "applied" research and scholarly activity to the extent that their resources from time to time permit.

Note

1. Under the Thompson Rivers University Act, TRU is also made responsible for serving the open learning needs of British Columbia, and the Act deals with matters relevant to that function; those provisions of the Act are not discussed here as they are not relevant for present purposes.

References

Dennison, J. 2006. From community college to university: a personal commentary on the evolution of an institution, *Canadian Journal of Higher Education*, 36:2, 107–24.

Garrod, N. and B. Macfarlane. 2007. Scoping the duals: the structural challenges of combining further and higher education in post compulsory institutions, *Higher Education Quarterly*, 2007, 61:4, 578–96.

Levin, J.S. 2003. Organizational paradigm shift and the university colleges of British Columbia, *Higher Education*, 46, 447–67.

Plant, G. 2007. *Access and Excellence: The Campus 2020 Plan for British Columbia's Post-secondary System*, http://www.campus2020-ThinkingAheadTheReport.pdf, (accessed April 5, 2007).

Province of British Columbia. 1996a. *University Act*, Revised Statutes of British Columbia 1996, Chapter 468, http://www.qp.gov.bc.ca/statreg/stat/U/96468_01.htm (accessed October 30, 2007).

Province of British Columbia. 1996b. *Royal Roads University Act*, Revised Statutes of British

Columbia 1996, Chapter 409, http://www.qp.gov.bc.ca/statreg/stat/R/96409_01.htm (accessed October 29, 2007).

Province of British Columbia. 2005. *Thompson Rivers University Act*, Province of British Columbia, Victoria: Queen's Printer. http://www.qp.gov.bc.ca/statreg/stat/T/05017_01.htm. (accessed October 29, 2007).

Province of British Columbia. 2006. *College and Institute Act*, http://www.qp.gov.bc.ca/statreg/stat/C/96052_01.htm. (accessed October 30, 2007)

Shanahan, T. and G. A. Jones 2007. Shifting roles and approaches: government co-ordination of post secondary education in Canada, 1995–2006, *Higher Education Research and Development*, 26:3, 31–43.

11
Careers

NEIL GARROD AND BRUCE MACFARLANE

Introduction

Several of the chapters in this book have outlined why it is important to challenge the boundary between further and higher education. Social justice, rates of participation in post-secondary education, and the demands of a modern economy have all been cited as pressing reasons. However, realizing these aspirations is heavily dependent on the cooperation and goodwill of academic staff. While many are committed to the social goals associated with providing students with a seamless educational experience, few are necessarily equipped or prepared to teach across the boundary between further and higher education.

Academic career structures reflect the divide between the sectors reinforced by different contractual conditions of service, education and training qualifications, and pension arrangements in a UK context. Research activity is normally expected of academic staff working in higher education while such expectations do not normally apply to lecturers in the further education sector. This is broadly in line with expectations in other national contexts, such as Canada, where community college staff focus on classroom instruction rather than research (see chapter 7). Breaking through these cultural and structural boundaries is one of the most, if not the most, important challenges of managing a dual sector or comprehensive post-secondary institution. Many of the issues lie beyond the scope of a single institution as they involve complex differences in academic career structures determined and reinforced by separate and long-standing industrial negotiations.

This chapter will draw on the experience of the authors as the Deputy Vice-Chancellor (Neil Garrod) and the Head of Educational Development (Bruce Macfarlane) at Thames Valley University (UK) during the four-year period immediately following the merger of the institution with Reading College and School of Arts and Design in 2004. The merger, which is explained in detail in chapter 6, brought together roughly equal numbers of further education and higher education lecturers into a single institution. Developing opportunities for staff to work across the sectors within the same institution and to develop their careers in flexible ways were recognized early on as paramount to the success of a comprehensive university (see figure 6.1, chapter 6). Part of the challenge was to develop a single academic contract. However, it was also fundamental to consider the way that the links between teaching and research could be strengthened to reshape perceptions of academic identity within the institution and help redefine the meaning of scholarship in the process.

Academic Contracts

Immediately following merger, Thames Valley University (TVU) comprised significant numbers of staff on either a further education or a higher education contract. These contracts contrast markedly in respect to conditions of employment. In common with other post-1992 UK universities,[1] staff on higher education contracts teach for a maximum of 550 hours per year and are normally expected to engage in "research and scholarly activity" (Robson 2006: 47). There is a nationally agreed contract: the Contract of Employment for Lecturers in Polytechnics and Colleges of Higher Education (hereafter, the "national contract") (Universities and College Union 2008), which pre-dates the expansion of the university sector in 1992. By contrast, staff within the merged university on further education contracts teach up to 850 hours per year on a locally agreed contract and have no parallel expectation of dedicated time to conduct research and scholarship. In a UK context, the distinction between a pre-1992 and a post-1992 university is significant in respect to the contractual conditions affecting academic staff. Staff in the post-1992 universities generally have higher teaching loads. The role of faculty in institutional governance tends to be weaker in post-1992 institutions, most of which are former polytechnics dating from the 1970s. This is because, in contrast with older universities, post-1992 institutions are legal corporations with Boards of Governors largely made up of "independent" members rather than faculty representatives (Evans 1999).

As a result of this history, the teaching function, rather than research, is central to academic identity at post-1992 universities such as TVU (Henkel 2000). This means that even among the higher education staff research is still seen by many as a developmental or aspirational part of their working life rather than key to their identity. While research activity as part of professional identity may be only weakly established among many higher education faculty, it plays an even more marginalized role among further education lecturers. The identity of further education lecturers is shaped more strongly by their first professional or occupational role outside the education sector. The concern of further education staff tends to focus on maintaining their credibility through keeping up to date with changes in working or professional practice (Robson 2006). They are also required to have a teaching qualification and to engage in continuous professional development activity, including "research and study related to professional practice" (Parry et al. 2006: 124). This contrasts with the position in higher education, where lecturers are not legally required to possess a current teaching qualification or to undertake continuous professional development. However, the position has been changing in recent years as the vast majority of UK universities now require faculty with less than three years' teaching experience to complete a certificate in learning and teaching (or equivalent nomenclature). These part-time postgraduate qualifications are subject to accreditation by the Higher Education Academy, which has a sector remit for raising the status of learning and teaching and the student experience.

Developing a Single Dual Sector Contract

As the merger between TVU and Reading College was achieved through the dissolution of the Reading College corporation and the assimilation of its assets by TVU (see chapter 6), the Reading College staff effectively had no contract of employment from the date of merger. There was therefore a pressing need to develop a new contract for these employees of the newly merged university.

Lecturers at the former TVU were employed under the national contract that is standard for all post-1992 universities. For those lecturers that taught on further education level courses there was a local agreement addendum to the national contract, which amended their maximum teaching hours on a sliding scale depending upon their volume of further education teaching.

At Reading College the situation was reversed. All staff were employed on the local Reading College further education contract, and higher education teaching—which composed about 15 percent of the College's curriculum—was accommodated through "grace and favor" reductions in their total teaching load. Thus, the further education lecturers at the founder TVU were seen to be in a much more favorable situation than their Reading College colleagues who had significant higher education teaching.

On merger, these contractual differences were recognized by staff as a significant issue. Naturally, differences in the further and higher education terms and conditions raised debate about the relative value of further and higher education. As the merged TVU had made an explicit and "equal commitment to further and higher education" (Garrod 2005: 57), questions were raised as to why terms and conditions for provision in the two sectors were different.

As funding levels for higher education are higher per student than for further education, there was never any possibility of a single contract with a single set of terms and conditions. Nonetheless, there was a deeply held conviction on the part of senior executive management that while external differences between the sectors would have to be recognized in different teaching hour commitments, there was a philosophical imperative to recognize these differences within a single contract—in other words, to blur the boundary of distinction between the academic staff in the two sectors in the same way that the merger was attempting to blur the boundary of distinction between its students.

This was achieved through the identification of three categories of lecturer: those that taught predominantly on further education courses (more than about 85 percent of their teaching at further education level), those that taught predominantly on higher education courses (more than 50 percent of their teaching at higher education level) and those that taught a significant blend of both further and higher education (i.e. any mix between the other two categories). The differences between the three categories related solely to teaching hours. Further education contact hours were limited to 850 hours per annum and higher education to 550, with the hybrid on a sliding scale in between.

Two critical points need to be made about the differences in teaching hours that are fundamental to the positive application of this contract. First, the sliding scale is not interpreted as a simple linear trade-off. Rather it provides a framework within which balanced workloads can be attributed to staff. Secondly, the decision as to which category applies to any particular individual is made prior to any teaching allocations. This avoids the temptation for staff to take on the teaching of particular courses in order to move from one category to another. Of equal importance, it provides a framework for planning and staff development.

Agreement on these three categories of lecturer with different teaching contact hours opened up the opportunity for a single contract for all academics. The wording of the national contract was found to be just as applicable to further education staff as it was to their higher education colleagues: yet another indicator that the further and higher education sector split is more bureaucratic than Platonic (see chapters 1 and 2). The one outstanding issue that needed to be resolved was that of research and scholarly activity. This formed an integral part of the national contract but was not mentioned in further education contracts. The relevant wording from the national contract in this regard makes it clear that engagement in research and scholarly activity is a "normal" expectation. According to the contract, this expectation should be accommodated throughout the academic year outside of teaching weeks and holiday entitlement. There is also an emphasis of academic staff self-managing their research and scholarly activity.

The history of TVU was as a teaching-led institution. Research and scholarly activity never played a significant role in staff appraisal and planning and "self managed research time" was interpreted largely as personal time for the academic. Some used this for research and scholarly activity but many did not. At the extreme, it was interpreted by some as an additional six weeks of paid holiday.

It is clear that there were research and scholarship issues facing the whole of the university and not just those that were previously employed on a Reading College contract. The resolution of these issues could not be achieved simply through the wording of a single contract. The subsequent work of the

Educational Development Unit and the Graduate School, detailed below, was critical in making a step change in the research environment at TVU. Nonetheless, the more embracing approach to research and scholarship adopted by the Educational Development Unit needed to be reflected in the employment contract. Two issues were central: the acceptance by all academic staff that research and scholarship was part of their academic identity; and the acceptance that current further education self-development activity should be explicitly recognized as scholarship.

Both issues were addressed directly in the final agreement. Research was recognized as occurring throughout the academic year and not just in pre-designated slots. It was explicitly recognized as forming an integral part of the workload of all academic staff, accepting that the balance and nature of the scholarship would vary between categories. Original research, or the scholarship of discovery in Boyer's terminology (Boyer 1990), would play a greater part in scholarship for higher education staff than for further education staff. For the latter grouping, scholarly activity was recognized as primarily directed at curriculum design and the development of teaching and learning materials. In addition, the need to ensure course team coherence and to facilitate student recruitment necessitated additional constraints on when staff could focus primarily on research and scholarship activities.

For the agreement to have operational meaning, there was a need to pursue and develop a clearer perspective of what was actually meant by research and scholarship within the context of a comprehensive post-secondary university.

Research and Scholarship

Teaching and research have often been perceived as opposite ends of the academic spectrum. Institutions commonly separate teaching and research both strategically and culturally through, for example, separate committees for teaching and research. Research development usually occurs in faculties or departments, while teaching development is organized centrally (Reid and Petocz 2003). The research-teaching divide is not helpful for academic practice because it encourages staff to identify either as teachers, who do little or no research, or as disciplinary researchers who teach. Academic identity is complex and is dependent on many factors such as discipline and institutional status (Becher and Trowler 2001). It is also common for faculty to perceive the teaching and research roles as competing for their time rather than as complementary activities.

The status gap between university and further education staff is closely associated with the research function. University lecturers, unlike teachers in schools or further education, are perceived to be involved, to a greater or lesser extent, in creating knowledge rather than just disseminating it (Hoyle 2001). This status gap is a particular tension that exists in a dual sector institution where there is a danger that research may be regarded even more as an exclusive and elitist activity than it is in a conventional university without a significant sub-degree-level provision.

One of the key career and development issues referred to elsewhere in this collection is the expectation that faculty at duals will undertake research and other forms of scholarship. Moodie argues in his chapter that to be a dual sector university an institution should have at least twenty doctoral completions per year (see chapter 5). In reality, however, many institutions making the claim to dual status fail to fulfill this criterion, including TVU.

In 2001, TVU was the most lowly ranked higher education institution in the UK Research Assessment Exercise (RAE). Less than one in five staff were selected as part of the RAE submission, and returns indicate that, at the time, there were just seven full-time equivalent research student registrations at the university. TVU also returned the smallest proportion of research-active staff of any university and, as a consequence, received the smallest amount of research funding in the sector. Subsequently, the university lost many of its research-active staff to other universities including a high-profile Centre for Food Policy. The poor performance of the university in the 2001 RAE and the more recent merger of TVU with Reading College provide an important context in understanding the concern of the university to reinvigorate its research and develop a fresh identity.

The merger between TVU and Reading College in 2004 meant that there was a new group of academic staff, employed on a further education contract and who had not, in the main, engaged with research. This does not imply, though, that further education lecturers do not do research, or at least have aspirations to do so (Hillier and Jameson 2003). At the time of merger, a number of further education staff were studying for master's or doctoral degrees that involve a substantial piece of independent research. Moreover, developing the higher education provision of some areas, such as technology, was recognized as being strategically important. Alongside such a goal was the need to ensure that the academic staff were provided with sufficient opportunities to engage in research and scholarly activity.

A New Language

A new strategic plan was created immediately following the formation of the new dual institution in 2004 (see chapter 6). This identified, inter alia, the need to build research capacity and led directly to the development of a proposal to create a Graduate School. The new strategic plan also reflected the desire to broaden understanding of the research role of the new dual institution through adopting an inclusive classification of scholarship, such as that proposed by Boyer (1990). This defines scholarship as one of four types: discovery, integration, application, and teaching (p. 16). While the scholarship of discovery refers to scientific investigation in a particular discipline designed to elicit new knowledge or discoveries about the world, Boyer's other categories refer to research activities that do not fit this conventional academic paradigm. Boyer defines the scholarship of integration as making connections across and between disciplines. This category pays due regard to the fact that much research, in reality, cuts across discipline fields. The scholarship of application concerns the use of specialist academic knowledge to tackle problems in their context of application and is a key category in recognizing the work of academics in applied and professional fields of study. Finally, the scholarship of teaching entails systematic inquiry into the processes of teaching and student learning, which in itself has grown to become a specialist field of study with its own academic journals, societies, and conferences. Essentially, the Boyer categories legitimize a much broader range of scholarly activity in the university, particularly that related to applied and professional fields. Other modern universities and duals, such as Kwantlen Polytechnic University in Canada, have also adopted the Boyer categories and sought to increasingly link them to reward and recognition policies (see chapter 7).

Adopting a clear, contemporary, and internationally accepted definition of scholarship was important for all academic staff of the new institution regardless of whether they came from a background in further or higher education. Even among higher education staff of the former TVU there was much vagueness and little shared understanding as to the meaning of scholarship. It was interpreted as anything from updating one's lecture notes through to publishing in a top-quality international journal. Subject heads, responsible for managing groups of academic staff within a cognate area, had no clear expectations. It was quickly recognized that developing a clearer and more inclusive language around research would be important in forging a new culture and common institutional language. Disseminating this new language, the Deputy Vice-Chancellor based his lecture at the 2005 Postgraduate Students conference on the Boyer categories.

Building a New Understanding

As part of the process of developing a shared institutional culture, the newly formed Educational Development Unit was located in the university-wide Graduate School with a remit to be a facilitator for and developer of academic research skills as an integral part of academic practice. This location and remit was broader than is conventionally associated with educational (or faculty) development. Most such units or centers tend be mainly concerned with the improvement of university teaching practices or supporting student development (Rowland *et al.* 1998; Badley 1998; Bath and Smith 2004; D'Andrea and Gosling 2001; Gosling 2001). A remit for developing the research capacity of academic staff is unusual except for mission-based projects linked to the student learning experience or the promotion of the scholarship of teaching (Bath and Smith 2004; Brew 2002). However, in the context of the newly merged institution, it was felt that such a broader role would be important especially given the need for the university to increase the strength of its research base and the identity of lecturers beyond that of a teacher.

The educational development unit embarked on a series of formal and informal initiatives designed to help establish research and scholarship as a mainstream part of academic practice at the institution open for both further and higher education academic staff (see figure 11.1). Some of these initiatives were focused on building educational research while others were more generically targeted at building research capacity across disciplines.

One of the first post-merger steps to be taken was the establishment of a university-wide Educational Research Group in 2004. This was designed to act as a focal point for members of academic staff with strong research interests in education who were scattered across the institution in the faculties of Arts, Health and Human Science, and Professional Studies of the former TVU. This included some staff from the former Reading College based in the Education and Languages subject group of the Faculty of Professional Studies. The group also included University Teaching Fellows, a small number of faculty identified since 2001 as excellent teachers. However, the potential of Teaching Fellows had not been fully exploited since the inception of the scheme, and their ability to influence colleagues and develop a suitable profile at a national level was felt to necessitate their development as researchers as well as teachers. As part of this strategy, the Teaching Fellows were provided with a modest level of funding to enable them to develop a stronger external profile and the concomitant strengthening of their capacity to provide consultancy and support for colleagues. They are also now leading the organization of an annual, university-wide teaching conference where research-informed teaching expertise can be disseminated.

The university established a Centre for Research in Tertiary Education (CReaTE), partly as a result of a grant from the English funding council for a research project focusing on the management challenges of dual sector education. The project enabled the university to learn more about its own institutional experiment as a dual and, through analysis, other models of dual sector management and education on an international basis (see Garrod and Macfarlane 2007; Macfarlane *et al.* 2007). Visiting professors, research

---

- Establishment of an educational research group
- Funding for pedagogic research by University Teaching Fellows
- Establishment of a Centre for Research in Tertiary Education (CReaTE)
- Research development workshops
- Book groups/Learning lunches
- Research-informed teaching environment initiative
- Building the research and scholarship capacity of the educational development team

Figure 11.1 Initiatives designed to embed research and scholarship.

associates, and doctoral students have helped strengthen the Centre and it has also acted as the organizational hub for the submission of a return in the Education Unit of Assessment in the 2008 Research Assessment Exercise.

Other initiatives sought to combine teaching with research development, a strategy advocated by Clegg (2003) and Reid and Petocz (2003), among others. These initiatives were designed for academic staff with research interests in any discipline. Research development workshops were established by the Educational Development Unit for the purpose of capacity building, such as applying for research grants, writing a book proposal, presenting papers at academic conferences, and writing papers for publication. Other workshops in this series focused on issues that link research and teaching such as research supervision and understanding the professional doctorate. The workshops appeal to both academic staff and doctoral students. Moreover, as many academic staff come from a professional background, a number currently have a dual identity as both faculty member and doctoral student.

Research and teaching was also linked through the organization of a number of book groups each year and associated learning lunches where authors would come to discuss their publications. While some titles selected were purely teaching-focused, others were new books about research in both a further and higher education context, such as *Empowering Researchers in Further Education* (Hillier and Jameson 2003) and *The Research Game in Academic Life* (Lucas 2006). The selection of books about teaching was based, in large part, on whether they contained original research. This, it was felt, was an important signal to staff about the integrative nature of academic practice. Book groups provide a means of organizing educational development activities that breaks with the formally timetabled workshop or seminar model. Allowing opportunities for such informal learning helps to build trust as well by promoting an emancipatory rather than managerial agenda (Land 2004).

The opportunity to further build capacity and understanding of research and scholarship arose, in part, as a result of the availability of funds for the development of research-led teaching through the English funding council. This is designed to strengthen the links between teaching and research and has added impetus to the aim of developing a more holistic conception of educational development. The funding was allocated to universities in inverse proportion to their performance at the 2001 Research Assessment Exercise (Higher Education Funding Council for England 2006). This means that many English institutions, such as TVU, with modest prior research returns received additional funding to support initiatives to build stronger links between teaching and research.

Prompted by the work of Jenkins and Healey (2005), a study leave scheme was established that embraced a broad range of interpretations of how teaching might be linked with research. These include getting students to learn about research findings ("research-led" teaching), teaching students about how to do research ("research-oriented" teaching), making inquiry-based learning central to teaching practice ("research-based" teaching) and encouraging pedagogic research among academic staff ("research-informed" teaching) (Jenkins and Healey 2005). Applicants for study leave needed to demonstrate how their proposed project would have a direct and demonstrable impact on student learning. This was often seen as occurring through some form of curriculum innovation. The initiative enabled educational development to appeal to a wider constituency of academics rather than those whose interest is confined to pedagogic research and built research capacity across the university. A number of projects have now been funded and the progress of beneficiaries is monitored and supported by a Senior Research Fellow appointed as a member of the Educational Development Unit to lead the initiative.

Finally, in leading the initiative to integrate teaching and research and providing development opportunities in both areas of practice, it is imperative that members of the Educational Development Unit are seen as legitimate agents of this change. This means that they must be able to demonstrate competence as researchers as well as teachers through success in attracting grants and publication. This requirement means that educational developers must be full-fledged meta-professionals (Webb 1996) rather than more limited service providers or "trainers" located in an administrative unit.

Conclusion

Shifting the identity of academic staff from backgrounds where research is tangential to their practice is a hard task and one that demands sustained effort over a period of time. The division between research and teaching is reinforced at a national and international level through the funding and audit practices of governments and the reward and recognitions systems employed by universities. However, blurring the boundaries between teaching and research is a positive way of demonstrating the fragility of this distinction at an intellectual level and promoting integration rather than separation. The single academic contract and the initiatives connected to educational development activity at Thames Valley University have only begun to scratch the surface of the teaching-oriented culture of both former institutions. Locating development for both teaching and research in the Graduate School, however, is a powerful symbol of a more integrative approach to academic practice.

Note

1. Predominantly former polytechnics before the abolition of the binary divide in the UK in 1992.

References

Badley, G. 1998. Making a case for educational development in times of drift and shift, *Quality Assurance in Education*, 6:2, 64–73.

Bath, D. and C. Smith. 2004. Academic developers: an academic tribe claiming their territory in higher education, *International Journal of Academic Development*, 9:1, 9–27.

Becher, T. and P. Trowler. 2001. *Academic Tribes and Territories: Intellectual Enquiry and the Cultures of Disciplines*, Buckingham: Society for Research into Higher Education/Open University Press.

Boyer, E. L. 1990. *Scholarship Reconsidered: Priorities for the Professoriate*, San Francisco: Jossey-Bass.

Brew, A. 2002. Research and the academic developer: a new agenda, *International Journal of Academic Development*, 7, 112–22.

Clegg, S. 2003. Problematising ourselves: continuing professional development in higher education, *International Journal for Academic Development*, 8:1–2, 37–50.

D'Andrea, V. and D. Gosling. 2001. Joining the dots: reconceptualizing educational development, *Active Learning in Higher Education*, 2:1, 64–80.

Evans, G. 1999. *Calling Academia to Account: Rights and Responsibilities*, Buckingham: Society for Research into Higher Education/Open University Press.

Garrod, N. 2005. The building of a dual-sector university: the case of Thames Valley University. In *The Tertiary Moment: What Road to an Inclusive Higher Education?*, ed. Duke, C., Leicester: NIACE, pp. 57–73.

Garrod, N. and B. Macfarlane. 2007. Scoping the duals: the structural challenges of combining further and higher education in post-compulsory institutions, *Higher Education Quarterly*, 61:4, 578–96.

Gosling, D. 2001. Educational development units in the UK: what are they doing five years on?, *International Journal of Academic Development*, 6, 74–90.

Henkel, M. 2000. *Academic Identities and Policy Change in Higher Education*, London: Jessica Kingsley.

Higher Education Funding Council for England. 2006. *Teaching Quality Enhancement Fund*. Available at http://www.hefce.ac.uk/learning/enhance/tqef.asp (accessed May 19, 2006).

Hillier, Y. and J. Jameson. 2003. *Empowering Researchers in Further Education*, Stoke-on-Trent: Trentham Books.

Hoyle, E. 2001. Teaching: prestige, status and esteem, *Educational Management and Administration*, 29, 139–52.

Jenkins, A. and M. Healey. 2005. *Institutional Strategies to Link Teaching and Research*, York: The Higher Education Academy.

Land, R. 2004. *Educational Development: Discourse, Identity and Practice*, Buckingham, Society for Research into Higher Education/Open University Press.

Lucas, L. 2006. *The Research Game in Academic Life*, Maidenhead, Society for Research into Higher Education/Open University Press.

Macfarlane, B., O. Filippakou, E. Halford, and A. Saraswat. 2007. *Managing Duality: The Role of Manager-Academics Working in a Dual Sector Institution*, Paper presented at the *Higher Education Academy Annual Conference: Engaging Students in Higher Education*, Harrogate International Centre, July 3–5, 2007, available online at http://www.heacademy.ac.uk/events/conference/papers.

Parry, G., A. Thompson and P. Blackie. 2006. *Managing Higher Education in Colleges*, London: Continuum.

Reid. A. and P. Petocz. 2003. Enhancing academic work through the synergy between teaching and research, *International Journal for Academic Development*, 8:1–2, 105–17.

Robson, J. 2006. *Teacher Professionalism in Further and Higher Education: Challenges to Culture and Practice*, London: Routledge.

Rowland, S., C. Byron, F. Furedi, N. Padfield, and T. Smyth. 1998. Turning Academics into Teachers?, *Teaching in Higher Education*, 3:2, 133–41.

Universities and College Union. 2008. *Contract of Employment for Lecturers in Polytechnics and Colleges of Higher Education*, http://www.ucu.org.uk/index.cfm?articleid=1972 (accessed April 2, 2008).

Webb, G. 1996. *Understanding Staff Development*, Buckingham: Society for Research into Higher Education/Open University Press.

12
Community

BRONTE NEYLAND AND LESLIE "SKIP" TRIPLETT

Introduction

This chapter considers the ability of dual sector, comprehensive universities to play a distinctive role in building an increasingly civil global society by working locally and internationally to bring the advantages of the "university experience" to historically under-represented groups. The chapter then considers the evolution of dual sector universities, how this process has shaped their role, and the challenges inherent in convincing members of under-represented groups that the benefits of a university education are substantial and attainable. The chapter will use the experiences and aspirations of two duals, one in Canada and one in Australia, as illustrations highlighting their efforts in working with local communities.

Defining the Civic Mission

Colby *et al.* provide a comprehensive definition of the "civic mission" of the academy.

> If today's college graduates are to be positive forces in this world, they need not only to possess knowledge and intellectual capacities but also to see themselves as members of a community, as individuals with a responsibility to contribute to their communities. They must be willing to act for the common good and capable of doing so effectively.
>
> (Colby *et al.* 2003: 7)

Using this definition, consider some associated questions: If the academy is a primary source of engaged citizens who have been prepared for local and global leadership and service, then what of those who have not attended the academy? (See chapter 2.) Are they a wasted, or at least an under prepared and therefore under utilized, resource? How much closer to a global civil society would the world be if all those who had the capacity to succeed in a university had been able to enter one? Further, in recent years many educators have expressed concerns that pressures to provide both private and public sector employers with a workforce that possesses sophisticated and relevant skills and individual students with an education aimed at equipping them for well-paid and satisfying careers have caused even research-intensive universities to lose sight of their "civic mission."

While many university leaders debate the veracity and the severity of this drift away from a mission essential to the development and preservation of civil society, some have taken it to heart. For example, the International Association of New Generation Universities, a group to which several dual universities belong, describes its members as institutions that draw strength from, and aspire to play transformational roles within, identifiable communities of inter-est. The governing board of one such institution, Kwantlen University College in Canada (in April 2008, Kwantlen University College was redesignated as Kwantlen Polytechnic University by the government of British Columbia), has incorporated this notion of a civic mission into a policy for which it holds its chief officer accountable and which it monitors closely. Its Global Ends Policy states that the university exists for the social, economic, cultural, and intel-lectual vibrancy of the region it serves and its board of governors requires its president to provide it with evidence that the university is pursuing and achieving this end.

This policy echoes the sense of purpose expressed by William G. Tierney:

> The project of modernism and the social role of the university have gone hand in hand throughout the 20th century. Broadly stated, proponents of modernism have assumed that rational, objective knowledge discovered by scientific inquiry ultimately will set humanity free, or at least improve the lives of men and women. Universities have existed to enable scientists and philosophers to study particular phenomena so that they might advance understanding and inculcate cultural truths into the young. In these respects universities have been seen as central organizations of the modern idea of the nation-state and a central tool for nation building.
>
> (Tierney 2001: 353)

However, some leaders worry that, even at universities where the civic mission is a primary one, too few citizens have an opportunity to engage in it because they belong to socioeconomic strata that attend university in very limited numbers or because they reside in areas with limited access to research-intensive universities. In two recent reports the Canada Millennium Scholar-ship Foundation, a Government of Canada initiative to remove financial barriers for academically qualified students, suggests that the most reliable predictors of university enrollment are family wealth, parents with higher education credentials, and non-aboriginal status. The reports suggest that since university participation rates of children from families with these charac-teristics are already acceptable, significant participation rate gains will likely be made only by concentrating on the most difficult segments of society to influence—those from barrier-ridden, disadvantaged backgrounds (Canada Millennium Scholarship Foundation, 2007a: 6–7, 2007b: 11).

The obvious conclusion to draw from these and similar reports is that a university education is still a privilege restricted to those who can afford it and that the best way to overcome this restriction is to make it affordable through low (or no) tuition and through scholarships, bursaries, and other financial support. However, a 2007 study by Statistics Canada, another agency of the Federal Government of Canada, "found only weak evidence that financial constraints were a direct barrier to attending university" (Statistics Canada 2007: 1). Instead, the agency attributed the propensity to attend or not attend university almost entirely to academic performance at age fifteen and to parental influence.

Assuming, in the absence of evidence to the contrary, that academic performance at age fifteen and parental influence are the key barriers to attending university, the question for educators concerned about extending the social role of the university to non-traditional groups becomes: how does one attract low academic performers who are members of families with low socioeconomic expectations?

A Canadian Response to Overcoming Socioeconomic Barriers

Kwantlen University College is a comprehensive, dual sector, teaching-intensive university and college in the Metro-Vancouver area of the Province of British Columbia's south west coast. Approximately 85 percent of its students are enrolled in university studies programs and the remaining 15 percent in community college developmental, vocational and trades studies. Kwantlen has taken three approaches to the problem of attracting students from socioeconomic strata with low academic aspirations.

The first approach is still experimental, but showing great promise. It deals with identifying high-school students who are "at risk," because they come from families with low expectations, while these students are in their final years of high school. Surrey, one of the cities in which Kwantlen University College has a major campus, is home to a large population of new Canadians with roots in the rural, agrarian areas of India's Punjab. Many of the families that make up this population have little, and sometimes no, formal education. The heads of these families were often manual laborers in India, are now manual laborers in Canada and expect their children to make their living through manual labor. Attending university is simply not part of the mindset of either parents or children.

In mid-2002, some prominent business leaders from Surrey's Indo-Canadian business community approached Kwantlen University College and expressed their concerns about the wasted human potential to which this situation gives rise. They expressed a willingness to work with Kwantlen to find a solution and to raise money for its implementation costs (mostly high school and university counselor time and university tuition). An experimental program, dubbed SPARK, was developed in consultation with these business leaders and with a local high school, Tamanawis Secondary School, with a large population of students from families recently arrived from the Punjab. In this SPARK program, Tamanawis counselors identify students in Grade 11 (the penultimate high school year) who are considered "at risk" of either not completing high school or not carrying on to university because of a combination of low academic performance and membership in low-expectation families. Typically, these students are fifteen or sixteen years of age and are from the Indo-Canadian community. However, membership in the Indo-Canadian ethnic group is not a criterion and the ethnic makeup of students in the SPARK program reflects that of the high school. These students and their families are then encouraged to apply for the SPARK program wherein counselors from both Tamanawis and Kwantlen will work with them and their parents for their final two years of high school and in which they will begin to take university courses with both academic and financial support.

In essence, the program works as follows. In the penultimate year of high school, students take courses designed to help them explore their interests and abilities and to develop time-management and study skills. The following year, in the final year of high school, they take university credit courses in each of the year's two semesters. The program is offered free of charge—including free university tuition at Kwantlen. Upon graduation from high school, the program also offers its students a 50 percent tuition scholarship when they enter higher education. Most students carry on their studies at Kwantlen but their scholarships may be used at the higher education institution of their choice.

As of 2007, five years following inception, the program has been remarkably successful. Fully 95 percent of SPARK participants graduate from high school, well over the School District and Provincial averages, and 80 percent make the transition into higher education. Again, these transition rates are much higher than School District and Provincial averages. Also, what began with a Grade 11 intake of twenty-five students in one high school has now spread to three high schools, each with an annual intake of twenty-five students. The program continues to be supported by the Indo Canadian business community through a charitable foundation that they formed. In 2007 this SPARK Foundation raised C$300,000 (Canadian dollars). Members of the Foundation also convinced the Government of British Columbia to make a one-time grant of C$800,000 to help fund the program. In 2007 the Government of British Columbia also agreed to help fund an extension of the program to the Aboriginal community.

The second Kwantlen University College program designed to attract members of families with low socioeconomic expectations is aimed directly at the Aboriginal community. Named the Kwantlen Capacity Development Camp, it runs two summer camps, each of two weeks' duration, for aboriginal children in the last three years of elementary school. Typically these children are ten to thirteen years of age, and the aim of the camps is to plant the seeds of learning in these formative years. The camps are also designed to encourage these children to develop interests in pursuing healthcare careers because British Columbia has critical shortages of healthcare professionals in its Aboriginal communities. The Aboriginal population is also worryingly under-represented in higher education classrooms.

Kwantlen University College's Faculty of Community and Health Studies organize the camps in consultation with Aboriginal elders. The camps bring the Aboriginal children to Kwantlen's Surrey campus for two weeks of full-day activities. These activities mix learning about Aboriginal culture through stories and participation in traditional visual and performance arts with carrying out experiments in Kwantlen's science laboratories and site visits to hospitals and other institutions. The Faculty of Community and Health Studies provides general oversight for the camps and Aboriginal teenagers directly supervise the children. Kwantlen provides these youth leaders with leadership training prior to the camps.

As the Camps have only been in operation for four years and work with young children, it is too early to tell whether or not they will be successful in encouraging their "graduates" to enter higher education studies in general and healthcare professions in particular. However, in 2007 there are three signs that indicate the outcome will be successful. First, the camps are very popular with Aboriginal parents and children; second, the camp's Aboriginal youth-leaders are very enthusiastic about their roles and keep returning, year after year; and third, one of these youth leaders is now bound for Medical School at the University of British Columbia.

Kwantlen University College's third initiative is much wider in scope. Kwantlen is steadily increasing educational options and pathways for students by purposefully and coherently integrating college and university programs. Eighty percent of Kwantlen's programs have bridging opportunities that allow students to complete a program with a credential and later return to higher-level studies with no repetition of material. Kwantlen's trades programs are distinctive examples of this flexible, student-centered option. Trades people who have completed their technical training and want to pursue other career options may do so by bridging into a diploma program and on to a degree. These pathways to degrees also help address how one attracts low academic performers who are members of families with low socioeconomic expectations.

In Kwantlen's experience, boredom, rather than lack of academic capacity, is the reason for the under-achievement of many high school students. They are often encouraged, by parents and high school teachers, to enter trades or vocational training programs in the mistaken belief that such programs are less intellectually challenging than university degree programs. However, once enrolled in programs that combine hands-on, practical training with the theoretical underpinnings that support the skills they are acquiring, such students often discover that their intellectual abilities are strong, and their interests and ambitions change as their confidence in their own abilities grow. The educational bridging opportunities between hitherto unrelated skills training and university level academic education allow these students to pursue their full potential without having to "start again from the beginning." Associated curricular reform also allows these students to earn academic credit in tandem with the acquisition of skill competencies and to supplement their skills training with academic courses, and thus benefit from the citizen-building, social role of universities while still enrolled as trades and vocational level students. Similarly, families from lower socioeconomic strata, without experience of a higher education, will often encourage their children to pursue trades or vocational careers simply because they do not believe a university education is attainable. As just described, these students, too, often discover latent interests and abilities once enrolled in challenging skills training programs.

Community Engagement in Victoria, Australia

In Australia's Victoria state, dual sector universities have evolved as a result of government initiation (see chapter 5). While Australian universities are by definition self-accrediting, the federal government, state, or territory governments and institutions share the responsibility, at a higher education level, for governance, regulation, and decision-making. Australian universities are established under either state or territory legislation, though the majority of their public funding is from the federal government through the *Higher Education Support Act 2003* (Department of Education, Science and Training 2003). The Victorian state government proposed the amalgamation of a number of technical universities with technical colleges or public vocational education providers to ensure the financial sustainability of the institutions involved. The amalgamation of these institutions and their evolution into dual sector universities occurred in Victoria in the 1990s.

RMIT University, formerly known as the Royal Melbourne Institute of Technology (RMIT), is a result of the amalgamation of RMIT and Phillip Institute of Technology in 1992, while Victoria University (known as Victorian University of Technology (VUT) until 2005) evolved from the amalgamation of Western Melbourne Institute of TAFE (Technical and Further Education) and VUT in 1998. Swinburne University of Technology was formed in 1992, having evolved from Eastern Suburbs Technical College and Swinburne Technical College. While the University of Ballarat was declared a university in 1994, it was not until 1998 that the amalgamation with the School of Mines and Industries Ballarat and with the Wimmera Institute of TAFE occurred. The only other Australian jurisdiction with a dual sector university is the Northern Territory, which established Charles Darwin University in 2003, much later than its Victorian counterparts. However, it was also created through a merger of differently mandated institutions: Northern Territory University, Centralian College, NT Rural College, and the Menzies School of Health Research.

While many of the dual sector universities in Victoria promote their dual sector nature as a unique selling point, highlighting the opportunities this creates for students who did not achieve the academic requirements for direct entry into degrees, there is still considerable work to be done at most of these institutions in terms of recognition for prior learning or credit transfer. Provision of credits from vocational education courses, which are predominantly trade-focused qualifications, into degree courses remains difficult across many fields owing to the training package requirements of vocational courses. The Office of Training and Tertiary Education, a state-based organization within the Victorian Department of Innovation, Industry and Regional Development, regulates the training competencies that must be met within each qualification awarded for a vocational and technical education course. Training packages require specific competencies to be acquired by students to ensure that they are able to perform the practical aspects of licensed trades, with these frequently requiring considerable hours of practical training. This focus on practical training often prevents significant credits being granted towards degree courses that have a predominantly theoretical focus. Canada's licensed trades have similar requirements and, as mentioned earlier in this chapter, Kwantlen University College has overcome much of the practical–theoretical divide by assigning credit equivalencies to competency attainments and by building university course options into its trades curricula.

Australia's student visa policies have had an impact on the activity of its dual sector universities. In certain cases, for example for Indian students, the requirements to obtain a student visa to Australia are less stringent if the student has an offer of a place on a degree course. It could therefore be argued that the international student market has driven the dual sector universities to increase the internal pathways from the vocational education courses to the degree courses and that this market has also forced the development of closer relationships between both public and private vocational education providers and universities and encouraged traditional universities to recognize a greater range of vocational education qualifications. Establishment of formal pathways, or documented recognition of prior learning, not only within dual sector universities but also between vocational education providers and universities, continues to increase.

Financial savings to the student or their family are also promoted by the dual sector institutions as the costs of vocational education courses are generally lower than the costs of a degree. If the duration of credit provided toward the degree course is similar to that of the vocational education studies, then financial savings will be achieved. This provides an attractive option to those who aspire to gain a degree but have financial constraints.

In recent years the Australian government has increased its promotion and support of vocational education courses and this has resulted in broader community recognition of the value of vocational education qualifications. In 2006 the Prime Minister announced a set of major new initiatives called "Skills for the Future." These initiatives, worth $837 million over five years, will focus on the need for continuous upgrading of skills over the course of an individual's working life (Department of Education, Science and Training 2007c). In many trades, there are opportunities to upgrade the initial qualification to a diploma or advanced diploma, which may then create opportunities for credit transfer into degrees.

One long-standing initiative introduced by the Australian Government, which continues to be successful, is the vocational education and training in schools (VETIS) programs. These programs, introduced in 1994, were developed to improve participation levels in post-compulsory education, which are Years 11 and 12 in most states in Australia. The program was also designed to meet the employment needs of industry. VETIS programs provide access and pathways for senior secondary students through the delivery of VET programs as a part of their Victorian Certificate of Education or the Victorian Certificate of Applied Learning. The programs require cooperation between schools, training providers, and industry. Students enroll in vocationally oriented studies or school-based apprenticeships that lead to a secondary school certificate.

Victoria University's participation in the VETIS program provides high school students with an opportunity to develop an affiliation with a university through their vocational studies in secondary school. Through this introduction the students gain a greater awareness of the higher education opportunities available to them after completing secondary school. This affiliation, particularly for those who may be first-generation university students, is important in introducing them to a broad variety of educational opportunities and also creating an environment that appears familiar to them.

While the Australian government continues to introduce schemes to increase the participation of Australian students in post-compulsory education, vocational education institutions have seen an increase in international student enrollments, particularly since 2006, in response to the Skilled Migration program promoted by the government. In recent years there has been a proliferation of private vocational education providers in Australia, established under corporations law, with many largely focused on the international student market, offering courses that will assist students in gaining permanent residence in Australia. While government vocational education providers recorded 14,730 commencing international students in October 2007 (year-to-date figures), non-government (private) providers recorded an astounding 54,810 international student commencements for the same period (Department of Education, Science and Training 2007b).

However, before this recent boom in the establishment of private vocational education providers, Navitas Limited (formerly known as IBT Education Ltd) established linkages with a university in most states of Australia. For example, Deakin University in Victoria has formal pathway agreements with Melbourne Institute of Business and Technology (MIBT), while Edith Cowan University in Perth provides credit towards a number of degrees for Perth Institute of Business and Technology (PIBT) graduates. While IBT Education Limited met market demand for international students who ultimately wanted to qualify with a degree, the programs were not designed to equip students with a trade as well as a formal qualification. The model's success was intrinsically linked to the clear and attractive credit transfer arrangements toward degree courses that were promoted to the international market.

According to AEI's 2006 data, 49,809 international students commenced vocational education courses. AEI's October 2007 statistics indicate that 9,289 commencing international students in Australia transferred year-to-date from vocational education courses to higher education courses. Until July 2007, the Australian government required students to complete at least twelve months of study at one institution, prior to transferring to another. Furthermore, with only five universities offering vocational and higher education courses and very few vocational education providers offering degrees before 2007, it is not unreasonable to assume that these figures represent transfers between institutions. These figures show that almost 19 percent of vocational education students aspire to graduating with a degree, clearly validating the mission of some dual institutions in providing a variety of access points to students aspiring to a degree.

While approximately one third of the universities' on-campus student population in Australia is diverse, and encouragingly there is greater representation of non-English-speaking Australians enrolled at universities, the representation of the indigenous community remains low. According to the Department of Education, Science and Training's (DEST) 2006 statistics (Department of Education, Science and Training 2007a), the cultural diversity of Australian universities consisted of: 12 percent of students who are non-English-speaking Australians, 1.0 percent indigenous students, 18.8 percent international students, 67.6 percent English-speaking Australians, and 0.6 percent New Zealanders. DEST Higher Education Statistics indicate that the number of indigenous students enrolled in 2006 was slightly less than the number enrolled in 2002, indicating a decline over the past five years (Department of Education, Science and Training 2007a). Milroy (2007: 1) comments that there has been little progress made over the past five years to improve indigenous education. Indigenous students represent approximately 1.2 percent of the domestic student population, or half the number for parity. The situation is also apparent at a staffing level, with less than 1.0 percent of higher education staff of indigenous origin. Indigenous representation amongst staff is even lower than that among the student body. While universities continue to employ such a low percentage of indigenous staff, it is challenging to provide an environment that supports indigenous students as these students require a culturally enriched and secure environment.

> When we consider current funding and expenditure on Indigenous higher education as a proportion of total higher education funding and expenditure in Australia, and within individual universities, then Indigenous people appear to have a disproportionately small share of the total resources. . . . Part of the difficulty is that there isn't a good understanding of what the cost drivers are for Indigenous higher education and where these might fit within university funding models.
>
> (Milroy 2007: 1)

With government funding models resulting in increased competition and encouraging research activities and differentiation in academic programs, there are few incentives for institutions to address the issue of indigenous education. However, the election of a new Labor government in late 2007, led by Kevin Rudd, has signaled a more sympathetic attitude to indigenous issues. On February 12, 2008, the Prime Minister apologized to the indigenous population of Australia, acknowledging the divide that exists between indigenous and non-indigenous Australians in life expectancy, educational achievement, and economic opportunity. University presidents across Australia were quick to acknowledge the apology and release a response supporting increased participation by the indigenous community in tertiary education. Since coming into office, the Prime Minister has restructured the education portfolio within the Federal Government, which may lead to post-secondary institutions being encouraged to allocate some of their funding to improving Indigenous higher education.

The lower socioeconomic status of indigenous communities does not appear to be unique to Australia. The World Indigenous Nations Higher Education Consortium (WINHEC) brings together indigenous cultures from across the globe, including those in Australia, New Zealand, North America, Norway, and Taiwan. According to Gerritsen (2008), higher education is being used by indigenous people to assist in keeping their culture alive and active, as well as to assist in improving their socioeconomic status. WINHEC provides a forum in which these cultures can share and learn from each other, addressing issues of language retention and educational underachievement. Institutions need to be aware of these specific priorities if they are to effectively support educational opportunities for indigenous communities.

While the evolution of the dual sector institutions in Australia was not intrinsically a social response to ensuring access and equity to those from lower socioeconomic strata, Victoria University has embraced this goal within its civic mission. Victoria University is the only university located in the western suburbs of Melbourne, a region that has traditionally been considered an area of lower socioeconomic strata, and thus the university welcomes a greater proportion of the non-traditional university students than many other universities in the state of Victoria. The commitment to this civic mission is highlighted in budget documents released by the University for 2008.

Victoria University's (VU) mission has been clearly defined around servicing the west of Melbourne, and in the university's recent strategies and initiatives community engagement is again identified as a key institutional focus:

> VU will resource three initiatives for a better life in Melbourne's western suburbs and to share this knowledge with other communities in Australia or overseas that may face similar challenges.
>
> (Victoria University 2007)

Through the "Making VU A New School of Thought" project, the university has indicated a commitment that at least 25 percent of each course, whether vocational or higher education, will comprise learning in the workplace or community. This will allow students to customize their educational experience to include a practical component and also ensure that graduates are better equipped to meet the needs of industry. Over recent years in Australia there has been a growing trend of degree graduates returning to study to obtain a vocational qualification, to enhance their career opportunities. The workplace and community focus will connect industry and students, bringing benefits to both groups, particularly in filling employment opportunities in future years. It will also provide opportunities for VU to provide upskilling and reskilling education for various industries.

These initiatives demonstrate the university's commitment to offering more flexible and relevant educational experiences to current and future students. The customized learning experience will facilitate students enrolling in subjects across both vocational and higher education sectors either in their diploma program or their degree studies, and will hopefully assist the university in leveraging off the benefits of being a dual sector.

As dual sector institutions remain clustered in particular regions rather than enjoying a national representation, the benefits remain limited to particular communities. Certainly in the case of Australia, until the election of the current Federal government it seemed unlikely that there would be encouragement to establish additional dual sector institutions. However, in mid-March the new government announced a review of higher education to be completed by the end of 2008. One of the key objectives of the review is to investigate and advise the government on a more integrated tertiary education system, including the development of proper articulation between vocational education and training providers and universities. This may have positive implications for dual sector universities. Furthermore, the current skills shortage in Australia, which has seen the expansion of the skilled migration program, has resulted in greater emphasis on vocational education. Dual sector universities, compared with single sector universities, are well placed to take advantage of this change in emphasis.

In Canada, a similar skill shortage has developed and its national and provincial politicians are also paying increased attention to vocational education and immigration solutions in their public statements. However, they are showing anecdotal and informal interest in British Columbia's dual sector institutions. In the main, Canadian resistance to the duals as a legitimate, new form of university comes from the country's oldest research-intensive institutions.

Conclusion

Internationally, many dual sector universities have mission statements that incorporate a civic element directed at the socially excluded. However, in both Australia and Canada, there is a strong argument that the existence of dual sector universities does not contribute nationally to increasing the access levels of first generation university students or those from lower socioeconomic strata. Four of the five dual sector universities in Australia are located in the state of Victoria, with the fifth located in the Northern Territory. All four of Canada's duals are located in the Province of British Columbia. Without the existence of such institutions in each Australian state or territory and each Canadian province or territory, it is difficult to argue from a national perspective their place in providing access to a broader spectrum of the community, as opposed to that of traditional single sector universities.

The new initiatives implemented by Kwantlen University College and the evolution of Victoria University into a dual sector demonstrate the capacity of dual sector institutions to offer a unique education experience. These institutions provide access to a degree for students who might not have otherwise been able to aspire to this level of qualification. However, further work is required to develop a broader range of pathways from vocational to higher education courses at both institutions, and in fact at most dual sector institutions (see chapters 3 and 13). This would create even greater opportunities for participation by under-represented groups.

The examples of engagement by both Kwantlen University College and Victoria University with their local communities demonstrate the capacity of tertiary education institutions to enhance the local education environment. While meeting financial imperatives, these institutions are contributing to the social enhancement of their respective communities. However, with increasingly competitive global and local conditions, the dual sector universities must remain alert to changes in their market environments and respond appropriately. Duals need to sustain their market momentum if they are to bring the advantages of the university experience to historically under-represented groups.

References

Canada Millennium Scholarship Foundation. 2007a. *Fast Forward,* available at www.millennium scholarships.ca.aboutus/AnnualReport.asp (accessed September 29, 2007).

Canada Millennium Scholarship Foundation. 2007b. *The Price of Knowledge: Access and Student Finance in Canada,* 3rd ed., www.millenniumscholarships.ca/en/research/price.asp (accessed September 29, 2007).

Colby, A., T. Ehrlich, E. Beaumont, and J. Stephens. 2003. *Educating Citizens: Preparing America's Undergraduates for Lives of Moral and Civic Responsibility,* San Francisco: Jossey-Bass.

Department of Education, Science and Training. 2003. *Higher Education Support Act,* http://www.comlaw.gov.au/comlaw/management.nsf/lookupindexpagesbyid/IP200402739?Open Document (accessed April 16, 2008).

Department of Education, Science and Training. 2007a. *Skills for the Future* http://www.skillsforthefuture.gov.au/about.htm (accessed December 30, 2007).

Department of Education, Science and Training. 2007b. *Statistics Relating to Higher Education,* http://www.dest.gov.au/sectors/higher_education/publications_resources/statistics 30 (accessed December 30, 2007).

Department of Education, Science and Training. 2007c. *Year 2007 Market Indicator Data,* https://aei.dest.gov.au/AEI/MIP/CurrentMarketInformation/NationalOffice/Statistics/2007/2007 Oct_0726_xls.xls (accessed December 9, 2007).

Gerritsen, J. 2008. Indigenous peoples seek their own answers, *University World News,* available at www.universityworldnews.com (accessed February 11, 2008).

Milroy, J. 2007. *Resourcing for Success in Indigenous Higher Education,* unpublished paper.

Statistics Canada. 2007. Study: Why are youth from lower-income families less likely to attend university, *The Daily,* February 8, 2007, available at http://www.statcan.ca/Daily/English/070208/d070208a.htm (accessed October 2, 2007).

Tierney, W. G. 2001. The autonomy of knowledge and the decline of the subject: Postmodernism and the reformation of the university, *Higher Education,* 41:4, 353–72.

Victoria University. 2007. *Making VU a New School of Thought,* 2007, http://www.vu.edu.au/home/Making_VU_a_New_School_of_Thought/index.aspx (accessed December 15, 2007).

13
Curriculum

NEIL GARROD AND LIZ WARR

Introduction

The impact of curriculum issues on student progression within the post-compulsory sector in England is explored in this chapter. UK government statements, policies, and initiatives regarding post-compulsory educational provision indicate significant support for greater progression from further to higher education and a curriculum that supports such progression (see e.g. Blunkett 2000; Department of Innovation, Universities and Skills 2008a). While many of these initiatives blur the further–higher distinction, in extremis they may recreate a higher education binary divide. It is unclear, at this stage, whether these increased progression opportunities will therefore challenge boundaries or simply relocate them.

In the next section some background to the historical curriculum differences between further and higher education is provided. More recent developments that have led to cross-sector convergence are discussed in the third section. Examples are drawn from Writtle College, one of three specialist land-based higher education institutions in the UK. Of the three, Writtle is the only dual sector organization, having been redesignated from a further education college to a higher education institution in 1994. In the fourth section specific innovations designed to bridge the further/higher—and indeed the school/post-school and sub-degree/degree—curriculum boundaries are outlined. A consideration of whether these developments represent a blurring or relocation of boundaries is offered in the fifth section, with concluding remarks in the final section.

Curriculum Separation

Further education and higher education curricula have historically reflected very different characteristics. Further education qualifications such as National Certificates and Diplomas are designed to provide education and training at technician level. They are based on a nationally defined work-related curriculum that reflects a primary focus on competency-based training, with knowledge and skills geared to the needs of industry. The wide geographical distribution of further education colleges facilitates local accessibility and close working links with employers. In combination these allow for flexible schemes of work and relatively small, mixed cohorts of full-time, part-time, and work-based learners. Assessment is criterion-referenced and is based, where possible, on the learners' work experience. Teachers and assessors must demonstrate technical competence and up-to-date expertise through the acquisition of relevant professional qualifications.

University degrees, in contrast, are content-based, with curricula designed by the academic staff and often reflecting their own research interests. Significant curriculum differences can therefore occur between institutions offering awards with identical titles. The emphasis has historically been on full-time cohorts of school leavers holding academic school-leaving qualifications and the development of learner autonomy has been a higher priority than the development of employability skills. Professional teaching qualifications for academic staff are optional.

More vocational, sub-degree higher education qualifications, such as Higher National Diplomas, exist but are rarely offered by research-intensive universities. While the curriculum of higher national awards (higher education) in specialist vocational subjects, such as agriculture, closely resembles the curriculum of the corresponding national award (further education), it reflects a stronger emphasis on underlying scientific and/or management principles and the disciplinary knowledge underpinning vocational practice. Assessment is criterion-referenced, as in further education, but with greater emphasis on its formative function. The work-based activity in higher education involves critical reflection on the knowledge and skills acquired rather than specific acquisition of technical competence (Clamp and Warr 2002).

Vocational qualifications in further education and higher education have been designed for two different markets: for technician level and supervisory or management level, respectively. As alternatives, progression from the former to the latter remains the exception rather than the rule. Where progression occurs, curriculum overlap between National Diplomas (further education) and Higher National Diplomas (higher education) can be a significant problem. It is difficult to imagine, for example, how a vocational competence such as tractor-driving could be developed differently in students on further and higher education programs and yet the skill acquired at National Diploma level is not normally recognized as a credit equivalent for the Higher National Diploma.

Progression and Curriculum Alignment

The differences between further and higher education curricula outlined above are less stark today. This is largely due to a convergence of higher education curricula. Credit-based modular curricula are now widely used within UK higher education and this has led to a greater focus on outcome-based curriculum models.

Higher education quality assurance systems have also contributed to increased congruence. In the UK, the Quality Assurance Agency for Higher Education (QAA) monitors academic standards and quality for the sector. Academic disciplines are now subject to a benchmarking exercise with the production of statements that describe the attributes that give a discipline its coherence and identity and define the abilities and skills that can be expected of a graduate in the subject (Quality Assurance Agency for Higher Education 2008a).

While these subject benchmarks are described as an overall conceptual framework rather than a national curriculum, their use in QAA review processes has undoubtedly given them significant importance. Guidelines on ten key aspects of provision (for example on assessment, on program design, approval, monitoring and review, and on work-based learning) are collectively known as the "Code of Practice" (Quality Assurance Agency for Higher Education 2008b). The requirement for providers to produce a program specification for every higher education program that describes the intended outcomes of learning and the teaching, learning, and assessment strategies through which these are achieved has created greater transparency in higher education curricula and contributed to greater congruence within the higher education sector.

Gourley (2007: 15) refers to such mediators of practice as "boundary objects" and describes bodies such as the QAA as "boundary organisations" (p. 17) as they link communities of practice and mediate discontinuities between institutions. While such mediation has also led to greater linkage with the further education sector, significant differences remain. Content, structure and outcomes may be drawing together but the pedagogies underlying curriculum delivery remain distinct. The major differences lie in the relative emphasis placed on autonomous learning and the support of students. Both these factors represent significant barriers to progression from further to higher education.

Current thinking about curriculum structures, connectivity, and progression is changing with the growing emphasis on lifelong learning. Government initiatives such as foundation degrees and lifelong learning networks, outlined below, highlight that further education should not only provide standalone qualifications but also educational progression to higher education (Higher Education Funding Council for England 2004). Nonetheless, this is still more evident in theory than in practice. Even in dual-sector organizations, where progression is a stated priority, Bathmaker and Thomas (2007) identify a poor match between National Diplomas and bachelor degrees. Little active promotion of routes between these qualifications occurs and curriculum alignment is weak.

Elsewhere in this book, Wheelahan (chapter 3) refers to the need for staff who can understand the cultures and demands of the two sectors to act as "boundary spanners" and develop collaborative arrangements that result in a "climbing framework" of qualifications that facilitate progression to employment and/or higher level study. A joint further and higher education Learning and Teaching Committee has been established at Writtle College as well as a working group entitled Bridging the Academic Divide. The prime purpose of this group is to facilitate boundary-crossing so that it becomes an integral feature of institutional practice through collaborative initiatives, curriculum alignment, and targeted staff development. Higher education taster days and master classes for further education students are built into the institutional action plan for widening participation. Higher education students are selected, trained, and paid as ambassadors and mentors to support further education students progressing to higher education.

Successful student progression from further to higher education requires a step change in learning experience for the student. There is a related change in the expectations of academic staff, the range of facilities on offer, and the type of study methods students will be expected to deploy. At the top end of further education programs there is a need to prepare students for higher education. There may be a tendency in some further education provision to over teach, resulting in students experiencing a duplication of provision as they progress to higher education study. Equally, a greater focus on teaching and learning strategies and student support in the first year of higher education would better support progression (Yorke and Longden 2008).

The non-completion rate in higher education has always been more pronounced in the first year of undergraduate study than in all subsequent years, and higher still in those institutions that have a significant number of entrants with vocationally based entrance qualifications (Higher Education Statistics Agency 2005). Watts *et al.* (2008) have identified that students feel better prepared to engage with the pedagogies of higher education when personal, professional, and academic development skills are incorporated into the formal curriculum rather than being offered as optional, extra-curricula skills development initiatives. This view is shared by a significant proportion of students with more conventional academic backgrounds.

Bridging Boundaries

Currently some 12 percent of higher education qualifications are gained in further education colleges (Higher Education Funding Council for England 2006). Without degree-awarding powers, colleges must form strategic alliances with universities to offer degree programs. Whether through partnership or less intimate validation processes, these links have naturally resulted in greater curriculum alignment between programs that sit at different levels within the National Qualifications Framework (Qualifications and Curriculum Authority 2008a). In this section we outline some of the major catalysts of this curriculum alignment.

Work-Based Learning

"Work-based learning" (WBL) in further education applies to competence-based programs designed for, and delivered in, the work place, such as Apprenticeship Frameworks (Training and Development Agency for Schools 2008) and National Vocational Qualifications (Qualification and Curriculum Authority 2008b).

In an extensive analysis of WBL in higher education, Brennan (2005) uses the term to denote that significant areas of the curriculum are completed in the work place rather than on campus with an emphasis on the process of learning rather than acquisition of vocational competence. The more embracing term "work-related learning" (WRL) is sometimes used as it also captures learning activities derived from the context of work or the work place (Hills *et al.* 2003).

Work-based learning in higher education is increasingly focusing on work-force development. Nixon *et al.* (2006) identify that a WBL curriculum is process- rather than content-driven and is strongly learner-centered, with learning outcomes identified and agreed by the student, employer, and university or college. In part the growing focus on WBL in higher education reflects the fact that almost three quarters of the 2020 UK workforce have already left compulsory education (Leitch 2006).

Leitch (2006) highlights the importance of the skills agenda to higher as well as further education. Within the review, however, skills at the higher education level are neither defined nor clearly differentiated from the need for higher-level qualifications in support of economic development in today's global economy. Subsequently, the UK government has emphasized the importance of vocational progression routes and sees employability as a core element of the university mission (Department for Innovation, Universities and Skills 2008b). Broad employability skills of communication, motivation, independence, analysis, and problem-solving, and generic competencies such as teamwork and entrepreneurship, are identified as important features of the curriculum and there is a clear intention to deliver future growth in higher education through greater employer engagement.

The employer voice is now largely channeled through the twenty-five Sector Skills Councils (SSC). Their remit from government is to enhance productivity and skills of the sector workforce and improve learning supply, including apprenticeships, higher education, and national occupational standards. They act as brokers between education providers, employers, and government, and their involvement is becoming a condition of funding for new curriculum-related initiatives.

The breadth of influence of SSCs is reflected in the work of the SSC for land-based industries. It has produced a Framework for foundation degrees within the sector and is currently leading the development of vocational diplomas in the compulsory (secondary school) sector. The Alliance of Sector

Skills Councils, created in April 2008, further strengthens the employer voice by representing all twenty-five SSCs in driving forward the employer-led skills agenda and the UK government's agenda for the co-funding of higher education qualifications by industry.

Quality Assurance Processes

As discussed by Barnsley and Sparks (chapter 10), higher education has a greater level of independence than does further education. This is reflected in terms of both curriculum and the separate quality regimes of the two sectors. Quality systems are particularly important in dual sector institutions as they can either reinforce further–higher education territorial boundaries or support integration.

Appraisal of quality in UK higher education is carried out by the QAA. This is a self-regulatory body with funding for the agency provided by subscriptions from higher education institutions (Quality Assurance Agency for Higher Education 2008c). The work of the QAA includes oversight of higher education courses taught within colleges of further education as well as those in universities and other higher education institutions.

Quality assessment of further education provision is carried out by the Office for Standards in Education, Children's Services and Skills (Ofsted). Ofsted is a statutory body that has a remit to inspect and regulate care for children and young people, and inspect further education and training for adults (Ofsted 2007).

Differences between the two regimes are reflected in their language and approach. Ofsted carry out "inspections" at "short notice." They "grade" against "national benchmarks" and develop "action plans" (Ofsted 2008). QAA carry out "peer review" on a "scheduled intervention." They produce "categorised judgments" against "national frameworks" and produce "recommendations" (Quality Assurance Agency for Higher Education 2008c).

These differences aside, commonalities do exist. Both bodies seek to ensure public accountability. They are responsible for the management of quality and standards. Moreover, they both utilize self-evaluation and external expertise and rely on an evidence-based approach in public reporting. Both are moving away from a strict quality assurance agenda to one of quality enhancement (the QAA term) or quality improvement (the Ofsted term).

All dual sector institutions in the UK are subject to a full Institutional Audit from QAA (at the same level of scrutiny as all universities) and an institutional inspection by Ofsted (as any general further education college). The two processes operate separately from each other. This creates an external environment in the UK that favors a more binary than unitary structure (Garrod and Macfarlane 2007). The divide is reflected at Writtle College, where further and higher education are operated as distinct divisions.

The challenge for dual sector institutions is to rethink and redesign quality assurance and enhancement in support of positive curriculum development. Helpfully, this is beginning to happen at the systemic level with greater strategic collaboration between Ofsted and QAA. There is some evidence that this reflects a conceptual convergence, for example in notions of enhancement and self-regulation, as well as some methodological convergence.

An example of this convergence can be found in the Integrated Quality Enhancement Review (IQER): a review method specially devised by QAA for higher education provided in further education colleges in England. It reflects elements of both QAA audits and Ofsted inspections. It is a peer review process with a focus on processes rather than outcomes, with a right to observe teaching and a formative developmental engagement prior to the summative review (Quality Assurance Agency for Higher Education 2008d).

With the government's desire to see an expansion in the number of higher education students taught in further education colleges (Higher Education Funding Council for England 2006), the IQER methodology may mark a blueprint for a more integrated quality assurance and enhancement system across the sectors. Perhaps more importantly, it may act as a model for an integrated concept of quality within dual sector institutions themselves.

Lifelong Learning Networks

Lifelong Learning Networks (LLN) are consortia of further and higher education providers established to improve the coherence, clarity, and certainty of progression opportunities for vocational learners in and through higher education (Higher Education Funding Council for England 2004). LLNs are dual sector partnerships rather than dual sector institutions. Previous widening participation initiatives sought to stimulate demand for higher education by raising awareness and aspiration (Higher Education Funding Council for England 2008a). In contrast, LLNs seek to stimulate supply, largely through the development of foundation degrees, greater curriculum alignment, and improved advice and guidance for vocational learners (Higher Education Funding Council for England 2008b).

LLNs are working to develop common approaches to credit transfer between partners with the accreditation of experiential learning as an important objective. Most are working on collaborative curriculum development leading to progression accords (similar to the "dual offers" described by Wheelahan in chapter 3), and agreements between senders and receivers of students to facilitate, and in some instances guarantee, progression opportunities. These developments are designed to transcend conventional boundaries between vocational and academic provision. A desk-based interim review concludes that "LLNs are working effectively to develop curricula and procedures that should, in due course, make a difference to vocational learners" (Little and Williams 2008: 4).

Foundation Degrees

The foundation degree is a new kind of qualification designed to integrate academic and vocational learning, partly through the inclusion of work-based learning. It is a two-year qualification, described initially as an associate degree but finally designated as a foundation degree (Parry 2006). The involvement of employers, employer organizations, and Sector Skills Councils in their design, delivery, and assessment helps ensure the incorporation of economically important higher-level skills in the curriculum (Longhurst 2007). The qualification is targeted at those in employment as well as those holding further education vocational qualifications. As such, it is an important transition qualification, providing a bridge between top-end further education qualifications and bachelor degrees.

To accelerate the initial development of foundation degrees, HEFCE funded the design and implementation of prototypes by consortia of higher and further education partners for delivery in 2000/2001. Writtle College was a member of one such consortium. The original intention to create a foundation degree using a basket of existing modules delivered by the collaborating partners proved too ambitious. Constraints imposed by different credit frameworks and regulations surrounding the accreditation of prior experience as well as learning and cultural differences between the partners were difficult to overcome.

Cultural disparities and diversity of expectations have been identified by Foskett (2003) as major barriers (see also chapters 3 and 6 in this volume) to effective design, organization, and delivery of foundation degree curricula. Differences between further and higher education resulting from the balance between teaching, administration and research, contrasting contracts of employment, holiday entitlement, and the rhythm of the academic year are all too real. These differences are reflected in reciprocal negative perceptions held between the sectors (Stoney 2005).

Nonetheless, Foskett (2003) also highlights the synergy that derives from diverse organizations bringing different perspectives to curriculum design. Design problems have been resolved through the adaptation of existing modules within an overall foundation degree curriculum framework. For example, academic, personal, and professional development skills are often integrated into a strand of generic modules contextualized for the relevant academic discipline, drawing upon knowledge embedded in, and generated from, the workplace (Hind and Warr 2001).

A required feature of foundation degree design at the time of their inception was the availability of a progression route to a bachelor degree via a follow-on year. More recently there has been a shift in emphasis away from specified bachelor-degree-level progression routes. A number of universities now offer more generic, potentially work-based, follow-on opportunities. These programs are given broad-based titles, such as "Professional Development Studies" and are designed to be contextualized for the individual learner in the particular academic discipline.

To promote employer engagement generally and foundation degrees specifically, the English funding council established Foundation Degree Forward (FDF), a national body that supports the development and validation of foundation degrees through advice and guidance (see http://www.fdf.ac.uk). As such it is an important boundary organisation (Gourley 2007), seeking to transcend sector mentalities that are so difficult to change (Parry 2007). Parry also highlights the fact that colleges and many universities are now competing for the same students at the same level, offering yet a further barrier to cross-sector collaboration.

14–19 Diploma

The UK government's agenda to involve industry in the design of educational programs is now extending into compulsory education with the development of new specialist diplomas. These will be offered alongside conventional school-leaving qualifications and have been described as a "once in a generation opportunity to tackle the historic divide between academic and vocational learning" (Department for Children, Schools and Families 2008: 19). They are being developed by partnerships, each led by the relevant Sector Skills Council. The full or Advanced Diploma is designed to sit between academic and vocational routes, offering general education within a context (Department for Children, Families and Schools 2008). An extended project is a compulsory element of the Advanced Diploma and is seen as valuable preparation for higher education study.

The diploma is being actively promoted to universities as an alternative entry qualification. The Advanced Diploma has been calibrated at a level slightly higher than the traditional modal entry requirement for most universities. Universities are being encouraged to amend their own curricula, particularly in the first year, to enable diploma holders make a successful transition into higher education.

The UK government is intent on establishing a more comprehensive and coherent qualification framework to provide better vocational progression routes into higher education. Existing further education vocational qualifications will be brought into the diploma structure, and learning undertaken through apprenticeships will count towards the diploma and vice versa. If implemented, these changes will lead to a blurring of the boundaries between the school and further education sectors.

It is intended that "14–19" qualifications will move to a credit-based qualification framework to be completed by 2013. This will identify qualifications by both level and volume of credit, unlike the current National Qualifications Framework. It is intended, in the longer term, to develop a single credit-based qualifications framework that will span compulsory and post-compulsory education (Qualifications and Curriculum Authority 2008c).

Blurring or Relocating the Boundary?

English, and to some extent UK, post-secondary educational provision can currently be characterized as having three main components: further education that is seen as vocational, reflected in National Vocational Qualifications and National Diplomas; sub-degree higher education that is seen as largely vocational, reflected in Higher National Diplomas and foundation degrees; and degree and postgraduate higher education that is seen as academic, reflected in bachelor and postgraduate degrees.

There is little doubt that the initiatives and structures described above have led to a much greater degree of curriculum alignment between further education and sub-degree higher education. The introduction of the 14–19 Diploma should strengthen this even more. However, the boundary between sub-degree and degree and postgraduate higher education, and indeed between further education and degree and postgraduate higher education, has to date been far less permeable.

For example, Higher National Diplomas (HND), awarded by national accreditation bodies, historically varied in the extent to which they were recognized by universities as providing exemption from, or academic credit toward, bachelor degrees. A plethora of progression routes existed, with some requiring one year's further study to achieve a bachelor degree while others required two. The resultant confusion was cited as a key justification for the introduction of the foundation degree. As a consequence, HNDs have increasingly become "nested" in undergraduate degree schemes, enabling seamless progression to university-validated bachelor degrees. Nonetheless, the actual progression rate has not been high. In 2004/05 over 35,000 HNDs were awarded (Higher Education Statistics Agency 2005), while the number of HND qualifiers entering degree study in 2005/06 was less than 8,000 (Higher Education Statistics Agency 2006), a progression rate of just over 20 percent.

Statistics regarding foundation degrees present an interesting comparison. While the percentage of Pre-92[1] universities offering foundation degrees has grown from 26 percent in 2001/02 to 44 percent in 2005/06, the equivalent figures for 2005/06 for Post-92 universities and further education colleges, respectively, are 85 percent and 91 percent (Higher Education Funding Council for England 2008c: 12). In 2005/06, 57 percent of foundation degrees were taught in further education colleges (p. 14). Of the 2004/05 foundation degree graduates, 54 percent progressed to a follow-on bachelor year in 2005/06. Of these, 76 percent graduated, meaning that just over 40 percent of foundation degree graduates successfully progress to a bachelor degree (pp. 44–5). This is twice the rate of HND awardees. The same source indicates that 90 percent of foundation degree awardees stay in the same institution for their follow-on year, suggesting that the majority of follow-on provision is also provided in further education colleges.

Thus while almost half of foundation degree graduates progress to a higher-level qualification, the provision of foundation degrees and, likely, follow-on years is dominated by further education colleges. This position will be solidified following the government's recent decision to enable the Privy Council to grant to further education colleges the power to award their own foundation degrees (Department of Children, Schools and Families 2006).

Parry (2006) reflects on the incentives that had to be offered to universities to engage with the foundation degree initiative. These involved additional funded places as well as development funding for institutions, employers, and employer organizations to work together in early curriculum development. The reluctance of universities to engage with the foundation degree directly, rather than through a franchise arrangement with a further education college, is illustrated in statistics regarding credit transfer from foundation degrees to follow-on years. While 87 percent of follow-on students are awarded a full two years' credit towards a bachelor degree when the student stays in the same institution, this falls to 60 percent if the students moves and as many as 14 percent of movers receive no credit at all (Higher Education Funding Council for England 2008c: 45). In the absence of any statistics it would seem safe to assume that, owing to geographical convenience alone, students are unlikely to move from one further education college to another, and that students who move will do so from a further education college to a university.

The developments described in earlier sections of this chapter have effected a blurring of the boundary between further and higher education. However, the statistics just presented also suggest that a new boundary is being created between sub-degree and degree and postgraduate higher education—recreating the binary divide dissolved in 1992 (Pratt 1997).

Even within evolving initiatives that are superficially "blurring" there are requirements that create new boundaries. For example, the quality assurance program for higher education provision within further education colleges, IQER, described above, requires colleges to articulate a separate higher education strategy in which they must set out their policies for creating a distinctive experience for their higher education learners. This is likely to sustain rather than transcend cross-sectoral boundaries.

Similarly, the involvement of Sector Skills Councils in curriculum development for the 14–19 Diploma and for foundation degrees will assist transition from one to the other. However, despite the importance placed by the current UK government on skills in post-compulsory curricula, Sector Skills Councils play no particular role in curriculum development for bachelor or postgraduate degrees, except in a handful of universities.

With a falling unit of resource for teaching, a greater concentration of research funding and additional funded student numbers being linked to LLNs and foundation degrees, there is a growing bifurcation of government funding for UK higher education. One track is research-focused and the other is access-focused. The growing integration of further education and sub-degree higher education speaks clearly to the access track but much less directly to the research track. Whether the blurring of boundaries will, in due course, penetrate the whole of higher education is a matter for speculation. The signs to date suggest that a blurring of the sub-degree and degree and postgraduate higher education boundary may not be well served by current structures and initiatives.

Conclusion

The systemic changes documented above facilitate seamless progression between further and higher education. However, current strategies present the possibility of simply relocating the post-compulsory boundary. Innovative teaching and learning strategies at institutional level will be pivotal in traversing whatever boundaries exist. Success in this is likely to depend on the design of aligned curricula and the evolution of advice and guidance systems that prepare learners for progression and that ensure successful achievement at the next level of study, whether in a further education college, in a university, or in the workplace.

Equally pivotal is research and scholarship. With a growing level of foundation degree activity within further education colleges, it is progression to bachelor degree and postgraduate study that is likely to become the next major sectoral boundary. In such an environment, dual sector universities can play an increasingly important role in the creation of a truly connected post-compulsory education system. The research aspects of the 20:20 rule (see chapter 5) will become increasingly relevant. Systemic change alone, in the absence of specific strategic focus, appears inadequate to achieve a holistic student learning environment. Curriculum design, alignment, and integration will all play strategically important roles in this context.

Note

1. The Further and Higher Education Act 1992 abolished the binary divide in UK higher education. "Pre-92 universities" refers those institutions that held university title prior to this date and are generally the more research-intensive universities today. "Post-92 universities" refers to former polytechnics and other institutions that have gained university title since 1992 and are generally the more access-focused universities today.

References

Bathmaker, A. and W. Thomas. 2007. Positioning themselves: an exploration of the nature and meaning of transitions in the context of dual sector FE/HE Institutions in England, paper presented at the *International Conference on Researching Transitions in Lifelong Learning*, University of Stirling June 22–24, http://www.shef.ac/furtherhigher/papers.html (accessed May 12, 2008).

Blunkett, D. 2000. Speech of the Secretary of State for Education, University of Greenwich, February 15, http://cms1.gre.ac.uk/dfee/#speech (accessed May 12, 2008).

Brennan, L. 2005. *Integrating Work-Based Learning into Higher Education: A Guide to Good Practice*, Bolton: University Vocational Awards Council.

Clamp, E. and E.M. Warr. 2002. Addressing employability through implementation of work-based learning, *Proceedings of 3rd Hertfordshire Integrated Learning Project Annual Conference*, Hatfield, England.

Department for Children, Schools and Families. 2006. *Further Education and Training Bill*, http://www.dfes.gov.uk/publications/furthereducationandtrainingbill/, (accessed May 8, 2008).

Department for Children, Schools and Families. 2008. *Promoting Achievement, Valuing Success: A Strategy for 14–19 Qualifications*, Norwich: The Stationery Office.

Department for Innovation, Universities and Skills. 2008a. *Higher Education Funding 2008–09*, http://www.hefce.ac.uk/pubs/board/2008/118/3a.pdf (accessed May 11, 2008).

Department for Innovation, Universities and Skills. 2008b. Consultation document on *Higher Education at Work High Skills: High Value*, http://www.dius.gov.uk/consultations/documents/Higher_Education_at_Work.pdf (accessed May 12, 2008).

Foskett, R. 2003. Employer and needs-led curriculum planning in higher education: a cross-sector study of foundation degree development. *British Educational Research Association Annual Conference*, Edinburgh, UK, September 11–13 (available online at http://www.leeds.ac.uk/educol/documents/00003182.htm).

Garrod, N. and B. Macfarlane. 2007. Scoping the duals: the structural challenges of combining further and higher education in post-compulsory institutions, *Higher Education Quarterly*, 61:4, 578–596.

Gourley, W. 2007. Higher-ness or further-ness, classifying higher education in further education in England (HFE) at the interface; boundary work, boundary objectives and boundary spanning, a working paper presented at the *International Conference on Researching Transitions in Lifelong Learning*, University of Stirling, June 22–24.

Higher Education Funding Council for England. 2004. *HEFCE Circular Letter Number 12/2004*, http://www.hefce.ac.uk/pubs/circlets/2004/cl12_04/ (accessed May 12, 2008).

Higher Education Funding Council for England. 2006. Consultation document on *Higher Education in Further Education Colleges* http://www.hefce.ac.uk/pubs/hefce/2006/06_48/ (accessed May 12, 2008).

Higher Education Funding Council for England. 2008a. *Widening Participation* http://www.hefce.ac.uk/widen/ (accessed May 13, 2008).

Higher Education Funding Council for England. 2008b. *Lifelong Learning Networks* http://www.hefce.ac.uk/widen/lln (accessed May 13, 2008).

Higher Education Funding Council for England. 2008c. *Foundation Degrees: Key Statistics 2001–02 to 2007–08*, Issue Paper 2008/16, available at http://www.hefce.ac.uk/pubs/hefce/2008/08_16/08_16.doc (accessed May 8, 2008).

Higher Education Statistics Agency. 2005. *HE Qualifications Obtained in the UK by Level, Mode of Study, Domicile, Gender, Class of First Degree and Subject Area 2004/05* http://www.hesa.ac.uk/dox/dataTables/studentsAndQualifiers/download/quals0405.xls (accessed May 8, 2008).

Higher Education Statistics Agency. 2006. *Non-Continuation Following Year of Entry: Young Full-Time First Degree Entrants 2004/05* http://www.hesa.ac.uk/dox/performanceIndicators/0506/t3b_0506.xls and *Projected Learning Outcomes: Full-Time Students Starting First Degree Courses 2004/05* http://www.hesa.ac.uk/dox/performanceIndicators/0506/t5_0506.xls (accessed April 20, 2008).

Hills, J., G. Robertson, R. Walker, M. Adey and I. Nixon. 2003. Bridging the gap between degree programme curricula and employability through implementation of work-related learning, *Teaching in Higher Education*, 8:2, 211–31.

Hind, A. and E. M. Warr. 2001. The "Professional Scholarship Programme": an integrated approach to skills development for undergraduates. *Proceedings of 2nd Institute for Learning and Teaching in Higher Education Annual Conference*, York, England.

Leitch, S. 2006. *Prosperity for All in the Global Economy: World Class Skills*, http://wwhm-treasury.gov.uk/independent_reviews/leitch (accessed May 12, 2008).

Little, B. and B. Williams. 2008. *Interim Evaluation of Lifelong Learning Networks*, London: Centre for Higher Education Research and Information, Open University.

Longhurst, D. 2007. Delivering Leitch, *Forward*, 12, 3–11.

Nixon, I., K. Smith, R. Stafford and S. Cam. 2006. *Work-based Learning: Illuminating the Higher Education Landscape*, York: Higher Education Academy.

Ofsted (The Office for Standards in Education, Children's Services and Skills). 2007. *Handbook for Inspecting Colleges*, http://www.ofsted.gov.uk/portal/site/Internet/menuitem.eace-3f09a603f6d9c3172a8a08c08a0c/?vgnextoid=96cdef7521322110VgnVC-M1000003507640aRCRD (accessed May 11, 2008).

Ofsted (The Office for Standards in Education, Children's Services and Skills). 2008. *Learning and Skills*, http://www.ofsted.gov.uk/portal/site/Internet/menuitem.455968b0530071c4828a0d8308c08a0c/?vgnextoid=c53a79d75892f010VgnVCM1000003507640aRCRD (accessed May 8, 2008).

Parry, G. 2006. Policy-participation trajectories in English higher education, *Higher Education Quarterly*, 60:4, 292–412.

Parry, G. 2007. Policy as chaos, order and experiment, *Forward*, 12, 16–18.

Pratt, J. 1997. *The Polytechnic Experiment 1965–1992*, Buckingham: Society for Research into Higher Education/Open University Press.

Qualifications and Curriculum Authority. 2008a. *National Qualifications Framework*, http://www.qca.org.uk/libraryAssets/media/qca-06–2298-nqf-web.pdf (accessed May 8, 2008).

Qualification and Curriculum Authority. 2008b. *NVQs* http://www.qca.org.uk/14–19/qualifications/index_nvqs.htm (accessed May 8, 2008).

Qualification and Curriculum Authority. 2008c. *Qualifications and Credit Framework and Higher Education*, http://www.qca.org.uk/qca_8154.aspx (accessed May 13, 2008).

Quality Assurance Agency for Higher Education. 2008a. *Subject Benchmark Statements*, http://www.qaa.ac.uk/academicinfrastructure/benchmark/default.asp (accessed May 11, 2008).

Quality Assurance Agency for Higher Education. 2008b. *Code of Practice for the Assurance of Academic Quality and Standards in Higher Education*, http://www.qaa.ac.uk/academicinfrastructure/CodeofPractice/default.asp (accessed May 13, 2008).

Quality Assurance Agency for Higher Education. 2008c. *The Quality Assurance Agency for Higher Education: An Introduction*, http://www.qaa.ac.uk/aboutus/qaaIntro/intro.asp (accessed May 8, 2008).

Quality Assurance Agency for Higher Education. 2008d. *Integrated Quality and Enhancement Review: England*, http://www.qaa.ac.uk/reviews/iqer/default.asp (accessed May 12, 2008).

Stoney, C. 2005. Improving HE/FE Partnerships: how far can streamlining quality assurance take us?, *Forward*, 6, 18–21.

Training and Development Agency for Schools. 2008. *Apprenticeship Framework Consultation*, http://www.tda.gov.uk/support/support_consultations/apprentice_consultation.aspx (accessed May 8, 2008).

Watts, M., D. Bridges and J. Eames. 2008. *Widening Participation and Encounters with the Pedagogies of Higher Education*, Cambridge: Von Hugel Institute.

Yorke, M. and B. Longden. 2008. *The First-Year Experience of Higher Education in the UK*, York: Higher Education Academy.

Index

6885 054

WITHDRAWAL